PRAISE FOR *THE GREATER GOOD*

"Madeleine is an extraordinary innovator whose ideas have had profound positive influence on so many lives. Her voice is a beacon for these times. Her stories will engage, inspire, and activate."

—**Joel Solomon,** author of *The Clean Money Revolution: Reinventing Power, Purpose, and Capitalism*

"Madeleine Shaw is a brilliant innovator, fierce feminist, generous collaborator, and persuasive storyteller—and is all of these things at once in *The Greater Good*."

—**Jennifer Weiss-Wolf,** author of *Periods Gone Public: Taking a Stand for Menstrual Equity*

"Run, don't walk, to buy *The Greater Good*. The old business models just give us the same results. Madeleine Shaw knows firsthand how to do good successfully. This is an essential primer for the new business world we need."

—**M.J. Ryan,** author of *Radical Generosity* and *How to Survive Change ... You Didn't Ask For*

"Madeleine Shaw's book arrives at the perfect time as a gift to future generations of social entrepreneurs who have dreams for a more equitable world. Shaw's decades of experience, insight, and wisdom are now available to all in a relatable format."

—**Vicki Saunders,** founder, SheEO

"*The Greater Good* is a master class that will welcome many more world-changers into the fold of social entrepreneurship."

—**Cory Ames,** founder, Grow Ensemble

"Madeleine Shaw is fiercely inspiring! And her book *The Greater Good* is a nurturing and inclusive guide to activistic entrepreneurship for the everyday human."

—**Dr. Melanie Rieback,** CEO/co-founder,
Radically Open Security

"Humane, intelligent, and deeply practical, *The Greater Good* is a guiding light for visionaries, innovators, and entrepreneurs ready to create a future where everyone can flourish."

—**Sarah Selecky,** author of *Radiant Shimmering Light* and founder of the Sarah Selecky Writing School

"With this book Madeleine captures the spirit of her in-person mentorship to guide the reader as they navigate creating their version of the greater good."

—**Emira Mears,** author of *The Boss of You: Everything a Woman Needs to Know to Start, Run, and Maintain Her Own Business*

"In *The Greater Good* Madeleine shares frank, generous, heartfelt stories and essential advice on how to avoid unconsciously upholding systemic biases."

—**Servane Mouazan,** founder, Ogunte

THE
GREATER
GOOD

THE
GREATER
GOOD

Social Entrepreneurship for
Everyday People Who Want
to Change the World

MADELEINE SHAW

WONDERWELL

Library of Congress Control Number: 2021910542

ISBN 978-1-63756-004-4 (hardcover)
ISBN 978-1-63756-005-1 (EPUB)

Editor: Allison Serrell
Cover design, cover illustration, and interior design: Morgan Krehbiel
Author photo: Felicia Chang Photography

Published by Wonderwell in Los Angeles, CA
www.wonderwell.press

WONDERWELL

Distributed in the US by Publishers Group West
and in Canada by Publishers Group Canada

Printed and bound in Canada

To:

Duncan and Pat, my greatest champions

Suzanne, the best of the best

Gigi, the future

CONTENTS

INTRODUCTION

ELLO AND WELCOME! I am sure you're eager to get cracking on ways and means to change the world, but I would be remiss if I did not share a bit about my background and perspective with you beforehand. I started my first social impact venture, a sustainable fashion line, twenty-eight years ago at age twenty-five, and I have since founded and co-founded three more. I have been part of countless social impact conferences, communities, and educational programs, have mentored dozens of aspiring entrepreneurs, and have spoken on the topic of social entrepreneurship internationally. While I have little formal business education, I would say that by this stage I have a "street MBA"—I earned my credentials through lived experience, rather than tests or degrees. All of my projects—some for-profit, some not-for-profit, and varying widely from reusable menstrual products to child-friendly workspaces—are motivated by a social change agenda.

As a general principle, I love growing things. This can include projects, businesses, relationships, plants, and ideas; all evoke a similar quality of creativity and nurturing to me. Nothing pleases me more than seeing something flourish and realize its potential, especially when it happens in unexpected or organic ways. This predilection informs my definition of entrepreneurship as something that is ideally generative, creative, and a profound act of self-expression. I should also add that my perspective is informed by my background as a white settler–Canadian cisgender woman living and working on unceded traditional Indigenous land (this book was mostly written on Kwantlen, Stó:lō, and xʷməθkʷəy̓əm Musqueam Nation territories), among other forms of visible social privilege. While my goal is to share the stories of everyday people and underrepresented leaders, I do not speak on their behalf. I am here to offer you inspiration along with accounts of lived experiences (rather than academic research) and practical advice, which I have endeavored to make as realistic and down-to-earth as possible.

My decades-long practice of starting and leading social change–driven initiatives has led me to a viewpoint of entrepreneurship that strongly differs from the tech-heavy, scale-oriented profile typically associated with Silicon Valley. Although, once upon a time, my creative, feminist soul would have dismissed starting an organization or company—especially a for-profit one—as restrictive and insufficiently political, I now hold the opposite view; today, my conviction is that founding a values-led enterprise of any size and type can be one of the most socially impactful things that you could set your heart, mind, and spirit to.

I see entrepreneurship quite differently than the way it's typically portrayed in the media, particularly in regards to who entrepreneurs are (or can be—hence the "everyday people" in this book's subtitle). Some common misperceptions that I want to address are the assumption that a business background or degree is necessary in order to start a venture, that a project must be "scalable" (in a state of constant financial growth), and that entrepreneurial projects must be for-profit.

I approach social entrepreneurship from an expansive perspective and, as such, am here to profile and champion a far more inclusive image of the entrepreneur than what you may be used to seeing. This includes people who, like me, may not have a business background, may not be white or male or driven by technology, and may not be seeking as their primary goal to "disrupt" anything, but rather to heal, nurture, and otherwise improve the world on any scale. Maybe you don't think of yourself as a businessperson, entrepreneur, leader, or changemaker—yet. That's okay. Maybe you primarily identify as an artist, parent, corporate worker, teacher, student, homemaker, tradesperson, or something else other than "entrepreneur." You might be racialized, female, transgender, or nonbinary, or a person with a disability who does not see many people who look like you on the covers of business magazines. What I am pretty certain of about you is that you are *curious*. Curious, possibly frustrated, and not one hundred percent down with "the way things are." I'm guessing that you'd like them to be different and could use a little inspiration, support, and encouragement to bring whatever is tugging at you to life. I wrote this book in order to encourage and support you in bringing your unique perspective, experience, and skills to bear on our collective challenges. The world needs you.

Social entrepreneurship as a concept has been around since the 1980s. The "social" part is shorthand for positive social and/or environmental impact. (There really is no separating them!) Under this approach, the core motivation for undertaking an initiative is to make the world a better place in some way. The initiative you end up undertaking could be as simple as a project or as vast as a full-blown multinational corporation—there just needs to be a vision, structure, plan, and desired outcome. Whether you decide to create an organic pet supply business, a nonprofit society to support people experiencing homelessness, a reusable takeout food container program, or pretty much anything else that represents *your expression* of world improvement, you've come to the right place to get started.

I was first introduced to this type of thinking via The Body Shop, Ben & Jerry's, and Patagonia. While these are large-scale examples, they were much smaller when they started in the 1980s and stood in stark contrast to the "greed is good" ethos of the day, as epitomized by the film *Wall Street*. They were remarkable in their approach and made a deep impression on me, all the more so as someone who came of age in an era characterized by conspicuous consumption and little regard for social and environmental consequences. These businesses were unique in that their charismatic founders genuinely wanted to do business in an explicitly progressive manner, finding creative ways to integrate initiatives like opposing animal testing, promoting environmental stewardship, and offering in-house child-care as part of their basic value propositions and business processes. In building their businesses this way, these founders—Anita Roddick, Ben Cohen and Jerry Greenfield, and Yvon Chouinard—gave their customers the ability to use their purchasing power to support meaningful social and environmental change.

These founders also shared the characteristic of coming from a nontraditional business background. Roddick was a mom looking for a sustainable way to support her daughters while her husband worked abroad; Cohen was a college dropout and Greenfield worked as a lab technician; and Chouinard was a rock climber and outdoor enthusiast. They also did not start their ventures with the primary aim of growing massive, internationally recognized brands; rather, their goals were to offer innovative people- and planet-friendly solutions above all else. They were everyday people who used the tools of business in service of the greater good.

The decades since have practically seen a revolution around environmentalism and other forms of social change activism, and how they intersect with entrepreneurship. In response to concerns about climate change, plastic pollution, and JEDI (justice, equity, diversity, and inclusion) on teams and in policies, consumers like you began demanding explicit and verifiable commitments to social and environmental justice from the organizations that you buy from and donate to. Some of the best-known, largest for-profit companies currently attempting to do this creatively (with mixed results, I should add—good intentions are not enough to *actually ensure* doing good) include TOMS shoes, Warby Parker, and Seventh Generation. Organizations like B Lab—a nonprofit that rigorously evaluates and ranks businesses' overall social and environmental impact and certifies those that pass as B Corporations (known as B Corps for short)—have arisen in order to create community, ensure transparency, and fight greenwashing, which is the practice of making false or misleading claims about a product or company's environmental impact.

Although large companies like these have the reach to effect more widespread change, to me, social entrepreneurship at the grassroots level represents the most potent means of remaking capitalism itself. We are small but mighty, nimble, creative, and canny. I realize that this may sound a bit grandiose, but imagine for a moment that you and everyone who has ever had the inkling of a social impact initiative actually went for it: it would literally change the world.

I firmly believe that it's time for *all initiatives of all sizes* to prioritize tackling social and environmental issues as their primary raison d'être. This is not just about taking some of the profits of a mainstream business and then giving back (as laudable as that can be), and it's no accident that "social" comes before "entrepreneurship": I am advocating for impact as the whole point, not as a nice-to-have. I also believe that it's time to recognize the value of projects and ventures of all sizes, not just those with the capacity to scale. (Scale, as you'll come to see, is something that I am borderline obsessed with unpacking and reimagining.) To date, scale—often even over profitability in recent years—has been the principal measure of successful organizational growth, with a focus on performance indicators like sales and number of customers. But should these metrics be the main or only ones? What about social and environmental impact: shouldn't these constitute part of how we evaluate and define success?

I started writing this book shortly before COVID-19 hit. Initially, I wondered whether it should be put on hold until the pandemic was over; then I realized that "over" was likely not going to be definitive, and if anything, the book's core message—essentially, *do what you can with what you've got to make the world a better place where you are*—was going to be more relevant than ever as we moved into a "new normal" (or as I like to think of it, "post-normal"). Sensing that our very definition of things like "normal," "work," "opportunity," "resources," and "community" were never going to be the same again, I decided to double down and recommit to seeing it through.

I think you'll agree that we find ourselves in a time of global reckoning. The structural and social flaws that existed before COVID-19 and George Floyd's murder were already there—there just needed to be a spark cast upon a bone-dry forest for the flames to erupt. Everything that wasn't working before has now been exposed and exacerbated.

Now, more than ever, nothing is certain (not that it ever was). This is the double edge of these times: they are so messed up and yet so rich in opportunity. One monumental example is the current urgent conversation unfolding about racism and other forms of social inequity. Now that white supremacy has finally been widely recognized as a systemic issue that demands far more than just having a "diversity lens" applied to it, the opportunity exists to dismantle, heal, or completely reimagine entire systems. While this may be overwhelming to some, personally, I find it thrilling. There are few organizations in existence right now that would not benefit from self-reflection, accountability, and action plans for addressing social equity. It's a massive undertaking that demands that all of us step up to do the work; so, let's do it.

Of course, you don't need me to tell you that these are desperate times or that we are living in an era where corporations and governments have largely failed the planet and its citizens. Broadly speaking, the power systems of the post-industrial age have left us in a huge mess. Can we still reasonably hope that these institutions will save us from climate change or fix social inequities? Of course not. As I see it, widespread social enterprise in all its forms has the potential to become a global paradigm for building a better future, if we can just let go of the assumption that bigger is necessarily better. To be clear, assuming that a venture has social impact embedded at its core, scaling it necessarily increases its benefit; what I am pointing to here specifically is an argument for there being more mission-driven initiatives started by a far more inclusive group of founders, rather than fewer, scale-driven entities.

Which brings me to you, wonderful everyday person who wants to change the world. Let's do this, together. My feeling is that when we include everyone, *especially those who have been marginalized or are underrepresented*, we start to see the most healing, innovative, and game-changing ideas emerge. It's an opportunity to redefine ourselves and what matters to us in order to move into a new era of inclusion, creativity, and values-driven entrepreneurial practices.

As famously put by the beloved author Arundhati Roy, "Another world is not only possible, she is on her way. On a quiet day, I can hear her breathing." Today, this post-COVID world, metaphorically speaking, is in that quiet day. As I'm writing this, it is literally quiet, with normally busy restaurants, retail businesses, libraries, and civic spaces empty and shuttered. Instead of airplanes, we are hearing birds; instead of traffic, we are hearing one another's voices. This is a time of immense possibility and potential.

So, here is my invitation: join me in exploring what it takes to open yourself up to acting as a changemaker. This book is for anyone who has ever felt scared, frustrated, or overwhelmed about the challenges of our times, from a global pandemic, climate change, and other environmental issues, to racial, gender, and economic inequality, and so much more. We have all had the experience of wishing that someone would *just do something* about the thing that drives us crazy, or imagined how great it would be if a certain thing existed.

Perhaps you have experienced having your back against the wall and needed to adapt to changing circumstances. Maybe you've had a full-blown vision but told yourself that you weren't the right person, or didn't have time, or were unqualified to achieve it. Or maybe you just wanted to make a difference but weren't sure how. Dear reader, this is the book for you.

HOW TO USE THIS BOOK

THIS BOOK TALKS ABOUT entrepreneurship in a way that is different from most standard books on the topic. It is my aim to be realistic and helpful without being jargony or intimidating, and to inspire you without creating false hopes. When I conceived of *The Greater Good*, I knew that I wanted to start with the inner self and work outward from there, building vision and making plans that grow from meaningful introspection.

I'm starting from the premise that you might not know exactly what sort of initiative you want to create or what your offering, product, or service will be. You may already be familiar, or even highly experienced, with the enterprise development and personal exploration concepts that I describe. What will likely be new and different is finding the combination of these things in one place. Throughout the book, I also offer stories and advice from other social entrepreneurs in order to illustrate a broad variety of enterprises, as well as to present diverse role models that I hope will resonate with, entertain, and inspire you. The first few chapters will help you to dream your purpose and vision into being with some exercises designed to encourage you to access your deepest values and understand your unique gifts. Later in the book, I'll walk you through the more nitty-gritty stages of making it real, from prototyping and connecting with a community to dealing with all manner of situations that will come up as you progress along your path.

Most business books don't start from this holistic place, but I believe that a priority shift of this manner is a major part of what needs to change to get us to a better place. If a certain chapter or part of the book does not feel relevant to you, I encourage you to approach it as a piece of narrative, as opposed to being instructive on a particular point. It's been my experience that sometimes all you have to do is witness someone's story for it to make an impression on you. The stories I've included in this book all demonstrate what can happen when you open up more fully to what is possible for you. I further encourage you to set aside expectations and simply sit back and see what comes up for you, as it may be surprising. If this seems frivolous, then absolutely jump ahead to wherever feels most relevant to you. I have a feeling that you may circle back another time. There is no need to approach this book in a linear way. I say this because it's been my experience that the journey of entrepreneurship is more cyclical than linear: a series of intuitive meanderings and unexpected outcomes that dictate next steps, rather than a plan that is strictly followed with a predictable result. I invite you to embrace whatever you undertake as an adventure that, rather than unfolding according to a plan, will reveal itself to you as it happens.

Whether you read this book from beginning to end or hop back and forth between chapters and exercises, I hope it will inspire you on the journey toward making your contribution to the greater good.

CHAPTER 1

Everyday People Doing Extraordinary Things

I BEGAN WRITING THIS CHAPTER in March 2020, a time many of us in the West now recognize as the pivotal moment when we realized the spread of COVID-19 was going to be devastating. It rapidly became clear that if we didn't work together as a global community, thousands—if not millions—of lives would be lost. "We're all in this together" became the common refrain. We learned that if we, as a species, did not stop tearing each other apart once and for all and turn instead to creating new systems of mutual support, we simply would not survive the crisis.

Hard-hitting as this lesson was, the basic principle wasn't new to me. A few years earlier, I was introduced to the revolutionary expression "collaboration is the new competition" by social entrepreneur Ilana Ben-Ari, and this new way of looking at the world has stayed with me ever since.

But let me back up a bit. In 2015, my and my business partner Suzanne Siemens's company, Lunapads, had been selected (along with Ilana's) among the top five applicants to receive a to-be-determined portion of a $500,000 interest-free loan pool. The fund was the creation of a remarkable new Toronto-based initiative to support and celebrate women entrepreneurs called SheEO (pronounced "She-E-O," a feminist spin on the CEO title). It was founded by Vicki Saunders, herself a former tech entrepreneur, in response to the pervasive gender bias she experienced in that sector. The money, rather than coming from a financial institution or venture fund, had been innovatively crowdsourced from five hundred Canadian women we called Activators, whose votes had then determined the top five recipient Ventures from a field of hundreds of applicants. Rather than the funds being allocated by a panel of "experts," we were summoned to Toronto with the other four top-ranked Ventures to negotiate which would receive what portion of the funds.

As if this wasn't unusual enough, the negotiation process was also completely novel and followed only two rules: the money could not all go to one Venture and also could not be equally divided. These metrics were unlike anything we had previously encountered in funding and entrepreneurial competitions. Most models presuppose a single winner, where the finalists, driven by self-interest, would essentially battle it out to receive the lion's share. The process in this case was the opposite. Our task instead was to collectively determine the *smartest* use of the funds for each business, with a goal of bonding us as a mutually supportive cohort. The exercise called on us to dig deeper individually and as a group to consider how much more successful we could be together, even as we sought to support our own interests. Central to the philosophical shift of "collaboration is the new competition" is the idea that individual success need not come at the expense of others. In fact, when we transcended a traditionally adversarial relationship, we were rewarded with better decisions and a broader network of support.

I share this story with you as a powerful example of the type of shift in entrepreneurial thinking and practice that I want to surface in this critical time of change and opportunity. The SheEO model is absolutely unique. Each year, approximately five hundred Activators each contribute $1,100 toward financing Ventures based on a set of sensible criteria that demonstrate basic financial viability, vision, and how the Venture's activities support the United Nations Sustainable Development Goals (SDGs). Having demonstrable social and environmental impact as a central motivating factor—or what I call being a "social venture"—is an essential prerequisite for being considered, alongside financial transparency and market viability. This non-negotiable primacy of making a difference is what I will spend the rest of the book arguing for and spelling out how to achieve.

So, what does this type of enterprise actually look like in practice? I'd like to briefly introduce you to the other SheEO Ventures with whom we shared this extraordinary experience, as a snapshot of the face of contemporary social entrepreneurship. These founders, as well as others highlighted in this book, are emblematic of how everyday people located their visions and found the courage to pursue them. My hope is that you will be inspired by, or even see something of yourself in one or more of them, as you begin to ponder what kind of project or venture you'd like to pursue.

These founders exemplify the type of values-led entrepreneurial ethos that I believe is becoming increasingly commonplace. As it happens, they are all cisgender women (meaning they identify with the gender they were assigned at birth), but this is obviously not a prerequisite. It's more like seeing a broader trend emerging where marginalized people—in this case women, many of them women of color—are bringing a different vision, lived experience, and set of values to the table than what has been considered "normal" to date. In addition to being simply great ideas that addressed issues that personally motivated each of them, their visions also have a far broader application toward the greater good.

Ilana Ben-Ari's Twenty One Toys teaches emotional intelligence skills like empathy, failure, and communication to children and adults alike. An industrial designer, Ilana originally developed her first product, the Empathy Toy, to facilitate play between blind and sighted children. Watching them play gave her the insight that the toy also had novel, universal applications for basically *anyone* who would benefit from enhancing their communication and relational skills. Just as Ilana introduced me to the expression "collaboration is the new competition," her toys essentially teach people to work together.

In Toronto, I witnessed firsthand how the Empathy Toy works. A pair of participants, one of whom is blindfolded, take turns describing what they are building with their identical sets of textured game pieces. The blindfolded participant tries to replicate what their partner is building without being able to see their partner's pieces, following only verbal descriptions. It was amazing to watch the cohort members find their way through explaining how to arrange the pieces; there was laughter, confusion, and even frustration. Ultimately, it was an exercise in trust, patience, and humility, and a perfect complement to the negotiation process we were engaged in. It was a moment that beautifully demonstrated the toys' power, as well as the human capacity to reach beyond our limitations, imagined or otherwise.

While Ilana's Venture focuses on empathy, **Sonia Strobel**'s promotes food security, sustainability, and economic justice. The shorthand way of thinking about her Venture, Skipper Otto Community Supported Fishery, is as a farmers market for seafood. It supports independent small-scale fishing in British Columbia, protecting valuable ocean resources while giving customers direct access to wild, sustainable seafood.

Sonia's community-focused Venture is taking on a powerful, well-established industry that offers little transparency about its supply chain. Sonia is steadfast in the face of challenging deep-pocketed competitors who do not share her concern for sustainability. Her background as a teacher could not be further from either fishing or entrepreneurship, yet she has risen to the challenge and now employs her profound communication skills in a new way. I highlight this as it's also true of the rest of the group: none of us started out in our careers with a goal of becoming entrepreneurs. Rather, we were called to it through personal circumstances and learned as we went.

Nadia Hamilton is the founder of Magnusmode, an accessibility partner for corporations committed to creating a more inclusive world for people with autism and other cognitive disabilities, which she started while still a university student. Inspired by her experience helping her brother Troy, who has autism, to manage daily tasks such as getting dressed and brushing his teeth, she created a set of hand-drawn cards to remind him how to perform his daily routine independently. When she realized that the cards could bring benefit to a far wider range of people with autism as well as an array of other cognitive disabilities, her Venture was born. Today, Magnusmode cards and the companion app help people like Troy navigate the world on their own terms. By marrying technology with her passion for accessibility and support from corporate partners, Nadia is delivering a meaningful solution for making daily life easier for individuals whose needs are not traditionally centered.

Toni Desrosiers is the founder of Abeego, a reusable beeswax food wrap. Abeego offers an easy way to reduce single-use plastic in our lives, while at the same time extending the freshness of our food and cutting down on waste. Toni's innovative products are born from her experience as a holistic nutritionist and are a great lesson in biomimicry. If you think of the natural, breathable skin of a lemon or avocado, as opposed to the sealed quality of plastic, you can see how this works in nature. Abeego is the same; it keeps food alive.

I would be remiss if I did not include in this list of inspiring entrepreneurs my business partner **Suzanne Siemens**, whom I have been working with since 2000 and who has been the company's CEO since 2013. Loosely speaking, I would call her a corporate dropout. Raised by strict immigrant parents who (understandably) wanted her to have a secure, prosperous career, she initially became a CPA and worked at several large firms. By the time we met at a community leadership course in 1999, she was nearing the end of her rope and feeling increasingly disillusioned by her then-employer's shareholder-first values. Meanwhile, I had recently closed my retail store and garment factory in order to focus on developing Lunapads, a line of washable cloth menstrual pads and period underwear that I had been developing alongside my artisanal fashion business. When the feminist fashion designer met the unhappy accountant, part of what attracted us to one another was how different we were. While we were working on a project together as part of our coursework, a friendship was created through shared values and diverse skills. We have now been working together for over twenty years. I have a great deal more to say about our partnership in general later in the book, but for now, I will simply convey that she is one of the best people I have ever known and that the company would not be anywhere close to where it is today without her skill and leadership.

Diverse points of individual inspiration provided the courage for these women to innovate, and in the process, they became new versions of themselves. Growing our Ventures has not been a completely comfortable journey, which I believe is true for many of us who did not start out thinking of ourselves as swashbuckling entrepreneurs, but rather as everyday people—as fashion designers, holistic nutritionists, teachers, students, and accountants, for example. Growing outside of your current identity and comfort zone is one of the most exciting and rewarding parts of creating your version of the greater good.

A major attribute I noticed about all of these entrepreneurs as I came to know them was that, while their Ventures were rooted in deeply personal motivations, when it came to their self-expression as leaders, it wasn't about *them*. Not that they were self-effacing—far from it—but I wasn't seeing a focus on personal branding, ego-driven behavior, or the need to be right or dominate discussions. These were grounded, self-aware grown-ups who wanted to get something done and intuitively recognized that we were going to go further together—that we were there as colleagues, friends, and allies, not competitors.

I have come to see this type of authentic, humble, get-it-done attitude as a hallmark of sincere social entrepreneurs. It stands in contrast to some recent examples of "rock star," "disruptor" types keen to appropriate the messages of social impact in order to drive their own desire for self-aggrandizement, with little regard for things like treating staff and colleagues respectfully. I am proud to call those social entrepreneurs my SheEO sisters and privileged to share their stories and wisdom.

RADICAL GENEROSITY

All five of the founders highlighted above have been immersed in a few core SheEO concepts, which I'd like to share as a way of helping you reimagine what entrepreneurship can be. You may be surprised, as I was, at how opposed these principles are to traditional business practices. The first is radical generosity, a concept rooted in a belief in abundance (as opposed to scarcity) as an underlying mindset. Radical generosity posits an open-ended belief system in terms of what's available to us, as opposed to the assumption that whatever we seek to obtain needs to be wrested away from someone else, and that resources overall—whether physical, imaginative, or intellectual—are limited.

Traditional business practice presumes a finite amount of opportunity, market share, and customers who must be acquired, converted, and prevented from being wooed away by wily competitors. Radical generosity takes a very different mindset—one that presumes abundance, celebrates good ideas over being right, and fosters creative approaches to partnership over "killing the competition."

In mainstream business thinking, when the presumption becomes an us vs. them, better/worse, winner/loser binary proposition, I feel like things go wrong, or at least become unhelpfully distracting. Do we really need to eliminate or otherwise beat out anyone with an offering similar to ours? And more importantly, in my opinion, is this the wisest place to put our attention? The core, visceral assumption that underlies this type of thinking is fear-driven scarcity that encourages an adversarial relationship with anyone else in our space (product or market segment). Basing our focus on this dynamic can be extremely reductive, in that we find ourselves defining our projects or brands based on how we measure up to these other offerings, as opposed to looking within and showcasing our unique light and story as well as those we seek to serve.

When we understand that we are actually *interdependent* and that our collective survival depends on preserving relationships, we can see the glimmer of a new perspective around ideas like competition. And for those who say that competition promotes excellence, I would argue that collaboration does, too. Competition has also shown itself to be highly damaging, inefficient, and counterproductive. It's time we gave a different mindset a shot.

I believe our economic systems can evolve and that the practice of business, and capitalism itself, have the potential to move from an extractive, transactional form into one that is regenerative and relational. The days when we assumed that the planet, its people, and resources were there to be exploited and leveraged for purely financial profit and growth at all costs (extractive) are dwindling. We are being regenerative when we create conditions not just for our own prosperity, but for the Earth's repair and renewal. Social entrepreneurs are at the forefront of this shift, and it's essential that we not just offer sustainable products and services, but that we do so in ways that reflect and embrace our humanity (relational). As an overall practice, we are creating conditions not only for our own prosperity, but for the Earth's. Think of yourself as a grateful houseguest in a beautiful home. You want to leave it better than you found it, right?

FOLLOWING THE ENERGY

Another core SheEO concept is "following the energy," which is about forms of wisdom and knowing that are nonlinear and not necessarily quantifiable—in other words, intuitive. Whether you call this gut knowledge or "just knowing," I feel like it's something that we all understand, yet is seldom, if ever, validated as a legitimate rationale for decision-making. When you are following the energy, you are awake to every conversation, feeling, and seemingly random interaction that comes your way. I think of it as following cosmic breadcrumbs (as in the fabled trail in a forest) or clues (as in a detective). Overall, it feels like openness, curiosity, and gentle anticipation: again, not things that are traditionally valued in a business context. After all, how do you quantify or qualify intuition? Yet it matters so deeply.

Another key SheEO practice, called Ask/Give, was beautifully exemplified in the organization's response to the COVID-19 crisis. In a show of community support and resourcefulness in action, weekly Zoom calls were immediately set up where Venture leaders rated their businesses' needs according to green (okay), yellow (unsteady) or red (crisis), and were given the opportunity to share their needs (Asks) as well as offer ways to support other Ventures (Gives). This practice was already a SheEO staple; it's understood that when we are clear about our needs, for the most part, we are already resourced within the network of Ventures and Activators to get what we need to keep going. In one case, a CEO was going to be unable to make her next staff payroll. (I should add that the staff are all individuals with barriers to employment and many were in precarious housing situations, so this intervention literally prevented them from becoming homeless.) Another Venture currently enjoying rapid growth stepped in to cover it. A third Venture, led by a journalist, set up a national petition calling on the Government of Canada to do more to support small and medium-sized enterprises, which went on to inform actual government policy. Others simply needed to know that they were not alone, to vent and share their fears. A great many organizations talk about values like trust, respect, and sustainability (wonderful!); I would argue that SheEO takes these to a whole other level of concrete expression.

As out there as "radical generosity" and "following the energy" may sound to you, whether or not the details resonate with you personally, these concepts, alongside a successful new financial mechanism of crowdsourced zero-interest loans, propose a fully articulated, viable alternative to the darker side of capitalism and business in a social impact–based, humane, and genuinely innovative way. SheEO sees the opportunity to build a different structure, with our own values and rules—a goal that I share in writing this book.

My hope is that by kicking off with stories about these real-life leaders and ventures and a powerful community, you will feel inspired, intrigued, and less alone. As I reflect on them, I remember how each founder made me feel as I came to get to know them. Part of me was inspired and kind of in awe, yet another part of me was resonating with a sense of kinship, of feeling met by a nourishing friend or teacher, and more encouraged to pursue my vision, as different as it was from theirs. I hope you will feel the same way as we dive deeper into reimagining entrepreneurship by looking at these inner "soul traits" in the next chapter. I invite you to consider which qualities resonate with you as you look at what may propel you toward your version of the greater good.

CHAPTER 2

Soul Traits of Social Entrepreneurs

As I shared in the last chapter, I knew that I wanted this book to be about more than just my experience right from the get-go. I wanted to learn more about the other Nadia Hamiltons and Ilana Ben-Aris out there, to illustrate the fact that social entrepreneurs can look and act in so many different ways, each with their own stories, gifts, and wisdom. My thinking was also that even if my own story did not resonate with you, perhaps someone else's might. Plus, as we have already started to see, these entrepreneurs and their journeys are just so inspiring. So, I wrote a simple survey and sent it out to my colleagues to gather more stories.

I received close to one hundred responses and was stunned by the diversity of personal backgrounds, ventures, and depth of passion that they reflected. I was rewarded with some of the most poignant, thought-provoking, and deeply personal stories that I could imagine. There were stories from artists, parents, fitness professionals, sexual health educators, journalists, musicians, scientists, designers, accountants, academics, and more. I should add that they were almost all women, mostly from Canada and the United States, though I did get some wonderful responses from participants in France, the Netherlands, South Africa, Australia, and New Zealand. Respondents ranged from college age to retirees. Although I did not ask about gender or sexual orientation (I did ask for pronouns), several mentioned that they were nonbinary and/or queer, and I had many responses from people who made it clear that they were Black, Brown, Asian, or Indigenous.

Their ventures and projects ranged from creative fundraising initiatives to innovative lactation support products, from inclusive technology ventures to adaptive vehicles. If anything, it made me think that social entrepreneurship was a natural place for marginalized people. It stood to reason, I thought, that if you were looking to make the world a better place, folks who have been oppressed or excluded by traditional power systems would have fresh ideas for something different, better, and more humane.

One aspect that stood out for me was that the respondents did not start their careers as entrepreneurs. They became entrepreneurs, often reluctantly. This transformation was one of the most exquisite and fascinating parts of writing this book: learning how these everyday people had become motivated, accepted a challenge, acted on it, persevered, asked for help, failed, flourished, despaired, and celebrated. This is why I wanted them to be part of the book; I wanted readers to see that if these people could do what they did, *so can any of us*.

As someone who was raised on the "bigger is better" notion of scale when it comes to business or project aspirations (*Go Big or Go Home!*), where the object is basically to get more of everything, the survey responses made me start to muse on the notion of lateral scale, or what I have come to call "radiance." This is a multidimensional, proliferative concept of growth and impact, which I will share in greater depth in chapter 11. What I mean by this is, instead of looking at an individual business and wondering how to make it as big as possible, what if you looked at a demographic and wondered how to create as many ventures out of their ideas as possible? In other words, creating more enterprises of diverse sizes instead of fewer, bigger ones. How would these two strategies compare in the long run if our metrics of success were not just top-line growth but also things like reduced greenhouse gas emissions and commuting hours, increased personal happiness, family well-being, job satisfaction, and social innovation, among other, more humane metrics? This became my new obsession; what would the result be if these people and their ideas were actualized and supported? What if, alongside all the good things that these ventures would surely create, an entirely new way of thinking about the purpose of commerce and nature of growth also emerged?

In creating the survey, I had hoped to understand not only what had inspired people's ideas but, vitally, what had motivated them to act on them. In reading people's answers to the questions and in follow-up interviews, several recurring themes emerged, which I have come to think of as the key "soul traits" of social entrepreneurs and which I'd like to briefly highlight here. Many of these stories will appear at greater length later in the book—this is just a taste. Perhaps you will recognize aspects of yourself in this list.

COLORING OUTSIDE THE LINES

Social entrepreneurs are so creative! Because their premise in starting a project usually comes from a nontraditional place and they themselves often fall outside the traditional profile of a business-person or entrepreneur, it's not surprising that they generate such unique, innovative ideas and organizational models. Some respondents with traditional business education and experience said that they had needed to unlearn their previous ways of thinking, while others who did not have this experience said that they felt unencumbered by limiting beliefs and expectations, which allowed them to try new things and be less afraid of failure. Social entrepreneurs are by definition "redefiners," in that they inherently question the accepted purpose of business-as-usual capitalism by putting the "social" part first. These folks go even further, though, coming up with their own definitions of goals, scale, profits, success, and more.

What am I talking about? Have you ever heard the expression "Together Everyone Achieves More" (TEAM)? The Five Ps of Marketing? The VUCA worldview? The 7 Habits of Highly Effective People? There are endless examples of these buzzy business acronyms. But are they inherently true, or did someone, once upon a time, effectively make them up?

Let's take as an example VUCA (volatile, uncertain, complex, and ambiguous), a post–Cold War US Army term that was coined to describe the worldview of the day and has regained popularity in common business vernacular in recent years. My question about VUCA is not whether or not it's true; it's about whether or not the concept is helpful, motivating, or inspirational. Personally, it just makes me scared, and scared is not a great place for anyone to create from. Fear is often dismissed ("Choose love over fear!"), but it can, of course, be a sensible and highly valuable reaction in critical situations. Yet fear triggers the fight, flight, or freeze mechanism in the brain, which is not helpful for getting creative or making decisions.

In early 2015, Suzanne and I were asked to give a presentation to an audience of women entrepreneur clients of a major Canadian bank in Calgary, titled "Entrepreneurial Ingenuity in the Age of Constant Disruptive Change." The Alberta economy was hard-hit at the time and the organizers were looking for practical yet inspiring content. I had read up on VUCA while attending the THNK School of Creative Leadership, and although I got the concept, something about it left me feeling hopeless, depleted, and frazzled. How were we going to do what was being asked of us while staying true to ourselves? I decided that we needed to reframe VUCA in a more positive and constructive light. Here is what we came up with: CODE.

- C = Colorful
- O = Opportunity-rich
- D = Diverse
- E = Evolving

We often forget, in our never-ending quest to keep up with the latest lingo and concepts, that we have the ability to see what's true for ourselves and express it in our own ways. Our audience loved CODE. Yes, we were saying, these are scary times. But what *actually serves us* when we think about that in terms of our personal worlds and businesses? CODE feels exciting while still acknowledging that the world is an unsettled place. Similarly, in response to the classic business concept coined by Jim Collins and Jerry Porras with the acronym BHAG (big, hairy, audacious goal), I prefer to use "beautiful, healthy, achievable, generative" as my personal success metric. I also came up with a cheeky reframing of the classic tech industry imperative "move fast and break things," to "move purposefully and nurture things."

TRUE GRIT

Social entrepreneurs with true grit have the patience, tenacity, and determination to persist, often in the face of immense challenges. Persistence, though unglamorous and underrated, is a common-sense ally for anyone trying to accomplish something that matters to them.

I love the word *grit*; it has a raw, honest quality that related terms like persistence, commitment, and perseverance lack. Grit implies edge, messiness, and overcoming adversity—being "bloodied but unbowed," to reference W.E. Henley's 1888 poem "Invictus." It acknowledges that there is a cost to our struggles and that entrepreneurial success is not as simple as getting a challenge figured out and then reaping the rewards. Grit also reminds me of dirt, which is deeply resonant to me as a devoted gardener. You can't grow plants in a garden without getting dirty, and you need to be unafraid of stretching yourself outside of your comfort zone in order to bring about something glorious.

Patrice Mousseau is an Anishinaabe woman and journalist from the Fort William First Nation in Ontario. When we initially met, she was in the earliest stages of growing her line of homegrown organic skincare products from a side hustle to a fully commercial business, and in the years since, I have been humbled to witness the challenges she has overcome as a businessperson, racialized woman, and single mother. She shared with me how often people suggest that her success is due to the fact that she is Indigenous and, as such, supposedly enjoys considerations not available to her white counterparts. This form of judgment serves to undermine the very real, sustained efforts she had to make to build her business in the face of multiple layers of oppression. I can only imagine how frustrating it must be to repeatedly confront systemic bias as you build your venture, only to be told that you effectively don't deserve the success that you achieve in spite of it.

In hindsight, when I think of every business book that I have read, precious few have offered even a shred of self-reflection about the idea that we do not all start from the same place in terms of access to resources and opportunities. I can't recall an example of one that explores the notion that for some of us, just getting out of bed in the morning (or even having a bed, for that matter) is not necessarily a given. Building our projects will not be an easy, flower-lined road of yeses and large checks. The grit required by people who are used to being underestimated in regular life will likely be doubly so as they undertake to bring their visions to life. Such people are the ones we collectively have the most to learn from.

MAKING LEMONADE

"If life gives you lemons, make lemonade." I am borrowing this classic adage that points to using personal trauma or adversity as creative fuel. This was one of the most common themes expressed by the entrepreneurs I interviewed, and also the most moving. Some of these people literally brought me to tears with their stories of courage and resilience in the face of unimaginable hardship.

Mary Letson is a perfect example. Following her recovery after a harrowing journey with breast cancer, she wanted to give back to others by raising funds for supplemental treatment and supports not covered by health insurance (including massage, physiotherapy, wig fitting, acupuncture, supplements, and meal delivery), which she credits with making a huge difference to her recovery. In addition to wanting to give others in her community undergoing cancer treatment the "extras" she'd had the privilege of being able to access, she also wanted to transform her relationship to the disease that had taken so much from her and redefine the notion of being a survivor to something, in her eyes, more empowered. A lifelong sports enthusiast, she hit on the idea of creating an annual fundraising swim event on the island where she lives in British Columbia, not only as a way to raise the funds but to assert herself in this new, post-survivor role. To date, she and her SwimBowen Society team have raised over $50,000 and reshaped a grueling journey for herself while benefiting dozens of others confronting their versions of it.

GIFTS FROM THE MARGINS

Part of this ability means using the unique perspectives brought about by being outside the dominant culture to inspire new ideas and insights. Lemonade makers' ideas are unique and valuable *because* they are outsiders, not in spite of it.

The phrase "gifts from the margins" relates to a story that Suzanne and I often tell as part of the Lunapads/Aisle story. As much as the brand has been praised for its prescient embrace of transgender and nonbinary individuals as part of its intersectional feminist values, the understanding and commitment did not come immediately for us on a personal level. Initially, despite the persistent championing of the issue by a key team member (who later came out to us as nonbinary), we hesitated about making significant changes to our language and product designs to be more explicitly inclusive of this "fringe" group. This was on the grounds that we had limited resources and needed to allocate them to our larger group of cisgender (people who identify with the gender assigned to them at birth) customers.

The team member patiently persisted. Coming to see the sense in their perspective as we became more educated, we gradually let go of our old fears and committed to removing gendered language from the website and developing a gender-inclusive product in the form of a boxer brief–style period undergarment. Until that point, all of our styles had been traditionally feminine, with color choices leaning that way as well.

It took us almost two years to develop the boxer brief, yet when we finally launched the product in early 2016, it was far and away our most successful product launch in the company's history. In case you're thinking, as I did, *Wow, there are a lot more gender-nonconforming folks out there than I thought*, give your head a shake. What the launch numbers showed us wasn't just that trans customers were buying the boxer brief; it was that *everyone* was. So much for thinking that the dominant majority is who you want to cater to—it turned out that the needs of marginalized people were actually pointing the way to *the future*.

Lots of marginalized and underrepresented people showed up to share their stories in the survey: people who felt like they didn't fit in as traditional customers, consumers, or citizens; immigrants, LGBTQIA+ individuals, and Indigenous people; those with uncommon skill sets, ways of thinking, and interests, who see that just because something is missing in the market, it doesn't mean that the world doesn't need it. It's more like an indicator of who has been in charge up to that point, who has decided what normal is, and whose voices and values are included . . . or not.

STRONGER TOGETHER

This trait involves not assuming or embracing an ego-driven, individualistic entrepreneurial persona. Instead, it means asking for help, working collaboratively, and building community. My respondents had great ideas to make their own lives better but also wanted to make life better for others, and often created new structures to embrace or celebrate these people. They defy the traditional "lone wolf" entrepreneurial stereotype. Given that the point of their enterprises is some form of shared social impact or equity, it makes sense that they would instinctively include others while building generosity and diversity into their leadership styles and the DNA of their ventures.

The largest-scale version of this that I can speak to personally is SheEO founder Vicki Saunders. Most entrepreneurs—even social entrepreneurs—build their ventures in order to serve a specific need or market gap, not to change something systemic. SheEO is a response to the fact that women are so drastically underserved and underrepresented in the business and entrepreneurial worlds. It exists to offer a new solution, one based on our needs and values. As I've watched her leadership over the years, Vicki has ceaselessly sought to elevate and make space for racialized and transgender women and those marginalized in other ways, both within her team and in the broader community. Beyond this, she embraces a distributed, nonhierarchical leadership model, all while exhibiting remarkable humility.

IMPACT IS THE NEW BLACK

This one may seem obvious given that the book is about social entrepreneurship, but it's worth noting that impact is not just a nice-to-have for these folks; it's their entire rationale and, as such, is an immense source of inspiration, energy, creativity, and drive.

My longtime colleague Amy Robinson typifies this soul trait. A lifelong environmentalist, she saw an opportunity to elevate the cause of supporting grassroots economic sustainability through education, awareness, and advocacy. She created LOCO BC, a vast network of sustainable small businesses located in the Greater Vancouver area that hosts events and encourages consumers to shop locally whenever possible. LOCO's research has been used to advocate for small businesses by groups across BC and in the rest of Canada and has resulted in more support from local city councils, as well as increased awareness from consumers.

IMPACT IS ALSO THE NEW CURRENCY

Given the current vogue for scalable businesses, it was surprising that financial scale as a motivation took a firm back seat to impact for my interviewees. What motivates them is the particular change they can make and taking it as far as they can, rather than just being big for bigness's sake. Further to that, scale of any variety beyond basic success (as defined by being effective and sustainable, as opposed to scalable) did not seem to be a hugely motivating factor. The biggest incentive for many was simply wanting to give it a try, with impact as the driver for taking the plunge.

WILLINGNESS TO TRANSFORM

This trait means being willing to change key self-perceptions in order to realize your vision. It goes beyond just getting outside your comfort zone; for many respondents, taking on their projects entailed significant personal transformation.

At Groundswell, Vancouver's alternative business school, they often talk about "nurturing entrepreneurs from the inside out," meaning that in order to start a venture, you first need to build a new sense of self. Many of the respondents to my survey needed to do some major mental and emotional shapeshifting to get their heads around starting a venture and did so with great success.

Margaret Magdesian, a Brazilian-born, Quebec-based biotech entrepreneur with a PhD in biochemistry, started Ananda Devices to maximize the impact of the research she was doing around increasing the speed and safety of animal-free drug testing through nanotechnology. Initially daunted by the idea of starting and running a company instead of being a successful laboratory scientist, she nevertheless persisted, fueled by the realization that if she did not take this step, the opportunity that the technology represented might never be fully realized.

Among the survey respondents, I heard stories from singers, videographers, marine biologists, fitness trainers, scientists, journalists, and more, all of whom courageously made the leap from their chosen career paths and identities into the world of social entrepreneurship. It was not always easy or comfortable, yet they let their desire to change the world override their fears and self-limiting beliefs to move their ideas forward.

HONORING YOUR CALLING

This phrase kept popping into my head so persistently that even though few of the respondents actually used this language, I knew that I had to include it. Other words for "calling" include vision, intuition, emergence, or whatever way you choose to express non-linear forms of knowing that someone was somehow meant to do a certain thing. I have heard it characterized as a small inner voice, "just knowing," or as a series of signs, coincidences, or events that consistently and irresistibly pointed to a particular idea.

Sabrina Rubli, founder of Femme International, a non-governmental organization that uses menstrual and reproductive health education to empower women and girls in East Africa, shared the following with me as an example:

21

I have always been passionate about women's rights and women's health. For me, using my skills and ability to empower women was not a question—I feel like it is my responsibility. Once I had the idea for Femme in my head, it was all I could think about, and I dove in headfirst.

DANCING WITH THE DEMONS

Demons that can arise as you begin a new venture include impostor syndrome, fear of failure, and profound self-doubt. I call it dancing rather than slaying, because many respondents found ways to be *with* their demons instead of trying to vanquish them. This key insight is more about making peace with yourself than trying to crush a part of you that may not actually need to be crushed for you to move forward.

Personally speaking, this is one of my biggest challenges. No matter how much experience and "success" I have under my belt, believing in myself is still hard to do consistently. Self-doubt is one of the more persistent and pervasive issues that came up for the entrepreneurs that I surveyed, especially for marginalized people.

What is clear to me about these people is that although their demons came at them full force, they grappled/danced with them and carried on. They did not let the demons win, which would have meant these brave souls never trying to realize their dreams in the first place. Their other piece of courage was having the humility and vulnerability to admit that they struggled at all. I can think of very few examples of a white, male business leader speaking openly about self-doubt or fear of failure. I wonder whether they actually do experience this and just don't talk about it, or whether they are, in fact, so sure of themselves that it never occurs to them to question their abilities.

For Elizabeth Sheehan—the creator of Climate Smart, a climate impact assessment tool for businesses—fear showed up as self-doubt, my personal Fear CEO. Internal voices would persistently question her ability to lead. "I had this crazy pattern where if things were challenging, the voice said that I was responsible and wasn't smart enough or doing whatever task at hand right," she shared with me. "I had to train myself (a work in progress) to curate a more welcoming and spacious attitude toward the inevitable ups and downs of a social venture." Whatever fear may look like for you, know that you're far from alone and that it's a natural internal response to the fact that you're considering taking on something you have likely never done before. We'll get much deeper into this topic later in the book and explore creative and compassionate tools for dealing with it constructively.

Before moving on, take a moment to consider how these soul traits land for you. Do you identify with any of them? Did they inspire more traits to add to this list? Perhaps you can already sense which of your innate qualities may be emerging as you consider taking next steps to express your vision for a better world.

CHAPTER 3

Finding Your Why

WITHOUT KNOWING WHERE YOU ARE in your journey to social entrepreneurship, I am going to assume that it may be as vague as a feeling of uneasiness or longing, or a sense of unmet potential in the world or aspect of your life. Perhaps you are already in a time of transition, in the liminal space between career or life phases. Rather than looking externally for direction, this chapter is about taking stock of your own lived experience as a way to access inspiration for your Why. Drawing from the term popularized by Simon Sinek in his classic TED talk and subsequent book, *Start with Why*, I am inviting you to consider your past as a potential pattern rather than a series of random incidents.

As we have begun to see already, each of the entrepreneurs highlighted so far found inspiration for their venture in their own life and experiences. Their personal history gave them cues for what to create as well as insights into their own strengths and gifts, and these became the tools they used to realize their goals. I invite you to begin to look at your own story and see what surfaces. Do any of your lived experiences provide an inkling of an idea? Perhaps you'd like to offer self-defense classes for girls and nonbinary youth, start a nonalcoholic spirits company to support the sober community, or import fair trade crafts or clothing to support artisans in the Global South. These are just a few examples of ideas I have seen in the universe of social entrepreneurship.

Looking within can tell you a lot about what venture or project may be calling you. Reflecting on my own life and the experiences that shaped my childhood led me to see how my adolescent rebelliousness paved the way to student activism, which eventually led to social entrepreneurship. This was extremely helpful to me as until I was able to draw those links, I had not seen myself as a "real businessperson," which deeply undermined my confidence, especially around people with commerce and MBA degrees. In this chapter, I'll share some of my experiences, as well as those of the entrepreneurs I interviewed. I'll also provide exercises to help you look at and bring to light the experiences, beliefs, and passions that have shaped you.

My own initial lightbulb moment in terms of entrepreneurship actually happened in slow motion, between 1992 and 1993. Until that point, the story that I had about my talents and career prospects was around social change leadership. I had had little to no exposure to anyone who called themselves an entrepreneur and imagined at the time that I might join the Canadian Foreign Service or become a social worker to earn a living. I should add that my childhood career dream of becoming a fashion designer also still tugged at me, which will become important later in my story. I needed to choose a career, or at least find a consistent way to support myself financially. Until then, I had held a series of unsatisfying office jobs and intermittently worked and traveled without really committing to developing a particular area of expertise. It was coming time to choose something that I could build as a career. A cosmic breadcrumb came when I was abruptly let go from a job and made a conscious choice to frame this time, which could have been scary, as an experience of self-discovery and resilience. I still remember thinking to myself at the time, *this is how you get to find out what you're made of.* I decided to take what I had been doing for years in generosity to friends and family (clothing alterations and diverse sewing projects) and start charging for it as a professional service. This also served to bolster my self-esteem as it affirmed that my skills were of value and gave me a greater sense of self-reliance.

As someone who came to feminist consciousness in my late teens, I had internalized the view that feminism and business were essentially morally irreconcilable. It was only through the lens of entrepreneurship—and thanks to Anita Roddick—that I found a way to situate myself as both changemaker and businessperson, where I could create what I wanted on my own terms. I had also realized at this stage that if you leave the people whose values you oppose in charge, then you can never expect change to happen. You have to get in there yourself if you want things to be different. Having my own business seemed like a wonderful way to challenge myself, express my values on my own terms, and see whether it was possible to sustainably monetize a social change agenda.

The final piece that motivated me to take the unusual step of starting everyware designs, my first company, at the relatively young age of twenty-five—and with no experience—was falling in love with a product that I made. As mentioned, I had been sewing since I was a kid, had always loved fashion design, and happened upon the idea of washable menstrual pads and period underwear thanks to my recurrent allergic reactions to the disposable pads and tampons I had been using until that point. As a feminist and budding environmentalist, I loved everything about the idea of reducing waste and rejecting the shame-based marketing culture of disposables. But it was the activity of using and washing the products that tapped into something deeper within me—a sense of self-love and liberation—and wanting to offer this feeling to other people with periods that made me go for it. Starting a business to make and sell my creations was the natural solution.

The company that is known as Aisle today (and was known as Lunapads from 2000 to 2020) was incepted in that moment. Little did I know that my unusual choice of focus was an early harbinger of what became a leading area of social venture innovation twenty years later: natural menstrual care. At the time, I don't think I thought of myself as a "social entrepreneur." It was more like I was an activist who was co-opting the tools of business to achieve my vision for a better world. It was only later that I became aware of the term and thought, *Yes! There is a name for people like me.*

We'll get back to my journey later in the book, but for now, I'd like to highlight a few of the inspiring stories from some of the entrepreneurs I interviewed. While not everyone necessarily had a full-on epiphany, all of these stories are examples of insight, motivation, turning points, and other major life experiences that sparked action.

As we saw in the last chapter, Nadia Hamilton's motivation for starting Magnusmode is one of the oldest and most primal of all: familial love. She grew up helping her brother Troy, a man living with autism, to complete everyday tasks like brushing his teeth. "To lessen his anxiety and support independence, I created hand-drawn step-by-step guides that he was able to follow along with and re-enact," she explains in her survey response. "Just simple crayon drawings on paper, the guides nonetheless provided the structure and foresight he needed to do things on his own."

When Troy graduated from high school, the homemade drawings were not enough to support him to participate in the world. Nadia explains:

> *I worked as a support worker throughout university, helping people with autism and other cognitive disabilities manage their day-to-day routines at home and school, or doing other activities in the community such as shopping. I realized that many families*

were facing a similar issue: that the world was not designed with the special needs of their loved ones in mind. That's when I decided to build Magnusmode, a company dedicated to removing the barriers that cause disability.

Nadia's venture exemplifies the "coloring outside the lines" belief system I spoke of earlier. In the past, the pervasive view has been that disabled people are somehow broken or unable to function correctly in a world that they have had precious little say in designing. Nadia asserts that this lack of an inclusive perspective and the limitations that it creates are the real cause of the disability, not the person. This insight, I would suggest, is a Why moment.

Magnusmode's primary tool, MagnusCards, is a digitized version of the hand-drawn solution Nadia made for her brother when they were younger. It's a strategy guide for life, with an ever-expanding library of guides in the form of card decks for home and community use. Companies across North America that share Magnusmode's vision of an accessible world sponsor the creation of branded card decks to help welcome and support customers with cognitive disabilities.

I don't think it's a stretch to say that Nadia's firsthand experience living with and loving her brother not only gave her the insights to see an opportunity to help, but further to offer a new perspective on how social biases are not immutable: they can be exposed, reframed, and leveraged to support a more compassionate and inclusive world-view and design process.

For Snugabell founder Wendy Armbruster, it was the experience of motherhood that triggered her to put her fashion design training to use in a new way. Wendy was working as a freelance apparel designer when she had her first baby and needed to pump breast milk because she didn't have maternity leave benefits. She describes how the challenges of early motherhood sparked a new idea for a hands-free pumping bra:

My then-husband would take the evening feed, which gave me a block of time to get some work done. The first time I used a breast pump, not only did my hands go numb because of postpartum carpal tunnel syndrome, but all I could think of the whole time was the dishes that needed to be done, the laundry that needed to be folded, and how there must be something on the market to hold the flanges for me. I Googled and found products that didn't impress me as a designer, that didn't have great reviews, and that were unattractive. I went to my sewing room and came up with a design that spoke to the design deficiencies reported online and then I intentionally chose beautiful fabrics, because I now know how extra important this is in the early days of motherhood. I saw it as an opportunity to not just solve a practical problem but also to help the user feel sassy, attractive, and more confident.

Beyond addressing a real, practical need and supporting positive self-esteem at what can be a fragile time in a person's life, Wendy is a proponent of the fourth trimester concept. In Western culture, the notion of pregnancy is limited to the traditional three trimesters and ends with the birth of the baby. The thinking behind the fourth trimester is more holistic and gives the message that the journey to motherhood actually takes longer and includes postpartum and nursing/breastfeeding. It's all a massive adjustment and can be hugely challenging. Wendy's business proudly embraces this with one of my favorite Why statements: "Snugabell empowers moms to rock the fourth trimester by designing and manufacturing high-quality, beautiful, and functional fourth trimester products that promote maternal and child health, and help moms retain a sense of individual style during a vulnerable and overwhelming time."

Finally, Wendy's story illustrates that there is never a perfect time to start a venture. There are very few of us with the time and resources to simply clear our schedules and devote the energy required to get it off the ground. Be prepared to do things gradually (which may frustrate the type-A personalities among us) and be creative and patient as you shift around the various other puzzle pieces of your life in order to make space to bring in this new element.

Parenthood showed up a few times in the survey responses as the Why behind a new venture. In Anthonia Ogundele's case, it was when her tween daughter arrived into her life that she became aware of the dearth of wholesome after-school activities, especially for Black youth, in her community. In response, she created Ethos Lab, safe spaces of culture and STEM-focused exploration where youth can co-create their experience to promote personal growth and development. She says:

> *My daughter arrived at eleven years old to our family and it was a great joy. When she asked me to go "hang out at the mall" with her friends, I immediately said no, and I asked myself,* Where can my daughter hang out where she receives social enrichment as well as intentional personal growth and development? *The next thought was,* How can this space reflect her intersectional identity as a Black girl with multiple needs and unique family/life experiences? *As such, I thought maybe I should give it a go.*

Interestingly, Anthonia's professional background is in disaster management. I can't think of better training to become an entrepreneur. Anthonia was also strongly motivated by wanting her daughter to have more Black women as role models in the STEM space.

> *There are few women of color, particularly Black women, in this innovation space. I thought by just taking the first step and trying that I might be able to inspire a younger generation of innovators. I have always done a lot of creative projects on the side and I felt like I was at the right point in my life to take the leap. But most importantly, I love my daughter.*

While the advent of COVID-19 has temporarily curtailed the vision for Ethọs as a physical space, the business has pivoted beautifully online, where it continues to build its following by offering innovative, youth-friendly programming. The first physical location of Ethọs is slated to open in fall 2021.

Vanessa LeBourdais, co-founder of an interactive environmental education program for children called DreamRider Productions, traces finding her Why as an environmentalist to her formative days spent on the wild west coast of Vancouver Island. After spending the first part of her career in the theater in Toronto, moving to the west coast of British Columbia awakened a deep love for the planet in her. She says:

> *The kitchen of where I was living at the time had big windows facing the backyard. Cedar trees in all directions, and ferns and mosses, grandfather's beard, crows, eagles, plus bears and cougars now and again if you didn't take proper care of your compost. As a Toronto-born girl, it amazed me.*
>
> *The day my landlady clear-cut the backyard, it began with a handwritten note on the kitchen table that said, "Don't go out back today. Trees falling." This from a woman who'd told us she'd prayed for each tree that was cleared for this house. Men came and cut the life down. Where there were fifteen shades of green, now there was mud and death. Then they burnt the stumps of these hundreds-year-old trees, so we had smoke for three days. Then trucks came and dragged the carcasses away. Then they literally paved paradise and put up a parking lot.*
>
> *I joined a dozen or so other young people who shared my outrage at some mass-scale logging that was taking place nearby and we got ourselves arrested to stop multinational logging companies from doing what had been done to my backyard. We sang songs that I wrote, we put our bodies on the line. We organized.*

The blockades were a lot like theater, I thought. Music, costumes, props, drama. I organized; I wrote songs; we sang.

I wanted to go back to the theater then. I didn't know why; it made no sense to me after helping save an ecosystem to go do musical theater. But I couldn't deny the call. So, I moved to Vancouver. I met my husband and we immediately began to write musicals together. Then in 1998, we were hired by the City of Vancouver to create a play about clean streets for elementary school kids. We made another one about recycling. In 2002, DreamRider Productions was born. Our work grew by word of mouth, municipality to municipality. We've reached over a million kids in fifteen countries so far.

Megan Sheldon started Seeking Ceremony to share ideas and stories from people who found unique ways to honor their life transitions through ritual. The idea had been forming for a few years, but it crystallized when she experienced a series of brutal life challenges and realized how the benefits of ceremony and ritual could be shared outside of their traditional religious confines. This is a classic example of making lemonade. Having found her Why through the experience of loss, Megan transmuted her pain into something that could be of benefit to others. She explains:

In a very short period of time, I experienced more loss than I had in my entire life. I had three miscarriages, lost my father-in-law, and my dad was diagnosed with lung cancer (he survived). It floored me just how isolating my grief was, and how most people stayed away because they didn't know what to say or do. I found great comfort in simple actions that I later realized were ceremonial. I lit a candle every morning. I wrote my wishes on stones and threw them into the ocean. I hosted fertility circles, inviting women to talk about their own fertility struggles. I wrote down my anger on paper and safely burned it in the forest. Nature became my cathedral, and ceremony became my way back to life.

I started to look at how the people around me grieved, but I also looked at how they celebrated. I realized there were so many rites of passage, so many moments and milestones, that we were missing out on. We weren't honoring our transitions—in school, in our careers, in our families and friendships. Other than marriage and childbirth, we were failing at honoring change and recognizing transformations.

My first initiative has been to connect with our local hospital and find ways to support grieving parents in the midst of pregnancy and infant loss by giving them ideas on how to start their grieving process. I also wanted to give our community better tools to support people going through this type of loss, as it's often hidden from plain sight.

I have seen time and time again how a personal experience, dream, or pain point can lead to gold when it comes to entrepreneurship. Part of the magic is that it is deeply personal. You have not just seen a gap in the market and exploited it; this is far more about the heart and right brain. I am talking about the ideas that call us, not ones that simply make sense.

Sometimes our Why shows up on its own, and other times it needs a little encouragement. Remember that the examples I cited took years in some cases to fully present themselves or were only clear in hindsight. Now I would like to give you a chance to consider what parts of your own life may reveal nuggets of inspiration for your project or venture. Here are a few tools that I have used and found to be simple ways to surface what may already be nudging you.

PERSONAL STORY DISCOVERY SUGGESTIONS

The types of insights that we are looking for can show up at any time, not just when we are intentionally seeking them. I have had major inspiration come when I was in the middle of other things and couldn't understand why this other idea kept showing up. As you start considering what your project or venture might be, pay particular attention to the stories that you are drawn to in the news, the events you get invited to but don't normally attend, or certain people's names that keep showing up. These types of things are easy to dismiss as random or distracting. Stay a bit more open and alert than usual, a bit more curious and less dismissive. Focus is great, but sometimes letting go of expectations and results can make space for whatever it is that wants to show up. Here is a fun introductory activity, a sort of self-reflection warm-up:

1. Assemble a collection of personally resonant objects, photographs, and mementos that you have in your home or that you collect in nature. For those of you who already have an altar, this is a good place to look. Scrapbooks, pieces of art or knickknacks that you find meaningful: it could look like literally anything, as long as it means something to you.

2. It's a good idea to document your thoughts during this process; personally, I am a big fan of large sticky notes and brightly colored markers. There are also some online virtual whiteboard tools such as Miro if you prefer to work that way. You may even want to listen to music or journal to help the flow of ideas as you gather.

3. Next, arrange these items on a table or comfortable floor space, considering each one. Where did it come from? Why is it significant to you? Did someone give it to you, or did you choose it? What is its story and why does that story mean enough to you that you keep this object in your home? Sit with the ideas and memories that come out of this and write them down. Are there any themes or patterns that arise? Any particular memories or feelings that surface? Pay close attention and write them down as well.

PERSONAL STORY MAPPING EXERCISE

Here are some ideas for looking more closely at your personal history:

- Do a bullet point inventory or map of your life's journey. What have the most impactful experiences been? In the past, I have used a wall-sized sticky note and done this in a spiral pattern with small illustrations. Don't feel like you have to simply stick with words; pictures or drawings may work better for you, or a combination.

- Create an autobiography with no particular audience in mind. This is just for you.

- How have you defined yourself in the past? Who do you see yourself as now? And how do you see yourself in an ideal future?

- What are things you love? Hate? Feel deeply curious about?

- What are your resources? This can include social in addition to financial capital—groups or particular relationships that can support you. Your skills and professional background are also relevant here.

- What are your constraints?

VALUES EXERCISE

Looking at your values is another good way to point your compass toward the kernel of an idea that may be meaningful. When we think of "values" as they apply to ourselves, I think we can often take them for granted in the sense that we think, *Of course I know what they are.* But do we? Have you given them a good thinking-through lately? It's definitely worth doing, especially if you have not articulated them recently. Some unexpected things may come up.

Values are a set of principles or beliefs that consciously or unconsciously guide your life choices and pursuits. They are the bare-bones, bottom-line things that matter to you the most and are the deepest expression of how you live your life.

I suggest setting aside a couple of undisturbed, meeting-free hours where you can focus without distraction. Start by meditating, doodling, flipping through magazines or photo albums, or journaling. One way or another, clear your mind enough to be receptive to the feelings that arise when you see certain words or images. Ultimately, you want a list of words or phrases; however, I am a big believer in noticing physical or emotional responses to images as well—these are all cues. When you look back at the personal story mapping exercise, what particular words, feelings, or themes emerged?

As an example, in a recent values exploration I did, I came up with the following principles that are most meaningful to me:

1. **Step up.** This is about leadership and being willing to be the first one to put myself out there. This speaks to my archetype, the Instigator. (We'll explore personal avatars and archetypes in chapter 4.)

2. **Stay open.** This means being with what is, as opposed to making things happen. I am receptive to other voices and experiences as I craft my initiatives.

3. **Let it flow.** It may have started with menstrual periods, but I see this as a metaphor for many of life's other processes. When I feel stuck or boxed in, I look to this value to find the way to move forward, the way that water navigates a streambed.

4. **Do the thing.** This one has two meanings: first, to do what you say that you're going to do; then, to take action instead of sitting on an idea or impulse.

5. **Make space.** This is about being mindful of my social privilege: how and where it shows up and how I can use it to

support others. Or just knowing when to get out of the way and be grateful for the opportunity to learn from others.

6. **Feel everything.** I am, to use V (formerly Eve Ensler)'s term, an emotional creature. Emotions are a very real form of intelligence. Be with your emotions, even when they are hard or scary. They have so much to teach us and bad things happen when we try to make them go away by ignoring them.

7. **Nurture.** How I love growing things! This includes relationships, companies, and plants, among others. I try to apply this value to everything that I do.

8. **Be strong.** I recently read Glennon Doyle's *Untamed* (which I highly recommend). One of her expressions that has stayed with me is "We Can Do Hard Things." Another source I take inspiration from on this front is A.A. Milne's Winnie-the-Pooh: "Always remember that you are braver than you believe, stronger than you seem, smarter than you think, and loved more than you know."

9. **Be awesome.** You don't need to be the best to be wonderful. Do your best and love your imperfect self without apology.

Here's one more example from the legendary design firm IDEO. Note that while I have just made a big jump going from personal to corporate values, I think this example works equally well in both cases.

- Talk less, do more.
- Make others successful.
- Learn from failure.
- Embrace ambiguity.
- Be optimistic.
- Collaborate.
- Take ownership.

Of course, your initiative will, in many ways, be a reflection of you. To begin your own list, brainstorm whatever comes up for you and write it all down. Take another pass and see whether you notice any related groupings or places where there is overlap in a similar vein. Values like respect, authenticity, honesty, and so on are great. However, if you can be more specific or add an anecdote to each that illustrates how you practice or recognize the value, so much the better. I would try to come up with a list of at least three to six that are the nearest and dearest to your heart, along with a short personal observation of why each one matters to you. Write them down and keep them somewhere handy; they will act as your inner compass as you navigate your journey.

Your values should inspire feelings of pride and conviction, with a touch of aspiration. If you are still feeling like the list is not perfect or is incomplete, I encourage you to move on, knowing that you can revisit this activity anytime. The missing pieces may come from activities that we explore later in the book as well.

By now, you likely have some rich material. Don't worry if it's not one hundred percent making sense yet. You have laid some important groundwork and given yourself a palette of values, areas of interest, core stories, and memories to draw from. Be sure to gather all of this material in one place—a notebook or file, for example. One of my favorite ways to do this is to get a large corkboard and literally pin anything to it that's relevant: old postcards, sticky notes, magazine articles, and so on. Either way, something that is accessible and easy to work with and rearrange is essential. Think of this as your sandbox of ideas that you can always return to as a key reference point as you embark on the next stage of your journey.

CHAPTER 4

Picking Up the Sword

I BELIEVE THAT THE desire to undertake a social impact–driven initiative reflects a deep impulse to address a higher calling, or purpose, than is normally framed by the term "career choice." The idea that we are all the hero in our own story at some point in our lives is so potent and wonderful. What if we all rose to hear the call, picked up the sword, or somehow summoned something deep, primal, and fierce in ourselves to go on an epic quest?

A quest by definition is a grand journey made in search of something or, in the case of medieval knights seeking to prove themselves, a myth-inspired expedition. "Quest" is a powerful word in and of itself, one that is ideally suited to the notion of social entrepreneurship thanks to its connotation with something great, even legendary. In fact, I chose the title of this book to reflect this idea.

If you find the metaphor of a sword to be problematic, allow me to explain my intended meaning. When I think of picking up a sword, I think of someone resisting oppression. It may be awkward at first and they may not have been given permission to use such tools to defend their own interests, yet here they are. For example, Angolan anticolonialist Queen Nzinga Mbandi and female samurai Nakano Takeko, among countless others. It's a strong metaphor, however one that I feel is apt for everyday people. We are not just choosing to take a stand for something that we believe in. Often, we are fighting to avenge, heal, or otherwise right an injustice.

There's something at stake for social entrepreneurs; we have something to prove, vanquish, or otherwise make a bigger point than dollars alone. Finding and exploiting this idea can be incredibly potent, not just for you as the hero-protagonist-founder, but for others whom you may call upon to join your quest or serve to liberate through it. Since stories are going to be a vital way that you will support your venture (or, if you will, quest), it's worth looking at how you relate to and share your own story. Trust me, it's a huge source of energy. Given that we are going after social change impact, the conversation that we are going to have with our users and supporters has to work on an emotional level, not just a practical one. The best, most memorable, and compelling way to do that is with a story, as opposed to facts or a convincing argument. We are trying to change the world, remember, and you are far more likely to motivate others by getting them to fall in love with what you have to offer. They also—vitally—need to be able to find or see themselves in it: your venture makes them heroes as well.

THE HERO'S JOURNEY

Let me be clear at the outset of this section that I am not an expert in myth or archetypes; however, I want to offer my thoughts and experience around their usefulness specifically as entrepreneurial and storytelling tools. There is a vast amount of information that can more precisely and extensively explain these concepts—these are just a few personal, anecdotal observations. The idea of the hero's journey is most commonly credited to Joseph Campbell's 1949 classic book *The Hero with a Thousand Faces*. Campbell was inspired by the groundbreaking work of psychoanalysts Carl Jung and Sigmund Freud, who—loosely speaking—posited that our dreams reflected human connection to a collective, universally shared unconscious. Stories about the hero's journey have been expressed in countless myths that draw upon these common human experiences and are used globally to make sense of our realities. They follow a similar pattern, roughly speaking: the hero-protagonist is going about their life when they feel called to pursue a new initiative, make a change, or rise to a challenge. While they may initially resist the call in a "Who, me?" kind of way (I have a feeling you may be at this stage), ultimately the journey ensues, during which they meet other characters, acquire tools or knowledge related to achieving their goal, overcome diverse challenges, and ultimately achieve their quest, having become transformed in the process. Examples that come to mind include the North American Haida myth of how Raven discovered the first humans and created the world, the Greek goddess Persephone's annual trip to the underworld causing seasonal change, and Buddhist goddess of compassion Kuan Yin's return from the gates of heaven to Earth to help assuage human suffering.

What's intriguing to me about myth is its universal attraction and moral instructiveness. In other words, we don't need to be a sword-brandishing, dragon-slaying hero to be on a meaningful journey of discovery and triumph, because really, myths are just metaphors for our own journeys as human beings. The reason I raise this is I believe there is not only something heroic in the journeys of everyday social entrepreneurs, but that it can also be very helpful to think of ourselves in this way. I don't know about you, but when it comes to the daily grind of emails, presentations, paying bills, and so on, thinking of these activities as being in support of something grander and more significant makes them feel richer and more interesting.

The idea that myths and stories shape us culturally is far from new, but what I'm pointing to is how they shape us personally. Examples of the hero story popularized in films include Frodo Baggins in *The Lord of the Rings*, the title character in *Mulan*, and T'Challa in *Black Panther*. These are all characters called to (reluctantly) take up a difficult challenge, who build relationships, endure threats and hardships, learn valuable lessons, and ultimately succeed in their quest. Their humble trappings make them relatable; they are everyperson characters called to a higher purpose. In undertaking their quests, they discover inner resilience, gifts, and strength they did not realize they possessed.

Many myths center on an underdog figure, and I feel these are particularly relevant to the path of the social entrepreneur. The unlikely hero uses their wits, unusual skills borne out of a lack of privilege, and sheer grit to overcome seemingly sure defeat at the hands of a larger, stronger adversary. The classic David and Goliath biblical tale, where a young shepherd defeats his mighty warrior opponent using his wits, is one example.

ARCHETYPES

Archetypes are central in myths and can likewise be useful as you consider your leadership journey. My understanding of archetypes is as a set of commonly recurring, iconic character types. The twelve classic archetypes as articulated by Jung are Innocent/Underdog; Everyperson; Hero; Outlaw/Rebel/Villain; Explorer; Creator; Ruler; Magician; Lover; Caregiver; Jester/Fool; and Healer/Sage. Many different systems have been articulated and, as far as I can tell, there is no one definitive set or number of them. If you are able to find or purchase a set of cards that depict various archetypes, this will help you to see whether the idea resonates with you.

The underdog archetype is a lovable character, which also appears as the Trickster in Indigenous storytelling traditions. These are characters who are underestimated and often marginalized, yet rather than accepting the status quo power system, challenge it where most others of their kind have failed to take a stand. Popular films that embody this archetype include *Rocky*, *Erin Brockovich*, *Slumdog Millionaire*, and *Seabiscuit*, among countless others. As social entrepreneurs we are often seeking to right a wrong or address something systemic that is far larger and seemingly more powerful than we are, making the underdog a valuable touchstone for us.

Looking back, I can now see how many of my pursuits have been motivated by a desire to avenge or otherwise heal a wound related to my gender identity that occurred when I was an adolescent. I can see the underdog in my choosing to take on massive corporate menstrual pad and tampon manufacturers as my "enemies," with my weapons of choice being feminism, creativity, and entrepreneurship.

Where archetypes started to take on practical meaning for me was when I learned about branding in a business context. I loved the idea that a brand could be representative of an archetype and as such be a powerfully attractive symbol to a certain aspect of human nature, often at an unconscious level. Big brand examples include Nike's Hero iconography and Apple's "Think Different" Innovator stance. Given that brands are reflections of the mission of their founders, you can easily see how we get from a leader identifying with an archetype to it being reflected in a brand.

Personally, I strongly relate to the Rebel archetype. This goes all the way back to a resistance to the conformity of my Brownies group (a junior Canadian version of Girl Guides). At the ripe old age of nine, I squirmed in the face of what I perceived as its silly names and rules and precious, antiquated etiquette. The fact that nobody questioned its top-down model, where none of the girls were invited to offer suggestions for projects or names for groups, made me want to jump out of my ugly brown uniform. Everyone else seemed perfectly happy (if a little bored) with our doings, but I wanted something more challenging and unusual.

At school, rebellion came naturally to me. I have always had a questioning nature and resisted the way things are. My identification continued as a university student where I was exposed to feminism and found my calling, realizing along the way that resistance to patriarchal authority was in fact a form of leadership and profound self-actualization.

ARCHETYPE DISCOVERY SUGGESTIONS

Archetypes are useful to us as entrepreneurs because they help us frame our own leadership style and journey. To do some discovery around your own archetypes, I would start by considering whether any figures or characters have popped up for you as part of this discussion; did anything come to mind? Revisiting your values can be a useful tool to discover archetypes when looking at what types of issues or situations these values show up in. Take a look at the values exercise we did in chapter 3—your answers might point you in the right direction. What matters enough to you that you are willing to risk something—time, money, reputation, failure—to obtain it? In my case, it's issues like reproductive choice, gender equity, family attachment, climate justice, sustainability, and creating economic opportunity for marginalized people. Heroes identify, take a stand and fight for, liberate, and protect the important things.

To find an archetype that feels right to you, look at the issues that inform your voting choices, political events you attend, organizations you donate to, brands you admire, or even things you would be willing to take up arms to protect. What stirs you about these issues and what personal connection do you have to them? Who are your personal heroes and why do they inspire you? What aspects of their character impress you the most? Ask yourself this question: If you had all the power in the world at your fingertips, what would you do with it? What change would you create and why? Start to notice whether there are patterns of behaviors, conflicts, relationships, or other aspects that persistently show up in your life. What are the lessons you seem to keep relearning? Are there recurring issues, dreams, dramas? What won't leave you alone?

As much as the Rebel lands for me, I wanted as an entrepreneur to recognize that I do more than take a stand against things, so I created a new option. I ended up inventing my own archetype (which may be out there already, although I have never seen it): the Instigator. The Instigator lands for me because of my patterns of starting things, of being willing to be the first to say something or to take action. This has always been true of my personality and I even have early childhood memories of proposing games, projects, or clubs to other kids and them following my lead. It's all about the action that I take, what I do. Other archetypes that resonate with me include Liberator, Mentor, Warrior, and Reformer. Do you resonate with more than one of them? There is no need to pick just one.

As an example of how myths can exert their power for social entrepreneurs in real life, I want to talk about Sofia Ashley, a survey respondent whom I have never met before. I was intrigued by the name of her venture, the Happy Vagina Project, which she describes as "a community of mothers who are reclaiming their sexuality to live more joyful, soulful and connected lives." As she was considering starting her venture, she read the Jewish legend of Lilith, a woman widely understood to have been Adam's first wife (before Eve), who was cast out of the Garden of Eden for refusing to obey (or, depending on the interpretation, have sex with) her husband, and was thus separated from sacred sexuality. Inspired, Sofia thought, *That's why I am here.* She says, "I come back to that legend over and over when I doubt myself."

PERSONAL HEROES

Other entrepreneurs draw inspiration from real-life personal heroes. Vanessa Richards, the founder of an inclusive, barrier-free community choir called the Van Van Song Society, cites Bernice Johnson Reagon, a legendary African-American civil rights leader and founder of the band Sweet Honey in the Rock, as someone who has always inspired her. She shared the following wisdom with me:

> *I draw upon the healing/coping/celebrating/common culture of song in African diaspora culture. I also draw upon the role of song in labor like the sea shanties, Scottish waulking, and the many contemporary songs coming from the community singing movement. Communal singing is like discovering there's a way to make all things better, and it's within, and it supports everyone tending to their own song and the collective song. That's the gift of song.*

Having witnessed Vanessa in action using her musical gifts as powerful, unique leadership tools on multiple occasions, I can attest to the profound impact of drawing on her role model to leverage shared song to unite, to work, and to resist.

As you think about embarking on your own quest in whatever project or venture you create, consider what tools, knowledge, and skills you'll use to fulfill your mission. Here are some exercises to help you discover—and summon—your own unique gifts.

GENIUS ACTIVITY

Karen Lam, a highly regarded executive coach, is a proponent of the Genius Quadrant tool. She generously facilitated a session with Suzanne and me at a time when we were re-evaluating our leadership roles at Lunapads.

This tool is about isolating the activities at which you uniquely excel and, ideally, will be able to invest the greatest portion of your time and energy doing. You can do this activity on your own or with a partner who knows you well. I found it very useful in our case as business partners to have it facilitated by someone outside our company, who could help us to clarify our respective roles. It's a very simple exercise; however, you need to take it seriously and be honest with yourself or else risk falling back into the same old stories about yourself.

Here's the basic idea:

- Get a piece of paper and make four quadrants or columns.
- Label each as follows: Incompetent, Competent, Excellent, and Genius.
- "Incompetent" is stuff that you either intensely dislike or are lousy at—the no-go list.
- "Competent" is so-so or mediocre. You can do it, but there are other folks who are better at these tasks than you.
- "Excellent" is for things that are easy for you, which you are skilled at, and enjoy. They are also skills that others likely have and may not truly light you up.
- "Genius" is your ultimate sweet spot. There does not have to be just one; what distinguishes this list is that it's unique to you. What do you bring that nobody else does? What's irreplaceable about you? What makes your heart sing?
- Each participant makes a thoughtful list of personal skills and attributes that they feel belong in each category.
- If you are working with a partner, compare your lists and discuss.

It was through doing this that I isolated my "Genius" abilities: the ability to inspire trust and confidence with others; to instigate action; to make team members feel valued; to cut through noise, buzzwords, and general BS to get at the core of an issue and vision. Vision meaning seeing patterns in seemingly random ideas or seeing the value in something old or lost and reimagining it. I enjoy public speaking and generally getting people excited about things. I love creating positive relationships and helpful connections for others. Conversely, I am helpless at details, managing people, "systems thinking," and conforming to many of the acronyms commonly found in business. Financial analysis, data of any variety, legal documents and the like, all make me want to jump off something high.

Seeing everything laid out like this was very liberating. Until that point, I had given myself a really hard time about not being "skilled" as a businessperson in the traditional sense and had underestimated the value of my contributions. In retrospect, I can see how this exercise was an important step in what ultimately led to restructuring Lunapads/Aisle's organization, from a co-leadership model to Suzanne becoming CEO and me assuming a more apt role as creative director. Knowing that this was a fit with my Genius profile calmed my ego and took the pressure off those places where I was feeling inadequate.

Letting go of judgment around where your skills and talents *are not* can be just as freeing as recognizing where they are, because it's all being done in the context of what you're amazing at. It's impossible to be great at everything and, in many ways, this exercise speaks to the need for collaboration and working with others to bring their awesome to the places that you can't. We cannot, and indeed should not, strive to be everything; this is another entrepreneurial myth that needs to be set aside, and yet another reason to consider collaboration over competition as you approach your venture.

HIDDEN SUPERPOWERS

Another way of framing Genius is thinking about superpowers, or the more subtle idea of *hidden superpowers*. While Genius is a great tool for understanding skill, hidden superpowers is about things that are less quantifiable. Having come up with a list of our Genius skills, our superpowers might look similar at first. So, what are some sources of power that are perhaps less obvious, or a bit strange, or flat-out weird? Again, exploring this topic is another opportunity to connect with a friend, or even a small group.

As an example, one of my hidden superpowers is having frank but gentle conversations with people about issues they are confronting in their careers or with their businesses. These conversations may start out being about a normal business issue but often quickly bring to the surface a deeper emotional dilemma or issue, which is what really requires attention. I cannot count the number of times that this has happened. It's almost like the person already knows that it's going to happen but doesn't have the language to ask for what they actually need. Which is fine with me—I'm used to it by now. It reminds me that so many of the things we do are not just what we perceive on the outside but manifestations of a connection to something much larger and not entirely under our rational control. When we are able to touch that connection, it creates an emotional response that can feel dissonant if you thought you were having a conversation about business. All of which is to say, stay open to your emotions; they have a valuable place, even in a business setting.

I am a frequent speaker and facilitator at Social Venture Institute (SVI) conferences, where I am often asked to lead small peer learning circles under the name "Random Intuitive Business Advice." I also do this more frequently on a one-on-one basis, although I don't give it any particular name. At SVI conferences, participants can choose all manner of more traditional topics like Raising Capital, Human Resources, Understanding Financials, and so on. They are definitely looking for something different when they join my circle. I ask participants to take turns briefly outlining what brought them there, and then I lead the group in a collective feedback brainstorm.

What happens is that I often get ideas, images, and questions popping into my head that are not necessarily directly related to what the person is saying. It's like I can hear a different voice, and I often surface questions that at first seem random (hence the "Random" part) but get at something underlying the surface issue being presented. In one-on-one sessions, people often spontaneously start crying when I ask them questions. Although I understand that this sounds terrible (it's not a scared or traumatized type of crying), it can actually be really lovely and it feels like an immense gift for me to be in this space with them, like I have the ability to open up an emotional frequency that does not often get touched. It's like there is a form of truth that may have been hard for someone to admit to themselves, and through conversation with me just kind of surfaces. Somehow, I have the ability to make people feel safe and not judged, and this allows us to work on a deeper level to understand the emotional or intuitive information that underlies whatever else is happening. Often the tears are about being overwhelmed and pass quickly; it's like a cloud passing by, and the people are like, "What just happened?" I think of it as emotional acupuncture.

As a way of looking for this in yourself, consider what types of reasons people are drawn to you or things they seek you out for. Do they ask you specific types of questions or seek comfort or counsel from you in certain situations? We often discount these types of knowing that we possess. Remember that emotion is a critical form of intelligence. Now's the time to identify and summon what this looks like for you. Again, make time, drop into a contemplative space, make a list of what comes up, and possibly discuss your insights with others. Developing self-awareness around these aspects of yourself will come in handy as you explore your vision and share your new narrative.

CHAPTER 5

Exploring Vision

IN THE LAST TWO CHAPTERS, we took an inventory that revealed what matters to us and why and investigated some useful frameworks and concepts. I'm hoping that by now, you can appreciate just how deep and personal this work can be. What comes next is formulating these insights into an idea that gives them shape. What will the long-term outcome of your initiative be, and what shape will it take to get there? This idea, loosely speaking, is what I'm calling "vision."

Many of the people I interviewed defined vision as how they imagined a better world would look and feel. This can involve seeing things that were missing or that could be vanquished or reinvented in ways that were more just or sustainable. I like to think of vision as social change make-believe, or what happens when we ask the question, "What if?"

One of the interesting things I like to be aware of is where the vision may be originating from, or if it's leaving a trail of cosmic bread-crumbs. Is it truly a random idea, or is it more a process of connecting the dots that are the chain of ideas adding up to a vision? Sometimes it's very direct, but it can evolve over many years or even decades. Just try to notice. My feeling is that vision is the single most compelling element of any venture. It motivates your constituents to take whatever action is necessary to move the project forward. People involved in a project simply need to be able to see, feel, and find themselves in its vision.

So, how do you move from story to vision? As an example, I'd like to share how my own vision for two of my ventures evolved from personal experiences. Then I'll move on to some exercises that you can use to help uncover and develop your own vision.

THE LUNAPADS/AISLE STORY

A lot of people ask me about the earliest points of inspiration for Lunapads. Where did the idea for period underwear and washable menstrual pads come from back in the early '90s, long before it hit the mainstream radar? The truth is that it evolved from a confluence of diverse influences and experiences over the course of many years.

My social entrepreneur story actually goes way back to being a preadolescent girl in the late 1970s. Like Judy Blume's title character in *Are You There God? It's Me, Margaret*, I was fascinated by the idea of becoming an adult woman. I was obsessed with all of womanhood's physical trappings: breasts, hips, hair, and of course, the ultimate indicator (in my mind at least)—periods. To me, the idea of becoming an adult woman was akin to becoming an astronaut or prime minister, a kind of "Who, me? I get to be one of them?" In my preadolescent imagination, adult women seemed like exotic birds—tall, confident, glittering, wise, and hilarious. Listening to them laugh at one another's witty comments at my parents' dinner parties, I ached to be included in their electric sisterhood.

As I approached menarche (the onset of menstrual periods), I secretly hoped for some form of initiation rite, where I would be warmly welcomed into their circle and shown the ropes of woman-hood. This never happened, but the yearning for it never left me.

My anticipation crumbled when my period finally arrived on a sweltering July day while on holiday with my family. I was in bed for days with what I thought was appendicitis (and my mom, bless her, gently rubbing my back all the while). When the true cause of my cramps revealed itself, I was mercilessly mocked by my younger brother and his friend, and I burned with humiliation. My cherished fascination quickly morphed into shame and disappointment. I let go of my childish imaginings and got on with the less happy reality of being a too-cool-to-care teenager. Remember what I said in the last chapter about vision coming from a desire to heal old wounds?

Within two years, I was taking hormonal birth control pills, which lessened my bleeding but more importantly, further eradicated my already tenuous relationship with my cycle. I started using tampons around this time in order to minimize my experience of bleeding and my consciousness around anything meaningful to do with my cycle and period was brought to zero. Rather than exploring and honoring my cycle, I internalized the idea that I was "liberated" from this monthly chore by pushing it as far from my consciousness as possible.

It's often said that our life choices can be the result of unresolved personal issues and in this case, it was absolutely true. Let's fast-forward to my early twenties when, thanks to a women's studies degree, I was waking up from my hormone-induced lull. I decided to go off the pill after ten years of continuous use and the impact was stunning. Suddenly, my body was so . . . wild. There was blood, lust, pain, energy, lethargy, creativity, rage—all of it. It was like being on a brand-new roller coaster at the emotional amusement park. I was fascinated. Another shift was that my trusty applicator-free tampons were driving me crazy, with bladder infections arriving pretty much regularly within twenty-four hours of the onset of my periods.

Another influential moment happened during a visit to the United States in the early '90s, when a friend showed me an article titled "The Truth About Tampons" from a now-defunct magazine called *Garbage*, and my curiosity and outrage were further stoked. Around this time, I also happened to see some washable cloth menstrual pads that were being made on a nearby island and was immediately intrigued. I bought some, but they were too large for me and required the hassle of sewing Velcro strips into my underwear. I found them to be bulky, uncomfortable, and unattractive. The basic idea still appealed to me, though, and I decided to make my own version, as well as an all-in-one pad/panty.

What happened next changed my life. Washing my own pads and period underwear (one of the grossest, most transgressive things imaginable in that day and age) was like being Alice walking through the looking glass, or Dorothy pulling back the curtain on the Wizard of Oz. Which is to say that I felt deliciously, thrillingly liberated. Once upon a time, I had sought to push my body's ebbs and flows away, whereas now, I was enthralled by a deep sense of awe and compassion for my cycling body.

What came to me was that disposable products, especially tampons, are the opposite of gentle. They are foreign, extractive, and even toxic. For the first time in my entire menstruating life, I was simply supporting my body in doing its thing on its own terms, without modification, judgment, resentment, or shame. I wept with rage and regret for not having realized this truth sooner, for having forced it into all manner of "choices" that were really about sanitized ideals of femininity, which were commodified and sold back to me as false "protection."

In this newly awakened state, I started to attend women's circles and track my cycle, as well as the cycle of the moon. I wanted to get to know not only my bleeding patterns, but also every other aspect of my cycle, from luteal to follicular. I became a rapt student of my sweet home: my fascinating, powerful, mysterious, amazing body. Menstruation had transformed from an irritating inconvenience into a fascinating gateway to self-knowledge, self-care, and personal liberation. What a gift!

It was this feeling of reverence, compassion, love, and awe that led me to want to commercialize Lunapads and Luna Undies. I wanted others to experience their own version of this feeling, if it was available to them. Our first mission statement summed the vision up: "To create more positive and informed relationships between women, their bodies and the Earth." I registered my first company, a sole proprietorship called everyware designs, in 1993; I then enrolled in a local entrepreneurial training course and wrote the first business plan for Lunapads in 1994.

THE NESTWORKS STORY

As another example of how vision can show up, let's look at Nestworks. It's a shared, family-friendly workspace concept that I have been working on since 2016, which originated from the indelible imprint left on Suzanne and me by bringing our children to work with us, from birth to approximately eighteen months old. Broadly speaking, we characterize our vision as "ReVillaging"—the idea of a welcoming, multigenerational space that supports family connection and economic resilience. We imagined a workspace with adjacent childcare amenities and a "We get it, how can we make life easier for you?" attitude toward integrating career and family needs. On my optimistic days, these spaces featured dedicated nursing spaces, ample stroller and bike parking, and skilled helping hands to keep small people engaged and well cared for, with easy access to parents as needed while parents are still able to quietly work. It had been pestering me for a while (as I kept earnestly telling others that they should do it), but one particular conversation flipped the switch on me saying yes.

For several years at Lunapads, we had a longstanding practice of renting out spare offices to other small, values-aligned entrepreneurs and organizations, on the understanding that we may one day need the space ourselves. One day, I was tasked with giving notice to a longtime tenant, a lovely woman with a thriving eco-friendly baby bath product business. When I gave her the news, she was naturally a bit unsettled, but recovered and took the time to share some thoughts about what working in proximity to the company and our team had meant to her. As I listened to her words, I was humbled and amazed to learn what a positive impact it had had for her. This was so much more than a shared space transaction; what she was speaking to was community, bonding, and acceptance—nontraditional business benefits that supported her as a woman and a mother, not just a businessperson. She shared how much it had meant to be able to easily ask for feedback on ideas or for service provider recommendations, to feel less alone when she was having a challenging day, and to have the freedom of bringing her kids with her when they were off school. Suddenly my own veil lifted. The experience and impact of what she was talking about—a physical space where what had been a happy byproduct for us would become the core intention—was what *I needed to create.* It was time to stop telling myself that I was too busy, or didn't have time, or whatever else. In that moment, I gave myself permission to let the vision in, to come to terms with the fact that it had been calling me all along, and to start working on a business case, give it a name, craft a story, and call on others for support.

It's interesting to note that we both cried during the conversation. Tears are often a sign of truth in my experience, as we saw in the previous discussion about hidden superpowers. Do not make the mistake of invariably associating them with sadness; they are an outward indication of something important landing or changing within ourselves. They are a form of surrender and acceptance and embodiment. We see what we are called to do and the moment when we stop resisting the call often feels fragile. We are becoming new people, after all, as we accept the call to pursue our visions.

FINDING YOUR VISION

Let's move on to looking at ways to uncover, summon, or otherwise access your vision. Taking intentional time to nourish vision is vital. It's amazing what can happen when you make space for it, rather than waiting for it to fit itself into your life. It's also helpful to take yourself out of the goal mindset, as it can be limiting and invites pressure to think in terms of deliverables or specific outcomes, which is not necessarily helpful at this stage. Instead, consider the idea of receiving whatever comes along without any particular effort. We are often so caught up in the idea of being productive without really being aware of it. Check in with yourself and see whether this might be true for you, and if it is, imagine talking to a child who is worried that their creative work will not be good enough, then try telling yourself what you would say to them.

VISION QUEST

What I mean by a "vision quest" is intentionally taking time out of your regular routine to open yourself up to receiving, or going deeper with, your vision. Here we're looking for whatever it takes to get out of your head, reflect on ideas or feelings that you may have pushed aside, or otherwise enter a different mental state outside of what is normal for you. These days, I tend to think more in terms of allowing visions to show up rather than making them happen, but whatever feels good to you in terms of making space for it is perfect.

Some general tips for a mini vision quest (no drugs involved!) can include:

- Spend time in nature.
- Look at or make art.
- Look at old photographs.
- Read old journals, blog posts, letters, or other pieces of writing that you have created.

- Do something unusual for you. This could be anything that is off your normal beaten path—basically, just trying something different. Examples could be a language or music class, exercise, meditation, drawing, or even writing with your non-dominant hand.
- Explore a part of your community where you don't normally spend time.
- Go away somewhere with the intention of letting go of old ideas and being intentionally open to new ones.
- Write a letter to your future self.
- Play games. They can shake up your thought patterns in interesting ways.
- Act quickly to record whatever it is you are seeing and feeling. What's happening? Are there any words, feelings, or images that came up? Don't forget to pay attention to what you may be experiencing physically. What's happening in your body?
- Create a voice recording on your phone or tablet, or make a quick video.
- Draw a picture or create a mind map of what you're seeing and feeling. This can be as simple as putting down a bunch of words or doodles that reflect whatever comes into your head. Indicate any relationships between the images or words. Let it be messy and don't worry if it's not linear. Imagine this as a cool, random road trip.
- Tell someone about what you experienced and invite them to ask questions to tease out details.
- Add anything you create to the work you may have already done in response to my earlier suggestions to this point and consider it in this context. Are there any patterns emerging?
- Notice how it feels in your body. I literally feel inhabited by visions sometimes, like a strong, warm glow in my chest.
- Freewrite by hand (not editing or second guessing, just write) about whatever is coming up for you.

- I have a folder full of old magazines that I use to make cards and vision boards, and something like that would also be handy for this purpose. Look at images and intuitively arrange them. Notice what words and images attract you.
- Visit a domain registry site and search URLs that come to mind. This is one of my favorite activities and it can ground your vision with a very meaningful yet practical step.

CULTIVATE CURIOSITY

Curiosity is an underrated source of power and creativity, along with intuition and receptivity. When we indulge our curiosity, it can bring us into a childlike state of "What if?" wonder. As adults, we become guarded, filtered, and potentially resistant to change and new ideas, whether we realize it or not. We think things have to be hard or challenging and that new ideas need to be big, bold, difficult, and truly novel. Sometimes my "new" ideas are actually very old (hello washable menstrual products, rite of passage events, and integrated work-family life), small, or simple. As an important sidenote, I would caution you against dismissing a vision for seeming too small or insignificant to be worthy of attention. Remember how I substituted "Beautiful" for the "Big" in BHAG earlier in the book? You are looking, as your first priority, for something that lights you up like this did for me.

We live in a world where bigger is taken for granted as being better, and with due respect to people who advocate for bold, disruptive, or audacious visions, I want to recognize that this may not feel true or comfortable for many of us—particularly those of us who are unused to taking up space or having our voices heard. What matters is that it feels true and exciting for you, that it makes your pulse race without feeling overwhelming. Visions can also grow and change over time; it's not a one-off thing, so don't be too hasty to write off a vision that may end up being a prototype for something else. The point here is to keep the energy moving and stay open and curious. And hey, if it ends up being massive, that's wonderful too!

A highly regarded person in my life recently shared that curiosity, in her view, is actually the antidote to fear. If this does not immediately land for you, consider the image of a child mesmerized by the sight of a nearby wild animal. In the absence of life experience or information that the animal may be dangerous, the first reaction is curiosity. The brain can work this way for adults as well. Make curiosity your friend and close ally on your vision quest.

DETECTIVE EXERCISE

I love the metaphor of being a detective and sometimes I even imagine myself wandering around wearing a cool hat with a large magnifying glass in hand. What does a detective do? They look for clues, often in unexpected places.

1. Keep a scrapbook of newspaper articles, photographs, postcards, business cards: anything that draws your attention or feels resonant with the insights you have already generated. This can also happen after the fact. Notice when something stays with you or keeps coming into your mind. It could be something you read, a conversation you had, or even just a few words or a phrase. Remember, you are looking for something that does not yet exist (at least, not your version of it!).

2. If you see something similar to what you want to create, find out as much as you can about it. This can look like many things, including conducting informational interviews with beneficiaries, leaders, or experts; Googling, rearranging pieces of information or images that you have previously collected into new patterns; and discussing your ideas with friends,

family, and colleagues. It's astonishing to me how often, when I'm telling someone about an idea or vision that I'm investigating, it leads to personal introductions and connections to others with valuable expertise and support.

3. Share your ideas liberally, never be afraid to ask for help, and remember that there are no dumb questions!

4. Again, check in regularly with how you are feeling. You are not just looking for aligned clues but feelings and a sense of flow, where one clue leads naturally to the next. I am a strong believer in being open to things taking on an interesting life of their own once you have started this process.

5. Pay closer attention to what you say than what you normally do, almost as though you are outside of yourself, listening. What do you notice? What words or phrases do you use frequently? What stories do you commonly tell? Do you notice any patterns?

Starting around 2010, I noticed myself often pitching the same business idea to friends and colleagues as a fantastic project that some of them might like to consider taking on. The idea was to lease a commercial space and share it with other entrepreneurs, kind of like an informal private co-working space for synergistic businesses. One further aspect about it that I loved was the idea that the partners, or members, or whoever, could *bring their children to work with them*. How cool would that be? By now, you know that this idea was Nestworks. It took the conversation that I shared earlier to wake me up to the reality that it was actually me being called by this idea that I kept trying to pass off to other people. If you notice a repeat pattern of telling others that they should pursue a particular idea, consider turning the mirror around and asking yourself whether the vision is in fact yours.

INNER CHILD MEDITATION EXERCISE

Another activity I have had loads of inspiration spring from is a regression meditation, through which you discover what your younger self has to tell you. It has always amazed me that we marvel at and celebrate creativity and imagination in children, yet can be so dismissive of these traits in adults. I, for one, have totally internalized the idea that as adults, we kind of "get over" our childhood imaginings in the name of adhering to a prescribed set of social norms. It's sad, because it's precisely that blue-sky thinking that will get us closer to what we desire. We only lose when we stop playing the game and close our minds to what might be possible.

I have done this exercise dozens of times and I find that taking time to revisit your former self (I think of these parts as timeless, inner versions of ourselves) can be extremely powerful. The benefit of finding out what your inner child or youth has to say is that it can provide great insight into things you may have forgotten, or become distracted from, as you moved through adolescence and adulthood. This can serve as a lens into our most pure, intrinsic self.

THE G DAY STORY

This is exactly what happened when I created G Day, a celebration series designed to honor tween girls from ages ten to twelve as they transition from childhood to adolescence. It was as though my inner girl had been waiting for the moment when she could break through to let me know what she wanted.

I credit the emergence of the G Day vision to a public speaking gig that I did in early 2013. I was invited to speak at PechaKucha Night Vancouver, a long-running and well-attended chapter of the widely celebrated global speaking series founded by architects Astrid Klein and Mark Dytham, of Tokyo's Klein Dytham, in 2003. PK Night has a distinct format where each presenter chooses twenty slides that are put on an automatic display function and change every twenty seconds.

As with many previous themed PK Nights, this one partnered with a local nonprofit; in this case, it was Women Transforming Cities, a feminist urban planning and development think tank. Speakers were asked to answer the question, "How would you change a city?" As thrilled as I was to be invited to speak at this prestigious event, when it came to answering the question, I was stumped. *I make period products, not change cities,* I told myself.

Then, as I allowed myself to contemplate the question of how I would change a city, a strange, fortuitous thing happened. I had a powerful flashback to *Are You There God? It's Me, Margaret.* Only this time, Margaret was me. Earlier, I shared how excited I had been about becoming a woman and that I secretly wished there could be some sort of celebration of the transition. When it came to PK Night, my heart went right back to my preadolescent self and her yearning for recognition, feeling welcomed and supported. Her voice raised itself inside me and said, "It's not too late." This is one of the most profound instances of vision that I have ever experienced.

As improbable as it may sound, my inner Margaret was literally calling to me from across the decades. Is there anything more hopeful than the phrase "It's not too late"? I collapsed into tears. This was how I would change a city: creating a time and space for this welcoming, this collective affirmation of our girls as they took their first steps on the metaphorical road toward adulthood. I wondered what places there might have once been for these types of occasions. What might this ritual look like? What vestiges of it could we find in urban landscapes? What would have given me and Margaret the feeling that we so deeply craved?

Having now produced twelve events across Canada that have welcomed more than twenty-five hundred people, as well as taken dozens of G Day volunteers through this inner child exercise, I can say with great certainty that girls (and inner girls) are far more self-aware, self-assured, and confident in who they are than we typically give them credit for. There is something very clear about their understanding of themselves, their basic likes and dislikes, what they are curious about, scared of, challenged by, and drawn to.

I think we typically have a very good sense of who we are at this age. However, we get sidetracked by what happens next in puberty, when all of a sudden (in the case of female-identified youth), the social messages that we receive about the ways we matter change, often abruptly. So, if during our childhood years we have been recognized for being good with animals, smart at science, and a loyal friend, for example, and suddenly the world at large seems more interested in our body shape and size, social popularity, and "hotness," it's easy to see why girls at this age often become depressed, moody, and confused. These confusing messages continue through our teenage years and can be hugely stressful—so much so that by the time we are in our twenties and thirties, many of us are still trying to find ourselves through therapy or personal development programs.

Events like G Day are designed to serve as internal touchstones of feeling valued in a community context without any judgment, where we give girls the message that they matter simply because they exist, without needing to meet any other criteria. My sense is that our inner girl/child/youth knows who we really are all along; we just get confused by the bad messages and forget the true ones.

I suggest you try your own inner child meditation. Set aside an hour or so at a time when you are feeling grounded and know you won't be interrupted. Take it slowly and see what comes up. I created these guidelines based on years of attending women's circles and yoga classes, and I use this meditation with all of the G Day leadership teams, volunteers, parents, and other adult G Day attendees.

INNER CHILD MEDITATION SUGGESTIONS

- Find a quiet, comfortable, and preferably private space.
- Prepare yourself with a comfortable seat, a pen, a notebook, and a glass of water or a hot beverage.
- Settle yourself and clear your mind.
- Take several deep, clearing breaths, imagining that whatever preoccupations have been in your mind are gently melting away from you.
- Feel your connection to the ground and chair beneath you consciously.
- Imagine a stem of light energy radiating from these points where your body connects with other surfaces, down into the earth.
- Imagine this energy also flowing through your body and out of the top of your head, up into the sky. You are glowing and full of beautiful light.
- Gently call into your mind's eye an image of yourself as a child or adolescent.
- Observe this self closely. What are they doing? What are they wearing? Are there any specific memories associated with this time for you?
- Going a bit deeper, feel for who they were at this point in your life. What amazed or intrigued them? What scared them? What did they love to do or create? Did they have particular dreams or aspirations?
- Gently approach them in your mind's eye and greet them. Pay particular attention to anything that they may want to share with you, and vice versa. Or just be together. You may want to hold their hand or hug them.
- Pause and just be in the moment for as long as you want, until you feel ready to let go.

- Knowing that you can revisit this person at any time (they reside within you, after all), gently let them go, and take a few breaths to come back into the present moment.
- Hydrate yourself and then write down what happened and what you noticed about this experience.
- Take your time and try to be in silence for at least thirty minutes after doing this, if possible.

As another option, consider getting a small group of trusted friends or colleagues together for a personal feedback session. Ask them what gifts and talents they see in you. There may be something that surfaces that you don't perceive in yourself, but others do.

MISSION STATEMENTS AND CREDOS

However you end up exploring your vision, I strongly encourage you, as part of this work, to come up with either something visual, a short (five to ten words is easy to remember) list, poem, statement (some people make their values into a mission statement), or credo. Remember, this is a work in progress and will be developed and refined as you move along your journey. I think of a credo as the statement that would be on your personal coat of arms, or the most succinct summary of what you're bringing to your time on the planet.

Looking retrospectively over my career, I can see there's clearly a feminist agenda, which when I parse further looks like social justice, anti-violence, community building, supporting attachment, sustainability, anti-racism and intersectionality, and ending economic inequality. The concept of labor is also extremely important to me, especially as it relates to creativity (another deeply held value), self-expression, and self-determination and autonomy. I also deeply value beauty and color, and I believe that both these things have more power than we typically give them credit for. I once had a personal credo come to me that still resonates for me: "To create and to lead." As I shared earlier, my earliest vision for Lunapads was expressed in its first mission statement, which was "To create more positive and informed relationships between women, their bodies and the Earth."

This statement was crafted in 1993, before it became more common practice to create distinct vision and mission statements. With apologies to readers who are more refined in their practice with respect to the nuances between these, for the purposes of this discussion, I am intentionally conflating them to illustrate the point that it's useful to write down what you are trying to achieve and, at a high level, how you plan to get there. If there are lots of feelings and ideas coming up for you that seem related, you may also consider writing a manifesto, which I think of as a longer, poetic style of expressing your values, vision/mission/purpose, and anything else you feel is key to your pursuit. You may want to consider doing something along these lines first, then refining shorter statements derived from it. As an example, SheEO's credo is as follows:

At SheEO we practice Radical Generosity, which we believe is
*   core to creating a new model and a better world.*
We have all that we need in this network to reach our potential.
If you need something, ask.
If you have something to give, please offer it.
We are all at different stages and ages and we come from
*   different experiences.*
We are here with our sleeves rolled up, ready to help one another.
This is a co-created environment built on trust.
We are creating a space for women to thrive on their own terms.
We take our time, and we consider the future.
We celebrate and embolden each other.
We amplify each other's voices.
We own our greatness.

Another wonderful example comes from CreativeMornings, a monthly breakfast lecture series for the creative community. Originally started in New York in 2008 by Tina Roth Eisenberg, Creative-Mornings now has chapters in over two hundred cities in almost seventy countries around the world. Here is their manifesto:

Everyone is creative.

A creative life requires bravery and action, honesty and hard work. We are here to support you, celebrate with you, and encourage you to make the things you love.

We believe in the power of community. We believe in giving a damn. We believe in face-to-face connections, in learning from others, in hugs and high fives.

We bring together people who are driven by passion and purpose, confident that they will inspire one another, and inspire change in neighborhoods and cities around the world.

Everyone is welcome.

I hope that these examples demonstrate that vision can show up in a multitude of ways. If you don't feel like you're there yet, it's okay. You never know what's around the corner and there are ways to help things along.

WHAT IF I DON'T HAVE A VISION (YET)?

Full disclosure: I used to hate the word *visionary*. It just seemed kind of arrogant, as though whoever claimed it as a title was full of themselves and basically got others to do the real work, while they lay around having their precious visions. It's tricky for me, though, because I actually am highly prone to visions—I just don't see it as a skill, exactly. So, it's taken me a long time to come around to owning my visionary-ness. (Is that even a thing?)

This is completely fine! Most of us don't have visions on a regular basis—it's actually pretty rare. My guess would be that if this is the case for you, it's likely just a matter of time. Consider what it was that made you want to read this book in the first place. Which words got your attention? What hope or other feeling did you have when you bought it? This feeling is a potential key to your vision. Maybe this book, or one of the stories in it, will become a cosmic breadcrumb for you. Just keep going on this path of curiosity, paying particular attention to events, conversations, and random things that pique your interest. Write them down. Turn them over in your mind.

It may also be the case that you're what's called an Integrator, which is no less valuable than a Visionary. The Visionary/Integrator model was created by author and entrepreneur Gino Wickman, whose book *Traction* spawned a widely used business management system called Entrepreneurial Operating System (EOS). The Visionary/Integrator model is one of EOS's core concepts and can roughly be understood as a right-brain (Visionary) left-brain (Integrator) synergistic dichotomy, where two different yet complementary personality types successfully combine their gifts to create something amazing. We have already talked a great deal about vision, which some people are naturally more gifted with than others. Vision is not an easy thing to "achieve," per se; it's typically more organic than that. Integrators are people who make sense of and ground visions in reality. They contain, translate, and otherwise create the necessary structure in order to get visions out of the Visionary's head and into the world. They are all about the indispensable structural and operational underpinnings of any enterprise, without which visions crumble. I should also add that Integrators make fantastic leaders and that Visionaries do not necessarily have the optimal skills for the minutiae of getting things done efficiently and effectively. (I am an excellent example!)

Everything in this chapter is relevant to you if you feel like you belong in the Integrator camp—things aren't one hundred percent clear-cut. However, I have seen this dynamic play out many times and there is abundant literature about it. Something is calling you either way, and my guess would be that reading this book will be a great foundation for knowing a good vision when you see one. My relationship with Suzanne can be read along these lines, and I have taken this interplay to heart in all of my projects. Other key Integrators for me include my amazing friend Hilary Mandel, who helped me launch G Day as well as Nestworks, as well as Sandra Nomoto, who has also been a longtime supporter and highly effective team member on both of these projects. I may have had the original vision, but successful implementation from an operational perspective would have been impossible without their contributions. In addition to being totally in alignment in terms of mission and values, these three women also possess tremendous analytic and organizational skills that I simply don't have. It takes all of us to not only see where we want to go, but also how to get there.

Having done all manner of internal work, it's time for us to shift gears into taking action. By now, I'm pretty sure that you at least have some ideas and feelings you are curious about and looking for more clues around. This will provide fertile ground for you to take your next step: creating a new story about you and your venture or project.

CHAPTER 6

Crafting Your Story

HAVING SPENT TIME IN THE VISION SPACE, I would now like to move to looking at what to do with the feelings, ideas, and images that came out of it, with the goal of crafting and sharing a narrative about your project or venture. There are two parts to this: formulating or laying out the vision as it stands and finding ways to express it. If you are still working on accessing your vision, please keep reading, as all of this will be relevant when it shows up and may further encourage it.

NAMING YOUR VENTURE

At this stage, you may already have a name or be thinking of one. Naming is such a powerful, evocative, creative act, which draws an obvious parallel with the naming of a child or pet. It confirms incarnation. A name is an essential component of a brand (a brand being everything that the name and all its associated assets represent). Naming and branding are among the most critical and potentially fraught areas of creating your enterprise, and you'll probably need to be very patient and flexible with the process. If you have resources to put toward getting professional help on this front, I strongly encourage it. Branding professionals are uniquely gifted and can help you get from a vision to a name, story, logo, and more. Assuming you find a person or agency who is a fit for you, they will likely be able to deliver something of higher quality than what you (assuming you are not a branding expert) or a friend skilled with design software could come up with on your own. Having recently advocated for a professional branding service, I must add that this can be extremely pricey, especially for those of us on a budget. I have seen wonderful logos (although not a fully scoped brand standards package) from websites like Fiverr.com, where independent designers offer relatively inexpensive, basic services. Otherwise, just do the best with what you have, knowing that it will evolve over time and as resources permit. Depending on the scale that you envision for your initiative, you would be well advised to do a preliminary online trademark search to see if other entities are using it, or something similar, in case there is a conflict later on.

HONING YOUR IDEA: KEY QUESTIONS

The first step that seems to work for many is to write your idea(s) down. Remember that it does not need to be final, and that at this stage at least, the purpose of the exercise is simply for you to lay out your thoughts and consider some key questions about your idea. Everything is a work in progress and this version is not for show. Don't let the perfect be the enemy of the good, as it can slow down or even freeze up the process in an unhelpful way. This is just about the concept; it can be as short as a couple of paragraphs or even just bullet points to start. This is the basic Why, What, Who, and How.

With a generous hat tip to Simon Sinek (if you have not watched his TED talk "Start with Why," please take a break and check it out), let's start with **Why**. This is the impact part. What problem are you solving? What are you trying to lift up, heal, or otherwise improve? To use Nestworks as an example for this exercise, our Why was to integrate career and family needs in order to support family attachment, mental health, local economic resilience, and sustainability. Put even more simply, to integrate work and life balance.

What is your good, service, solution, or idea? Our What is a family-friendly shared workspace, where parents can access quiet working areas while their children are cared for nearby.

Who is you and whoever else is on your team or otherwise supporting you, such as mentors, advisory board members, consultants, etc. The Nestworks board of directors is a team of parents who are also experienced entrepreneurs, civic leaders, and experts in design thinking and the sharing economy. Who should also include who you serve: your customer, donor, or beneficiary. The Nestworks user is a parent of children ranging in age from infant to school-aged, who is working as an independent consultant, remote worker, or entrepreneur, and who needs a workspace with connected childcare. We are also serving children, who value being proximate to their less stressed-out parents and feeling safe and cared for in a fun environment.

How is your plan for achieving What. We held several public gatherings to learn more about our user needs as well as to build awareness and interest, which led to pop-up events that have acted as valuable prototype experiences. Through these, we are validating our concept and building content for a crowdfunding campaign to raise funds to open our first permanent location. Alongside these activities, we have crafted a detailed architectural functional program to understand how the space would need to be designed and conducted dozens of interviews with leaders in related fields including property developers, childcare advocates, civic leaders, and operators of co-working spaces.

ARTICULATING YOUR IDEA

I personally favor creating a short PowerPoint, or other slide format presentation, to flesh out these basic ideas with some supporting images. This is a simple, handy way to share your vision which, once polished, can be attached to an email or even become the basis for a creative brief, presentation, website copy, or business plan (this will be more thoroughly discussed later in the book). If you created a credo, manifesto, or mission statement in the previous chapter, use this as a starting point. Include things that you found in your detective work, for example, whether or not there are already similar offerings, social or market trends, or other conditions that point to why your solution has merit.

Once you have a rough concept document of some sort, start working up to a more comprehensive deck, i.e., a slide format presentation. Below is a common format typically used by businesses. Don't worry if you do not yet have all of these elements, but keep placeholders for them and assume that they are relevant to your enterprise. You can also think about creating a slide library based on this that you can draw from to create more focused versions, depending on the audience and format.

Basic Deck Sequence

1. **Name and description.** Use a logo and website address if you have one, or an attractive, related image if not.

2. **Why.** This is often framed as the problem that you are trying to solve, or pain point you are addressing. Put another way, in what way do you want the world to be different? What is the story behind your initiative? What impact do you seek and for whose benefit?

3. **Your solution.** How will you fix the problem and make the world a better place?

4. **What.** Details of your product, service, or other offering.

5. **Who.** Your team. This includes advisors, mentors, and organizations who have offered to support you, as well as customers, donors, volunteers, and beneficiaries (those who will benefit from the impact that your initiative creates).

6. If applicable, add an **industry or segment overview** that shows related offerings and "whitespace" (the places where others in your field aren't) that shows where you have the strongest opportunity to differentiate your offering. This should illustrate an overview of related products, services, or organizations in your orbit. Further to my earlier comments about competition, this overview may reveal prospective partners, not just others with related offerings.

7. **Your unique selling proposition (USP) or value proposition.** In one sentence, what makes your offering different from others? In the case of Aisle, our USP is that we are the most ethical, sustainable, and socially inclusive brand of menstrual products in the world.

8. **Money: your business or revenue model.** This absolutely includes grants, donations, and so on, if you go the nonprofit route. How will your project be sustainable from a financial perspective? We'll go into this in more detail in upcoming chapters, so you may just want to create a placeholder for this now.

9. **Go to Market strategy** is how you'll be reaching your beneficiaries. How will people hear about you? How will you maintain relationships with them? We'll pick this up again in chapter 8.

10. **Resources and needs.** What are your assets and what are you missing? This could include people, money, and relationships—anything that is crucial to put all of the pieces together.

11. **Next steps and call to action.** What are you going to do next and what do you want whoever is looking at this to do? It's amazing how often I see social entrepreneurs talk all about their great idea and then forget to ask for something. This could include asking for social media follows, e-newsletter signups, volunteer hours, introductions, mentorship, petition signatures, donations, or investment. To think about this in a slightly different way: how does your venture bring whoever is seeing or receiving this into your quest? We'll refine the elements of this deck or document in chapter 8, so a draft is fine for now.

MIND MAP

A mind map is a less linear way to capture your ideas, which illustrates all of the different forces and stakeholders at play in one place. Start with your beneficiary in the middle and place all related aspects of their lives around them. Draw lines connecting things that rely on, relate to, or intersect with one another. Part of what you are looking for is partnership opportunities or key relationships that will support you in achieving your mission. For example, are there ways to reach beneficiaries through organizations that are already serving them? In the case of children with cognitive disabilities, this could mean schools, related charities, educational or recreational programs, or healthcare providers. Remember that this will be a work in progress for some time as you continue to learn about these people and their needs. As much as possible, find actual people with the needs you want to address (if you are not already well versed) and interview them. This will be discussed more thoroughly in chapter 8 and can be a basic outline at this stage.

SHARING YOUR STORY

Once you have these items in draft form, it's time to start thinking about how you will share your ideas in your own words—that is, when you are actually speaking with people, not communicating with slides or via email. This is commonly known as a pitch. Start by throwing away the notion that the purpose of this pitch is to *convince* someone of something. We all know about thirty-second elevator pitches, where you have someone's attention for a very short time and must convince them of the merit of paying further attention to you, or else lose them forever. I have no idea how often this actually happens (it must sometimes), but it has become a dominant paradigm in gathering support that I would personally love to see diversified.

While you need to be able to succinctly describe your vision or venture, my experience is that cultivating a relationship of trust with other human beings is what really matters, first and foremost. I cannot overstate this point; emotion is literally the ball game. Do not be swayed by the lure of impressive statistics as the primary way of getting someone's attention. As relevant as they can be to back up your offering, they have nothing on the power of touching someone's heart. Again, this goes back to your vision, why it matters to you, and the story you tell about it. Get clear on these three things and everything else will follow. And when I say emotion, I don't just mean getting someone to realize how bad a certain problem is. It's more about conveying a sense of excitement, possibility, and connection. Think in terms of offering someone an experience, rather than a result. If I am going on a trip, it's not just about getting to the end. What kind of a trip will this be? How you deliver the story, the emotion that you bring to it, and (thanks to the magic of human empathy) how it will land with your listener are what you should focus on. This is why I got you to do those inner child and vision activities earlier. You need to be able to tap into this energy and emotion. How will you inspire the listener's inner hero to join your quest?

As an example, when I am talking to adults about the G Day

celebration series for tween girls, I often ask the simple question, "What do you remember about who you were at ages ten to twelve?" Then I pause. Contrast this to rolling out alarming statistics about how girls' self-esteem and participation in sports start to collapse after age ten and how neurological research shows that intervention with in-person events creates an emotional imprint that can serve as a positive touchstone as they move through their teenage years. Not to mention how this, in turn, can improve family relationships and build empathy, connection, and resilience. Whew! Confused, yes; excited, no. This torrent of information is too abstract. But by asking the above question, I am inviting someone on a trip—one that will have a guaranteed emotional response ("Oh, my adolescent years were perfectly happy and uneventful," said no one ever).

What I am offering them is the opportunity to either re-experience positive feelings or to heal negative ones; either way, you have someone, and they get it because it's now *about them*. Then, rather than barraging them with more information, I usually wait for them to share something, or I ask a follow-up question, like "What's coming up for you?". Based on what they say, I'll then pull out a thread that somehow relates to explaining more about what G Day is, why I created it, what it's like, who attends, and so on. Finally, I am ready with my ask. If they do not have a girl in their lives who might be able to attend, I suggest that they volunteer at the next event, ask them to tell a friend who has a daughter or niece, or suggest that they attend one of our fundraisers. I would say that well over fifty percent of these conversations end with the person saying something along the lines of "I wish I had had something like this when I was that age." At a bare minimum, I have shared a powerful moment with someone, which is wonderful in and of itself regardless of future outcomes. As a gardener, I often think of this type of small yet meaningful interaction as being akin to planting seeds. Even the mightiest trees start off as tiny seeds; do not underestimate their potential long-term impact.

CENTERING EXERCISE

Assuming you are able to prepare yourself energetically prior to your storytelling opportunity (as these are sometimes spontaneous), I want to share a brief exercise that I have found to be very helpful. Wendy Palmer is an Aikido sensei (master practitioner and teacher), who works with the unique energetic principles of this Japanese martial art to shift and manipulate force, rather than meet it head-on. She founded Leadership Embodiment in order to bring these ideas to bear on leadership and communication. Prior to engaging with others, she recommends a practice of centering. Centering is different from grounding, in that it encourages elevation and a sense of rising to an occasion. This idea resonated with me as a potentially valuable tool for everyday people, who may benefit from the experience of their energy going up, out, and expanding outward in all directions to take up more space than they are accustomed to.

Here's how it works:

1. Start by standing as tall and strong as you can, feeling your breastbone broaden. On an inhale breath, place one of your hands on the top of your head and gently compress it, then feel yourself spring up when you remove it.

2. Slowly exhale and feel your chest soften and open. Think of something that delights you or makes you smile (I think of kissing my daughter's forehead).

3. Spread your arms out into the space around you, imagining beautiful light emanating from your hands. Imagine this light as a sphere that surrounds you, taking up as much space as you feel like.

4. Settle into this energy and become aware of your surroundings.

A streamlined version of this is to breathe, remember your posture (think "strong spine, soft heart"), expand your personal space, think of something that delights you, and look into the space around you. Once you have completed either version, imagine welcoming whoever it is you will be speaking to into your sphere.

CREATIVE APPROACHES TO PITCHING

Wendy's exercise is a perfect way to prepare yourself energetically before doing something—such as pitching your idea—that can be extremely challenging. Pitches of any variety, and particularly pitch competitions, can bring up strong feelings of anxiety for me, and research has consistently shown that the metaphorical deck is definitely stacked along social privilege lines when it comes to the judges of these events and any supposed meritocracy or objectivity. Sooner or later, you are going to need to share your offering in this way, so I recommend finding as many ways to support yourself through this as possible. And while I have issues with what I'll call the harder-edged *Shark Tank* version of pitching, doing it can actually be quite exhilarating, depending on your audience and setup.

As I mentioned earlier, crafting a shorthand oral version of your vision (the pitch) is not about convincing others; it's about seduction, hope, optimism, engagement, trust, empathy, and motivation, among other things. And remember, your story is never just about you—it's also about helping whoever hears it to find their role and inspiring them to get on board, whether as a partner, team member, funder, supplier, or volunteer. These types of relationships also usually take longer than thirty seconds or three minutes to establish, so please continue to hold the idea of crafting a story, rather than a pitch, even when this is the terminology being used.

As a final tip, try to come up with something evocative or tangible that people can visualize as they are considering your idea. With Nestworks, I usually ask whether someone is a parent right at the beginning. If the answer is yes, I'll then ask, "How's work-life balance for you these days?" This typically surfaces some form of challenge. From there, I invite them to imagine the easefulness (parents crave this in their hectic lives) of being able to have their workspace and child-care in the same place. This will produce more questions and, usually, a sense of hopefulness. I often close with the observation, "We only need to balance things that are separate and far apart from one another," stretching my arms wide to suggest the great distance, physical as well as psychological, that we have placed between work and our kids. Closing my hands slowly together, I say something like, "Nestworks is about integration. Imagine being able to leave your child somewhere safe and fun, head next door to a meeting or for some quiet work time, then meet up again with them for lunch or just to check in." Sold.

Maybe you are perfectly comfortable with sharing your story or even thrive on traditional pitching; if so, that is awesome. I am still inviting you to consider new ways of framing and executing it, which may improve your results. This could look like challenging yourself to start your pitch with a brief story or provocative question, or saying "I believe . . ." as your first two words. Either way, sharing your vision, telling your story, and asking for help are activities that are absolutely essential to bringing your vision to life, so the more comfortable, committed, and excited you are about them, the more likely it is that others will be, too.

STORYTELLING TIPS

I always find it helpful to do the following when considering sharing my vision:

- Remember the hero's journey. Consider the basic narrative arc of what you are presenting, the emotions you are trying to evoke, and ways you might help whoever is listening to you to find themselves in the story. Most people's brains are hardwired to think about themselves and how whatever is being presented to them relates to them personally.

- Don't overgeneralize or hyperbolize market potential for your idea. The fact that the furniture industry is worth however many billion dollars annually has almost nothing to do with how many organic throw pillows you think you can sell.

- Resist the temptation to bombard people with facts and statistics. Nevertheless, keep one or two relevant statistics in your back pocket.

- Ask potent questions that will draw your listeners into your story. This is typically something that most people can relate to: "How many of you have ever struggled with (the pain point you are solving for) or know someone who has?"

- Tell the story of where your idea came from honestly and succinctly. Mary Letson's story about coming to appreciate the value of extra support and pampering as central to healing from her experience of breast cancer is a good example. There is nothing more moving and credible than direct personal experience.

- Close with a specific, actionable ask. What do you need and how can the person who is listening help you? Examples can include social media follows, writing reviews, getting referrals to other contacts, follow-up calls or meetings, or an agreement to provide feedback.

Practice on random people or do some role-play with a receptive friend, colleague, or mentor. Pretend your role-play partner is many different people: investor, neighbor, politician, random stranger, and so on.

Notice how you feel when you are telling your story; your body can give you valuable signals about when you are hitting your mark. This is why we often talk about gut reactions. What's happening in your tummy? Do you have butterflies or feel nauseous, or calm and grounded? Some people report tingling sensations in their hands, and I discussed earlier the important sign that tears can be. Tune in and see what's there, rather than pushing past or trying to ignore what your body may be telling you. Pay close attention to any verbal slips or turns of phrase that seem to come out of nowhere. Write them down and think about them. Pay close attention as well to the person you are speaking to, as though you are imparting something personally important to them that you may never have the opportunity to share again. Imagine literally holding on to their attention, in the most respectful manner. Be open to their responses and questions. Make it a conversation. Avoid steamrolling.

For Jeeti Pooni, a motivational speaker, author, and documentary filmmaker, sharing her story came in the form of breaking her silence about surviving sexual abuse when she confided her long-buried secret to her husband and family. I would like to say that Jeeti's story is an extreme example of the value of speaking your truth, but these types of stories are sadly all too common, so it isn't. As we have witnessed in recent years with the #MeToo movement, Jeeti found healing alongside the calling to several creative projects—writing a book, making the documentary film *Because We Are Girls*, and launching a public speaking career—as acts of resistance; in this case, against an older male cousin who had abused her and her sisters for years as children. In her words:

Breaking my silence and telling my story had a huge impact on me as a person and a leader. It changed me profoundly. It allowed me to find my own healing, become a better other, see myself as a leader, rise as an advocate to inspire and help heal others, and to educate communities worldwide. Speaking out helped to heal the trauma passed down from generation to generation in my family system and allowed me to become a voice for the oppressed, including my mother, great-grandmother, and other ancestors who endured great suffering and died in silence. It allowed me to see the richness in my story, the power my story had in helping heal others, the power of storytelling, the difference one person can make to serve humanity, and what selfless service is. It allowed me to be thankful for all of life's lessons and experiences and to see myself as a greater leader who steps up higher and higher to lead further.

By telling my story, I have become a stronger and more loving role model to my daughters. I am more open-minded, self-accepting, compassionate, and empathetic, and have an even bigger voice. I have become an entrepreneur with a greater social purpose, a more conscious human being who embraces and honors all her qualities to live a better life and fulfill her purpose in serving humanity.

For Jeeti, finding her voice and sharing her story were more than just expressing an idea. These acts demanded bravery of the highest order. If she could rise up against layers of trauma, cultural taboos, shame, and the threat of family ostracism to share her vision and bring it into being, then who are the rest of us to not stand up for whatever is calling us?

PUBLIC SPEAKING

Public speaking can be a major opportunity for you to share your vision. Just how powerful can this be? As I recounted in the previous chapter, G Day's vision traces back to a public speaking gig that I did in 2013. I got up in front of a sold-out crowd of twelve hundred people (I have never before or since addressed that many people) to tell the story about my menstrual health advocacy, Margaret, and my vision of a day and a place where we could bring our daughters, put flowers in their hair and, as I put it, "welcome them into the grand feminine mystery." It was awesome and I was elated.

Like a pebble tossed into a still pool of water, this was the moment of inception for many other ripples. A few weeks later, I was at a fundraiser for a civic politician when I was approached by a striking woman who recognized me from the event. She looked like Annie Lennox and I was immediately attracted to her alpha female confidence. She asked me how serious I was about the event idea I had explored in the presentation.

Until that moment, I had not fully given myself permission to commit to planning an actual event (I did not have a name for it yet, but that was only days away). Yet the more I talked to Catherine Runnals (a highly accomplished event planner, although I did not know this at the time), the more excited I became. We talked about how these types of rites of passage, at least in Western culture, are largely overlooked, and speculated about how our lives might have been different if we had had such an experience. As committed, professional women and entrepreneurs, we had both struggled to prove ourselves and move our ideas forward at times. Could this have been easier if we had had the benefit of this kind of community support— tangible evidence that we mattered beyond our parents and families? As the mother of a son, she further shared that she felt drawn to the idea as a way of supporting girls, since she did not have a daughter of her own.

Later that night, thrilled by this new acquaintance, I went home and Googled her and learned that her version of event planning was masterminding music and fireworks festivals attended by hundreds of thousands of people. This was who wanted to help me, thanks to me getting up on stage and sharing my vision. I was awestruck.

I continued to meet with Catherine, as well as attend more events with an eye to gleaning design and production ideas. One of my favorite colleagues, Melody Biringer, was planning an intriguing-sounding event in her hometown of Seattle, so I took it as a research opportunity and headed off. I should add that Melody is responsible for a bit of wisdom I enjoy sharing far and wide: "Relationships are the true currency." We'll get into just how valuable this currency can be in the next chapter.

Urban Campfire was a gathering of around 250 women in business which, thanks to a unique circular stage, managed to feel intimate. The focus was on personal journeys and featured many well-known speakers. The basic idea was for them to share their inner journeys as women, not just their surface formula for success. The participants then moved into smaller groups to discuss their own stories and responses. At the end there were s'mores (one of Melody's hallmarks) and a dance party. I loved it and started planning to adapt it for what I had begun calling "G Day."

The day after the event, I went for coffee with Melody, as well as Susan Gibson, an intriguing friend of hers. From the moment I met Susan, I knew that I was in the presence of someone special and powerful, despite the fact that I knew nothing about her other than that she was Melody's friend. It was just the way she looked at me, so kindly and with such great care and attention.

I shared with them my vision of a special time and place to honor girls as they transitioned from childhood to adolescence, as a way to support their self-esteem as they entered their challenging teenage years. We all shared stories in turn about what that age had been like for us, and they were very encouraging. At some point, Susan asked whether I needed capital to bring the project to life. I said yes and she offered to help. There you go: relationships are the true currency.

I hope it's becoming clear by now why I am such a huge proponent of sharing ideas and stories. This was one of the longest chains of serendipitous events I had ever witnessed in my career. The more I talked about G Day, the more amazing people kept showing up and offering to help. None of this would have happened had I not shared my vision in a way that touched the hearts of the people who heard it.

There are a multitude of ways to land a speaking gig. You can volunteer to do a presentation in a group you're part of, submit an application to a speaking event you feel drawn to, or even create your own. Lots of people don't think of the latter option but it's easier than ever these days, given the new Zoomed-up world we now inhabit.

I realize that public speaking is a fear for many of us and I know that almost every time that I do it, I wrestle with anxiety as well as excitement. To calm myself down, I remind myself of the following:

- Your audience has chosen to be here and wants to see you succeed.
- We are all human beings and none of us is perfect. We do not trust people who are "bulletproof."
- Some of the most compelling speaking presentations I have ever seen have been ones where the speaker wrestles with authentic emotion brought about by what they are sharing.
- When I say public speaking, I'm not talking about some abstract subject that I have had to research extensively and memorize facts on. It's just a story I am telling about things that are part of my life experience.
- Every group, gathering, and space has its own energy that you cannot fully control the outcome of. In other words, whatever happens is largely out of your hands anyway. All you have to do is show up fully as yourself and speak your truth. The rest will take care of itself.
- Try to work without notes as much as possible. I find that having a slide deck is useful, not just to illustrate your points visually to the audience, but also to give you cues about what you want to say at that point in the presentation.
- Some of my best moments in public speaking have happened spontaneously, when I have gone off track or followed the energy in the room instead of my planned script.

ASKING FOR HELP

Your story-sharing skills will inevitably be needed when you ask for help with your project or venture. Lots of people have issues with asking for help as it can make them feel weak, inadequate, or ashamed. If you experience these feelings, I want to invite you to take a moment to remember the last time that you helped someone do something and consider how you felt. Did you judge that person or think of them as weak? Did you resent them, or did it make you feel good? My experience is that most of us want to feel useful, especially when it comes to creating something meaningful. Over the years, I have actually come to love the practice of asking for help. Not only is it essential for getting things done, but it's an amazing way to get to know people, too. It's also kind of liberating. Why should we be ashamed of inviting others to join us in making the world better off?

Vancouver-based menstrual equity leader Dr. Selina Tribe describes what it was like to ask for support from her local school board, to address the need for access to free period products in her daughter's school:

> *Talking to the parent advisory council chair was the first time I actually spoke to someone "official" about the issue, and I was nervous! I remember being afraid to call her and bring up my issue. I imagined she would think it ridiculous. I gathered my strength and made the call. You get to the point where you just say, "F**k it, I'm gonna do it anyway." She was very sympathetic and gave her full support. And I was off to the races.*

I love this story because it shows us that the support *was already there*, ready and willing; Selina just had to ask for it. Sometimes getting results is easier than we think.

Note that "help" is not only going to look like roll-up-your-sleeves physical work. More often, it's about asking for information, contacts, social sharing, and so on. Let's take a deeper dive with what I call "wisdom harvesting," as many of its tips and tactics are relevant here. Wisdom harvesting is my personal reframing of the common concept of brain-picking, an activity which, while extremely useful, can have a dark side if not executed respectfully. Which is not to say that I have never "brain-picked"—I totally have. It's a quick and inexpensive way to get the benefit of a more experienced person's "pickings": contacts, information, trade secrets, whatever magic is the currency in your field. It can be a gold mine.

At some point several years ago, I started to feel like I wasn't actually getting what I hoped for in my brain-picking activities. I had the astonishing realization that business wasn't just about having the right contacts or information; it was about *quality relationships*. So, how do you mine gold sustainably and in good faith? In my case, I changed the name to wisdom harvesting, which felt more positive. The other realization was to see the object of the exercise as not just about the extracting part but what could be repaid or exchanged. There is a strong power dynamic underneath the concept of brain-picking that I believe is actually disempowering to the picker; namely, the idea that we have nothing and that someone else has everything. The truth is that we all have something and, as with much of what we have looked at so far, we are better off sharing it.

WISDOM HARVESTING TIPS

- Check your motivation and expectations, watching particularly for an underlying belief that you can find the keys to the kingdom, which someone else has essentially done the work for. We are all about sharing, but ultimately, you need to do the work one way or another—a fact that should be a source of pride and the essential point of your practice.

- Be discerning about who you ask. Resist putting the "harvestee" on the spot if you are in a competitive field. Even though you may share goals and values, don't assume they will want to support your project or endeavor.

- Consider paying them for their time or make a different ask—something smaller and specific, such as an introduction, or feedback on a particular idea. Are you looking for free consulting or information that you are not taking the time to look up yourself, as opposed to the benefit of someone's personal experience? Ask yourself, if you were them, would you say yes? Another option is to consider asking for an ongoing mentorship relationship (which we'll go into in the next chapter).

- Be prepared. Read as much as you can that has been written by or about them. Prepare specific, thoughtful, nonobvious questions (the answers to which do not already appear on their websites or in a Google search).

- Be willing to tell your whole story. Once upon a time during a brain-picking session, as the pickee, I was asked for a cherry-picked version of more than twenty years of my best business advice, only to be told that I was not to be trusted with a crucial piece of the picker's business story. I have no problem with being asked to sign an NDA in advance of a call or meeting; however, the assumption that her idea was so original (and that I, while being asked to offer up all manner of my valuable information, was not to be trusted with hers) frankly ticked me off and reduced my ability to actually help. Which brings me to the next tip: don't take yourself too freaking seriously. Never lose sight of the fact that we are all just humans playing a game called life together.

- Practice active listening. This seems super obvious; however, hearing feedback can be less than fun if you are not willing to listen. On another brain-picking occasion, I spent the better part of an hour feeling like the picker was defending themselves against every question or piece of advice I offered them. At the end, it honestly felt like they didn't want me to help them at all; they were too busy trying to look like they had thought of everything already. Trust me, you have not thought of everything yet. I haven't thought of everything yet—nobody has. It's okay!

- Be open to feedback and possibilities. Further to this point, be especially open to ideas or outcomes that you didn't think were relevant to your enterprise. There are likely pet theories about your venture lurking at the back of your mind that you secretly want harvestees to validate (which is also okay, just be aware of it). Having these outed or questioned can be fun and surprisingly valuable. Remember, you are not in this to convince this person you are right. Be humble.

- Show gratitude and presence. Time and attention are the greatest gifts of all, so appreciate and use them well. Be transparent when you outline your vision and goals, as you need to build trust with harvestees for them to feel comfortable sharing with you. The more excited they are about your project, the more support you will get.

- Don't apologize or minimize the opportunity that you are offering someone in being part of your project. This can show up as using language like, "Sorry to be a pain, but . . ." or "I know that this is a tiny project, but . . ." and so on. Give yourself credit for having stepped up to the plate. If people don't get it, or don't have time, or whatever, that's also okay. We are all grown-ups and it's as fine for them to say no as it is for you to make an ask. Don't take it personally and trust that you will get what you need elsewhere (or, possibly, already have the answer within you).

- Give to get. Consider (or even ask) what's in it for a prospective harvestee to connect with you. The exchange does
  not need to be one hundred percent equal, but there needs
  to be some meaningful attempt at reciprocity. There are
  things you know that they have no idea about and many
  other ways you can bring value. Watch for what they might
  be and offer them in return. As another way of doing this,
  have a supply of small, sustainable, useful gifts to give
  people who help you. My personal go-tos are organic cotton
  handkerchiefs, wool ankle socks, and small bits of oyster
  shells that I am obsessed with, which I call "yois." Although
  they cost me literally nothing, I have created a small bit
  of mythology around the yois that people seem charmed
  by. Recently, I have started making collaged postcards and
  giving them to friends and colleagues with short, personal
  messages. They carry meaning and my appreciation and can
  be a fun piece of desk or fridge art. People remember these
  things and are more likely to keep you in mind as time goes
  by. Call it energetic swag.

- Follow up. I am surprised at how infrequently harvesters
  follow up to keep us posted on what impact we may have
  had. It's lovely to hear those stories, so be sure to tell them.

There will be dozens of other asks that come up as you pursue
your venture. Always remember to put your story first, be specific
about what you need, invite others into the story, and think in terms
of exchange as much as possible.

HONORING TRANSITIONS

As I have attempted to show here, stories have the power to literally change reality from one state to another, to birth ventures and
change lives. As you hone and share your vision, notice that you

may well be moving into a new phase of your life and, possibly, a new self-definition. Again, this is a special and powerful thing that deserves recognition, as well as support, on all available fronts. You may also be transitioning *away* from something else—an old job, identity, or something that was holding you back. Either way (or both), ritual is one of the best tools I know of to mark this kind of change. It can be as simple as creating a time and place, either on your own or with people close to you, to share and celebrate what you're doing—literally making space in your life to pause and reflect, before barreling ahead as most of us do.

Here's a pared-down example that is not as elaborate as a full-on ritual, but which nevertheless brought a sense of sacredness and witnessing to a pivotal moment for me. When it came time for me to sign the contract with my publisher to write this book, I was in the Aisle office and needed someone to witness my signature. The idea of writing a book had been calling me for several years, which, true to the "Who, me?" underdog archetype that we discussed earlier, I had pushed away, telling myself that I didn't know enough yet or that nobody would find value in it. When the time came to actually go for it, it was a big, no-going-back step, and feelings of fear and excitement were having a pitched battle within me.

Christa Trueman, our amazing Aisle customer service leader at the time, was at her desk nearby and I asked whether she would be willing to help me with something. Christa is a very special person who is, in my eyes, the heart of the company, and one of the most patient, wise, kind people I know. I explained the book (which I had been fairly shy about discussing with the team until that point, for fear of backing out) and she looked me straight in the eye and said, "I can't think of anyone better to write that book." We both got a little teary, recognizing that this new step would also mean less of my energy going to Aisle. With those words, she witnessed my signature, and I knew that I had crossed the threshold from being my old self, who was not a writer, to a new self who was. By picking up the pen, I had picked up the sword. I felt seen, supported, and set free to move on and make my team proud by realizing my dream.

If you find the ritual idea appealing, take a look at the following suggestions from Emily Antflick, a former G Day Toronto community leader, founder of Shecosystem.ca, and an accomplished teacher of ritual:

- Be clear with yourself and your guests/participants/witnesses about the purpose and intention behind this ritual.
- Anchor the ritual using tangible objects, special garments, and symbols. This can mean anything related to you or the project that feels meaningful.
- Ground it in nature or the elements.
- Be intentional about who will be there and who will speak.
- Choose a meaningful time and place.
- Create a container for the ritual with a clear opening and closing of sacred space.
- Remember that you have a body; weave in breath, movement, food, or other sensory experiences.

In this chapter, we have seen that our story is basically a calling card for an actionable vision, as well as our credibility as a leader. The next step is to put yourself out there, whatever that means to you. There are literally hundreds of ways to do this, many of which will not necessarily be directly related to what you seek to create. It might be a public speaking or writing class, a meet-up of people with common interests, or a business advocacy group. In the next chapter, we'll look at building relationships and community as supports for furthering your project or venture.

CHAPTER 7

Relationships and Community Building

As I discussed in chapter 1, I am of the firm belief that a new ethos of collaboration, collective well-being, reciprocity, regeneration, and relational thinking needs to define our practice as social entrepreneurs. This stands in stark contrast to the stereotype that was hitting its peak in the pre-COVID era of the rock star entrepreneur: the solitary, driven visionary who works ceaselessly to realize his goals of disrupting entire industries, moving fast and breaking things, "crushing the competition," and "killing it" on social media. I strung together a few of the more common buzzwords—disrupting, crushing, breaking, killing—to illustrate how what was normal in the entrepreneurial vernacular, an article of faith and even cool, was actually pretty negative and ugly. I choose masculine pronouns in order to underline the distorted "toxic" masculine nature of this type of framing, even though it was absolutely practiced by people of all genders. If such activities are the presumed goals and metrics of success, what does this say about how we view our fellow human beings?

If the purpose of our pursuit is to carve out our market share and defeat others seeking to pursue similar goals, this type of adversarial language makes sense. But assuming that human creativity is finite, resources scarce, and a competitive win vs. lose framework is inevitable, is not a helpful mindset as we seek to rebuild a sustainable economy in the post-COVID world. One of the more productive insights surfaced by COVID-19 was the stark revelation that we are all in it together, and that real, lasting solutions could only be found through mutual support. Our job as citizens, activists, entrepreneurs, and change agents is to regenerate, heal, and nurture. I think it's safe to say that we have all had enough of disruption, whether by design or as an "act of God." If our goal is to support the greater good, then we need to see ourselves as colleagues and builders, not competitors.

As I discussed in the previous chapter, the reality TV show *Shark Tank* presents entrepreneurs in front of a group of merciless prospective investors (the Sharks), for gladiator-in-the-arena-style entertainment. The clear dynamic is that the Sharks are the ones with the money, influence, and last word; they set the terms of an offer or decide to be "out," meaning that they won't invest in the venture. Pitch competitions are often scaled-down versions of the same setup—sensational winner-takes-all circuses of triumph and humiliation. Something inside me always shrank when I watched these shows and events, realizing from firsthand experience how severely they minimized the entrepreneurs' efforts, exaggerated their imperfections, and virtually negated the opportunity to develop meaningful relationships between the entrepreneurs and those assessing them. *Why does this need to be adversarial?* I often wondered as I watched.

Let's imagine for a moment how a helpful reframing of this model might look. I would call it something like "Barn Raisers." The narrative would be that entrepreneurs (Barn Architects, if you will) would present their ideas to an audience of Raisers (investors, mentors, and supporters of multiple varieties). Rather than judging or negotiating, the competition would be to see which solutions or resources the Raisers could offer to help the Architects to further their ventures. "Winning" would be the successful implementation of the venture based on this collaboration.

Let's return now to you and your venture. In case you still think that you will be able to successfully bring your vision to life on your own, you can probably guess by now what I'm going to say: forget it. I'm not even going to bother with trying to convince you that this is true, so let's just move ahead with some thoughts on creating flourishing relationships, which will not only help you to make your dreams come true but will be their own reward.

First, let's look at your relationship with yourself. How's it going? Keeping in mind the inventory you took of your values, skills, and preferences earlier in the book, what I'd like to point to here is what a pillar of support we can be to ourselves. I can tell you right now that self-doubt will almost certainly plague you at some point in this journey (which we'll discuss later in the book), so a gentle reminder to be your best friend and champion at this early stage will serve you well. Know that you are just one imperfect human being who is undertaking an enormous challenge. Have compassion for yourself, even as you push yourself beyond your boundaries and into experiences that may be uncomfortable, or even painful. I can guarantee you there will be times on this journey that you feel lost and in despair. Promise yourself right now that no matter what happens, you will remain committed to being loving and gentle with yourself.

JOINING LIKE-MINDED COMMUNITIES

Support is critical when starting any new venture. Bonnie Foley-Wong, a CPA and founder of Pique Ventures, a boutique investment firm specializing in women-led, impact-focused ventures, shared her experience of this in an interview:

It is very important to have support, whether that's a financial safety net (your own that you've built up or from others), professional support, or emotional support. Perhaps the most obvious benefit is that it makes less work for you, while dividing the emotional load. This is true about starting a family and doubly true if you're starting a family and a business at the same time, or even starting a new venture that is super challenging for you. Support is critical. Having support from all sorts of sources helped me get through a very challenging time in my life and career.

Social impact organizations like Social Venture Institute (SVI) and SheEO, my two primary, indispensable business communities, offer support in the form of mentoring, education, funding, and community. There are dozens of others that I have engaged with in a variety of ways, all of which have brought and taught me something. If you take nothing else from this section, know this: you will always learn something or otherwise derive benefit, even if it's only to learn about what does not work for you, when you put yourself out there. Doing this these days will most likely mean joining an online community of some kind, but in the past, it centered around conferences and other events. While SVI and SheEO may not do the trick for you, don't worry—there are many other worthy organizations to look to for support. Thanks to COVID-19 forcing everyone to migrate online, these types of communities are more globalized and accessible than ever.

One of these is Zebras Unite, a community where pretty much anyone reading this book would find value, whose growth I have been excitedly watching since its inception in 2016. Zebras Unite is an extraordinary organization dedicated to championing mutualistic, cooperative, values-driven enterprises of all sizes, along with their founders. The Zebra name and concept were created in explicit opposition to the much-ballyhooed tech "unicorn" (a startup company with a billion-dollar valuation independent of revenue or profitability), the darling needle in the haystack of Silicon Valley venture capitalists. Zebras are a metaphor for more abundant and realistic ventures that are more colorful (as in, for profit and purpose), yet do not get nearly the level of attention, or dollars, that unicorns grab. If you have not read the founders' 2017 manifesto (all women, it so happens), aptly titled "Zebras Fix What Unicorns Break," please feel free to take a break, go to their website, and do so right now.

Here's how Zebras Unite illustrates their concept:

	UNICORN	ZEBRA
THE WHY		
purpose	exponential growth	sustainable prosperity
end game	exit, liquidity event, 10x	profitable, sustainable, 2x
outcome	monopoly	plurality
THE HOW		
worldview	zero sum, winners and losers	win-win
method	competition	cooperation
natural model	parasitism	mutualism
resources	hoarded	shared
style	assertive	participatory
seeks	more	enough, better
THE WHO		
beneficiary	private, individuals, shareholders	public, communities
team composition	engineer heavy	balanced: community managers, customer success, engineers
user pays	with attention (opaque)	for value (transparent)
THE WHAT		
growth direction	hockey stick	regenerative growth
metric	quantity	quality
priority	user acquisition	user success
obstacle	product adoption	process adoption

zebrasunite.coop

I don't know about you, but this resonates with every fiber of my entrepreneurial being. More practically speaking, Zebras Unite is a vibrant online community that boasts over seven thousand members from across the globe housed in a creative hybrid structure. Their nonprofit arm, www.zebrasunite.org, supports a more inclusive, equitable, and ethical environment for early-stage businesses, while their cooperative (www.zebrasunite.coop, launched in 2021) provides a path for entrepreneurs to own and govern the movement. Until the COVID-19 crisis, it also hosted an annual gathering (brilliantly named DazzleCon because, as everyone should know, a herd of zebras is called *a dazzle!*), and now has even more excellent online content, including podcasts. Go and sign up, look around, and be inspired. Zebras are the future, so I hope you'll meet me there. It's going to be dazzling.

Events and conferences, to the extent that they are available these days, are also a great way to make contacts, get leading-edge information, and find learning opportunities, thanks to the ability to meet people face-to-face. As much as Zoom has given us an easy way to reach one another, I am still a fan of the irreplaceable connections that can only happen in real life. Attending the SVI conference in 2000 was a pivotal moment for me, which has led to literally hundreds of meaningful conversations, relationships, and self-insights. Being among a community of dedicated, self-declared entrepreneurs who put social impact first, I finally understood just what I was and that I was not alone. I still consider the SVI community and events my spiritual home as an entrepreneur.

BE Alink, founder and creator of the Alinker walking bike, learned as much about what BE did not want for the Alinker business as what BE did want by being immersed in the social venture startup world. I should add, as a bit of a preamble, that BE is a self-described "gender weirdo" and has one of the most unique, determined minds that I have ever come across. I would call BE a visionary's visionary. The Alinker is a revolutionary walking bike that has changed what freedom means for thousands of previous wheelchair users and presents a radically empowered vision for people living with disabilities. To me, BE represents the classic profile of a social entrepreneur. Like most of the entrepreneurs highlighted in the book, BE's calling started outside of the business world: in this case, as an architect and woodworker. In terms of soul traits, I would say that BE is part "Gifts from the Margins" and part "Dancing with the Demons." Rather than trying to fit the Alinker vision into a traditional business mold, BE questioned and resisted it, and in doing so, found BE's voice and community.

I built my business in loneliness and through depression, with my vision about the world I would want to live in as a guide. Everybody said I was nuts, that I set myself up for failure, that I was all over the place and should try to comply with the systems, and that I would be crushed.

Nevertheless, there was a series of Angels (private investors) along the way who made it possible for me to survive, and I managed to build what I envisioned. Not just the Alinker bike, but a company that is a vehicle for social change, a movement where a huge diversity of people feel they belong, are heard and seen, and together we move differently. Since I learned about SheEO, everything changed. I found people who I resonated with, a network that is relational (not transactional), that comes together in radical generosity. Then my world opened up and everything became possible.

Reflecting on BE's experience, I want to pause for a moment to discuss the idea of giving ourselves permission. I feel like a lot of us are waiting for someone else to give us permission to act or approve of our idea. (For the record, BE was definitely not waiting for anyone's permission!) This may be due to the fact that we are not part of the dominant power structure or feel like because we don't fit in, our ideas are not valid or won't succeed in the current landscape. One of the most powerful aspects of BE's story is that initial feeling of not fitting in, even within the social venture community. And yet this is precisely the community's—and BE's—brilliance. These are exactly the types of products and models that are harbingers of a better future. Not only did BE create a socially impactful product: BE insisted on doing it in a nontraditional way. I want to make it clear that I believe it's essential for social entrepreneurs to not fall into the mindset of simply feeding progressive products and services into a traditional approach to business and competition. To fully express the opportunity that we have, we need to interrogate traditional mindsets and practices and be unafraid to imagine our own, based on our values and commitment to the greater good.

People did not "get" BE because BE saw an opportunity not visible to others with a more fixed mindset. I would personally concur that the social venture community is still gender and racially imbalanced and can also fall into the trap of being self-congratulatory, or thinking that no further social justice self-interrogation needs to happen because we are all so "woke." Nothing could be further from the truth and this is why organizations founded and led by women, people with disabilities, racialized people, LGBTQIA+ individuals, and others who fall outside the dominant white/cis/het/young/able-bodied male paradigm, are so critically important. How this all relates back to putting yourself out there is: 1) It's not easy, especially for "underestimated" people (to respectfully borrow Arlan Hamilton's term); and 2) There is nothing more essential if we want to build a better world.

EDUCATION AND INCUBATORS

There are increasing numbers of innovative entrepreneurial courses, programs, and incubators out there these days, some of which are specialized by type of venture (tech, food, social impact) or demographics (youth, women, etc.). In 1994, I signed up for the Venture Program, an entrepreneurial training program at the British Columbia Institute of Technology. Being part of the program gave me structure and showed me what I didn't know. My academic experience up to that point was in liberal arts, so even basic business concepts were entirely new to me. I enjoyed the program thoroughly and even walked away with a cash prize for "Most Promising Business Plan."

Caroline Thibault, the founder of a reusable coffee cup venture called the Nulla Project, entered an incubator to develop her idea for replacing disposable coffee cups.

I was working a government job that made me feel stale. I wasn't growing anymore and I felt the work didn't fully match my values. I took some time to think about my personal values and what I really wanted to try to accomplish. I applied for an entrepreneurial incubator called Project Zero and got in! I couldn't believe it at first, but I allowed myself to finally think: Why not me? I can do this! *The mentors at Project Zero believed in me and my business partner. The focus was on helping entrepreneurs develop the circular economy on Vancouver Island. I took every opportunity I could to network with as many people as I could even when I really didn't feel like it. At the end of the program, I launched our pilot project. I still can't believe it! I have felt like giving up more often than I want to admit. But every little success and the special moments that we have had and continue to have outweigh the difficult ones, from registering a partnership to having our website going live to securing our first customer to doing our first TV interview. These have been some of the most amazing moments of my life.*

VOLUNTEERING

Volunteering is a common theme that came up among my survey participants. This is a kind of low-risk way to "try on" the issue you want to address, which also serves to educate you and build your community and can even lead to partnerships. Here's a wonderful example of how showing up in a volunteer capacity led to the formation of a business partnership from Kai Scott, co-founder of TransFocus Consulting, a consultancy dedicated to promoting understanding of transgender issues in workplace settings:

> *In 2013, I was part of a volunteer working group of community members tasked with developing recommendations to support greater inclusion of transgender and nonbinary people at the Vancouver Park Board. We undertook a nearly year-long consultation process to develop a comprehensive set of seventy-seven recommendations that the multiparty board unanimously passed in April 2014. Afterwards, we got invited to speak on the recommendations at several conferences. The information we shared inspired many other organizations to raise their standards and practices and they wanted us to help them out.*
>
> *Another member of the working group, Drew Dennis, had recently left their long-term position as an executive director and was exploring options for next steps in their career. So, on a brisk winter night in 2015, we sat on my couch talking about life—I can still see it crystal clear in my mind's eye. Drew was sharing about their idea to create a foundation to promote trans issues and that it would take about two years to create a plan and fundraise operating costs. Then I casually pondered out loud: "What if we started a consulting practice that addresses trans issues?" This would allow us to start almost immediately on a cost-recovery basis. There was a sudden shift as a spark was lit. We were instantly giddy with excitement.*

I especially love the beautiful progression, from how Kai put himself out there to the pivotal conversation with Drew, to the founding of the enterprise. At the risk of being repetitive, tell everyone you know—and especially people you don't know—your ideas. They are contagious in the best possible sense.

Debbie Roche, founder of *Uncomfortable* the podcast, also got her spark from volunteering. Her podcast is subtitled *Comfortable*

Conversations around Uncomfortable Topics, and features themes including menstruation (an episode on which I was a guest), divorce, death, illness, and money, among many others. She created it to combat feelings of shame and social isolation. Here, she recalls getting started:

> *I volunteered at an event put on by a women's leadership non-profit. Women of different age groups, communities, and industries shared stories of failure and success. I'd never experienced being in a room where people openly shared their stories with an audience who were so open and supportive. I realized how powerful this was. Feeling inspired, I started a video blog where I interviewed women on "success" and what it means to them. The vlog was great and lasted a couple of years, but I started to crave conversation around more taboo topics—ones that had a stigma surrounding them. I wanted to create a safe space for those conversations to happen and realized that podcasting was a better option than video, as interviewees could choose to be anonymous.* Uncomfortable *the podcast was born.*

MENTORSHIP

Another key relationship I encourage you to cultivate is one with a mentor. Mentorship is so powerful and personalizes the "If you can see it, you can be it" axiom. Although what a mentor brings in terms of knowledge and experience is crucial, for mentorship to be truly effective, you also want to cultivate a bond of human empathy. I say this because, again, relationships that are merely transactional never yield the same kinds of rewards (not to mention pleasure) as those that are reciprocal. The other thing that's valuable about this type of relationship is accountability. Having someone to report back to about your commitments and progress—who actually cares, because you have built trust and empathy with them—is huge. When it's just us by ourselves, we can get sidetracked. When someone else is watching, we're more likely to follow through.

As someone who has mentored dozens of early-stage entrepreneurs, I can tell you what's in it for me. As a feminist, I know that it's not a meritocracy out there and that a large part of my success has to do with my social privilege, even set as it is against a backdrop of systemic gender bias. I am committed to lifting others as I rise, as a matter of principle. It also gives me the greatest pleasure when the things I have learned are "upcycled" by others, deriving additional benefit for them and many more, not just for me. As a mentor, it's like I have the ability not only to pay it forward, but to be someone that I wish I had had in my life as I set out on this path.

So, how do you find a mentor? I have been in successful mentoring relationships that were formally organized by business advocacy and training groups, as well as in more organic ways, and they both have merit. The point is to keep an eye out for someone who you respect, trust, and feel a sense of connection to. Good places to start looking are speakers at events that you are drawn to attend, LinkedIn searches, and media spokespeople whose commentary resonates with you, as a few examples. When you find a candidate, do your homework on them. Google them, read their LinkedIn profile, watch videos of their presentations, and research the organizations that they are connected to, so as to avoid asking them to repeat answers to questions that they have likely heard many times.

Once you have located a prospect and done a bit of homework on them, craft an invitation that includes what you are up to, why they and their work resonate with you, and a specific ask in terms of time and expectations. An example of what this has looked like in my experience is follow-up from a guest lecture at a local university, where the student (who asked several brave, smart questions at the lecture, making herself memorable) asked me via email for an in-person meeting to discuss her career prospects. It has also looked like meeting someone who was interviewing me online in the lead-up to an event speaking gig and just having a spark moment. Other meetings have been more formally organized by groups with whom I am affiliated. Sometimes things just work, other times not; there is no formula other than showing up and being in tune with yourself about how you feel drawn to others. At least in the beginning, set up biweekly calls or meetings (this should be up to the mentee), and "design the alliance" (to use a coaching term)— this means spelling out the desired engagement terms and desired outcome, either in a document or as an oral agreement.

It's important to cultivate and appreciate your mentors. Here are some guidelines:

- An important tip for a successful relationship of this type is for the mentee to assume the emotional labor of setting meeting times, creating calendar invites and video links, proposing meeting locations, etc. Make it as easy as possible for your mentor to help you out.

- In terms of structure, I suggest starting with monthly two-hour meetings over the course of a year. That way there's enough time to see the fruits of everyone's labors, balanced with a relatively small ask in terms of time spent. Discuss this with your mentor before you start your meetings so that expectations are clear. I should add that I have also seen these types of relationships be far more sporadic and organic, but that speaks more to the way I work personally. Eventually, most of my relationships with mentees have evolved into friendships, where the rigid roles kind of dissolve and we grow into mutually supportive peers and allies.

- Acknowledge your mentor's time with small gifts and abundant gratitude. What feeds mentors is being listened to and having their mentees take their advice. Which is not to say that you need to follow everything that they say, but if you are finding that you're not agreeing with what they have to offer you, then it may be time to look elsewhere.

Speaking of peers, it's a common assumption that mentors are always older than mentees. This obfuscates the potential of peer mentoring, or between other entrepreneurs who are on similar but different journeys of their own and could be of any age. I cannot say enough about the value of this type of relationship. The benefits are massive. It can be like having another brain working alongside yours that can nimbly share information and tips, saving you heaps of time. The kicker here is that you need to show up as well, to understand that what you are learning on your path is valuable to others and be willing to share it. In other words, the dynamic is more equal than with traditional mentorship and you will need to do more work yourself in order to support the other person.

START YOUR OWN MENTORSHIP GROUP

If this feels like a good idea to you, it's time to start looking! Good places to begin are communities like the ones I discussed earlier. One of my favorite peer mentoring groups is called The Breakfast Club—a cheeky reference to the movie, as well as the fact that we convened for several years at monthly breakfast meetings. The Breakfast Club has its origins in SVI. At any given meeting, there would be six to twelve of us following the basic format of a roundtable catch-up that was part personal and part business, followed by a (friendly) hot seat focus, where one of us would present an issue that we were facing and receive feedback on it from the group. The group would then ask clarifying questions and offer advice about how to deal with the issue. Attending dozens of these meetings cemented our bonds and from there, we were able to call upon one another at any time with quick questions, recommendation requests, feedback on ideas, and so on. The relationship with my and Suzanne's SheEO Venture cohort is very similar. Having invested time and energy into getting to know the person and their venture, we are able to give speedy, frank, and helpful feedback. Plus, we are all emotionally invested in one another, so it's not just about smart tips. These are people and projects that we want to see succeed; they are making a better world for us too, after all.

COACHING

When done well, coaching can be one of the most rewarding invest-ments you will make. I have the immense good fortune of having one of the most experienced life coaches ever as one of my closest friends—Signy Wilson, a Co-Active Training Institute faculty member and Master Certified Coach. I have benefited from her insight right from the get-go, when I was one of her earliest practice-clients in 2001. I have learned so much from her during my journey. Understanding the relationship between my personal values and career path, the willing-ness to have tough conversations, and the value of accountability are all related to the early work that I did with her.

To back up a bit for folks new to coaching (whether it's per-sonal coaching, executive, career, relationship—basically anything nonathletic), it looks pretty much how you might imagine: a highly skilled individual who is in your corner beyond "You've got this!" and who is similar to a supportive friend or family member, except that their primary focus is *your agenda*. (No matter how much they love you, friends and family members still have their own personal objectives running in the background.)

Coaches focus on goals and accountability, and invariably ask awesome questions. They hold the perspective that people are natu-rally creative, resourceful, and whole, meaning that they do not try to fix you because they do not see you as broken or a problem to be solved. Instead, they work to help you discover your own answers to the challenges that invariably come with pursuing a dream by acti-vating the part of you that comes up with your own solutions.

To be clear, coaches are not the same as therapists or counsel-ors. A coach is there to help you achieve whatever it is that you are committed to, not so much to hear the personal issues that are getting in the way. They are also not consultants who give you advice based on their experience. They are there to help you get where you want to go, while holding you accountable to a plan that they support you in designing.

Vanessa LeBourdais, the founder of DreamRider Productions, shares her experience with coaching:

> *I have the incredible privilege of having an executive coach who has walked me through much darkness, pain, and uncertainty for ten years now. "Coach" is the wrong word. There is no darkness I can enter that he is afraid of. He literally saved my marriage, helped transform my board, and made it possible for me to lead a small nonprofit without following my family members into heart disease. Last week, he led me by the hand out of the panic and anxiety I was immobilized by as ninety percent of our revenues are at risk because of COVID-19. Liberated, over the next two days I began new initiatives to turn the organization around.*

I will add that this example is a longer list of issues than most coaches typically deal with, but you get the idea. I would also say that coaching is especially beneficial for social entrepreneurs because of our deep attachment to the Why behind what we undertake. It's not always a straightforward "read the market, make the product, get the margins right, execute" type of strategy. There are typically other layers in there that can complicate things. Truly knowing ourselves—what motivates us, how we work best, our strengths and weaknesses—is what will increase the chances of succeeding in our endeavors. Coaching helps with that. Furthermore, when choosing to step into a new space like social entrepreneurship, one part of the process might be needing to redefine ourselves. We can do that most effectively by understanding where we have come from, how it relates to this change, and where we ultimately want to go. Having a trained professional helping to proactively navigate alongside us makes something that can often be challenging both richer and easier. That said, coaching can be pricey, so that's another reason why it's worth being discerning about who you work with.

SIGNY WILSON'S TIPS ON WORKING WITH A COACH

For coaching to be most effective, you need to have a rapport or chemistry between you. To be clear, rapport is not about being similar in terms of personality, but about being able to let your guard down with them and to feel comfortable bringing all of yourself. If you are trying to look good in front of your coach, impress them, or "get it right," the coaching will be less effective. Ask yourself these questions: Would it feel easy to give this person straight feedback? Would you feel comfortable receiving feedback from them? Will they bring out the best in you, as in bringing out your authentic brilliance?

How a coaching engagement typically unfolds:

- Sample session: A free thirty-minute introduction where you meet the coach and get a sense of their coaching style.
- Agreeing to work together, usually for a specified time period (often six months, but there are many options).
- Discovery session: A longer fact-finding session to get clarity on your business and life goals, values, and coaching goals, as well as to design the working alliance between you.
- Ongoing, regular coaching sessions: The frequency and length will vary, depending on the coach and what you need. Having two forty-five-minute conversations per month is not uncommon.
- Regular interactions via email or text throughout the month: These exchanges could be about suggested articles, books, websites, etc.
- Some coaching engagements will include evaluating your results from an assessment tool together (the Myers-Briggs

Type Indicator® personality inventory is a classic example, although there are dozens of others).

- Completion session: This comes at the end, to look back over your progress and decide if you want to keep working together for a second engagement.

Here are Signy's top six tips for success in working with coaches:

1. **Know what you are getting into**. Professional coaching is not the same as "business coaching." Generally speaking, business coaching is code for consulting about your business (the word *coaching* has become so hot recently that it is being integrated into lots of different, unrelated job titles). That said, professional coaches can put just about anything in front of the word *coaching*, and this is so you know their specialty; for example, leadership coaching. Be sure that you are clear on what they are offering and how they will support you. It is less important that they have specific experience doing what you are trying to do (which tends to result in a lot of consulting conversations where giving advice is the focus), and more important that you feel like they get you and have the skills to help you achieve your objectives.

2. **Be coachable.** It is the coach's job to help you grow as a person as you grow a business idea or passion project. This means being open to feedback, including on your blind spots, which can be hard to hear but can also change the trajectory of your work and life. It is your job as the client to be deeply curious and willing to experiment, and to give your coach feedback on what you need more or less of (e.g., challenge, support, or accountability). So, pick a coach whose style you like (whether that's more direct, informal, process oriented, spontaneous, etc.) and who you trust enough to let past whatever armor you might have on.

3. **Have well-defined coaching goals.** Coaches can be a part of the process of identifying and refining these goals, but if it's something you need help with, be explicit with your potential coach about this in the sample session. Coaching without a clear goal is like sailing without a rudder.

4. **Bring clear topics to each coaching session.** These will often relate to your original goals but sometimes will diverge. With coaching, you are not buying a set program (although that also exists) where the coach takes you through certain prescribed activities. More typically, it is customized to you. To that end, you, the client, are the one guiding the process by intentionally selecting topics that will advance your work.

5. **Be willing to be real.** If you are not able to bring your whole self, the coach has less to work with. Part of their work in coaching is to help you excavate your deeper motivations, your dreams, and what holds you back. If you are only telling them half the story, you will only get half the benefit.

6. Speaking of stories, it can be tempting to start each session with a long-winded retelling of how you got to the point that you want to address in that session, or else what your week was like. Usually, the coach does not need that information. They are working to move you forward, so the past is less of the focus. **Bottom-lining to get to the heart of the matter** will help you make best use of your coaching time.

PARTNERSHIPS

The Lunapads/Aisle story is as much about the relationship between my co-founder and CEO, Suzanne Siemens, and me as it is about social impact. Whether or not you have the good fortune to find a reliable, skilled, energized business partner you are able to maintain a harmonious and productive relationship with, the takeaway is this: the success of your enterprise will largely be determined by the quality of relationships that you create to support it. This includes suppliers, investors, customers, team members, and others. They are all people first.

I first met Suzanne in 1999, when I was transitioning my first company, everyware designs, from garment manufacturing, retail, and custom clothing to focus solely on Lunapads. Having worked with a small but tight-knit team of five members for the previous three years, I was on my own again, with the exception of the intermittent support of an excellent production manager, Judy Ho, and a prescient web designer, Henry Faber. I closed my store and factory and moved into a small office in an eclectic building downtown, dedicating myself to pursuing wholesale and online sales for Lunapads. While I had left the stress of carrying too many diverse activities behind me, I was lonely and missed working with others.

One day, I was visiting my parents and my mom suggested that I enroll in a local community leadership course, which she had heard about through her own career as a social worker, volunteer, and nonprofit board chair. Even though I didn't know any of the details, I had an instant intuition hit about signing up and was subsequently invited for an interview. By the interview, I had realized through various subtle signals that as a small-scale creative entrepreneur, I was definitely an outlier. The program was designed to recruit and train corporate executives to become active as nonprofit board members. Feeling out of place and disappointed, I walked away assuming that I would not be selected to attend.

I was amazed and delighted when I got the news that I had in fact been admitted, and was soon packing my bags to attend a weekend retreat on a nearby island. Within the larger class of sixty or so participants, we were convened into smaller groups for the purposes of project-based work. Suzanne was in my group and I instantly liked her. We were about the same age and I was immediately struck by her energy, intelligence, and kindness. For her part, she tells the story of how, at the retreat, we were all given polar fleece vests embroidered with the program's logo. I politely refused mine, citing the fact that I did not need it (stylish, logo-free polar fleece vests being a specialty from my design days), which somehow impressed her. She recalls thinking that seeing me refuse the vest made her desire to befriend this "rebel entrepreneur."

By the end of the weekend, I had an important new friend, and I remember telling my then-boyfriend (now husband) Tim about her. In the past, people had often suggested to me that I should consider finding a business partner, which always frustrated me. While it was clear to me that my skill set was, shall we say, uneven, the implication that such partners were easy to find if one only looked was irksome to say the least. But at last, I had found someone who felt like exactly the type of person I wanted to work with.

And work together we did. We had ongoing meetings about our project thanks to the program, the purpose of which were to create a marketing plan for an organization with the mandate to maintain girls' participation in sports as they entered adolescence. For anyone new to this issue, there is a devastating trend of attrition in girls' sport participation and commensurate drop in their self-esteem starting around the age of ten. I remember being so impressed when we had meetings at Suzanne's company's office, located high up in a downtown skyscraper. She just seemed so grown-up and powerful to me with her smart suits and business savvy. I felt like some kind of a hippy ruffian artist freak by contrast, yet there we were, rapidly becoming fast friends.

It's worth noting that the basis of our relationship was collaborating on a project together, rather than something more common like meeting at a social event. Thanks to this, we were able to see what it was like to actually work together, rather than "just" being friends (friendship is no small thing!). As you saw in chapter 7's example of Kai Scott and Drew Dennis coming together as co-founders after volunteering on a community project together, this type of framework can be a wonderful test case for a business partnership. This is very different from a situation where you start out as close friends and assume that everything will go well as business partners because you love each other so much. Not that that can't happen— you're just starting from a different place, which can make it harder to accurately see flaws and address stressful situations as they arise.

Another thing to note is that, in my experience, when we look for a business partner or any other figure key to building our under- takings, we often default to seeking people who are similar to us. This makes sense in terms of values and vision, but what you need to keep an eye out for is when things overlap too much in terms of skills, background, and areas of interest. If, for example, I'm a fashion designer who wants to start a fashion design business, does it neces- sarily bring value to have another designer as a business partner? We both love fashion, so why not? Why not is because you need to occupy different seats and bring different strengths; in other words, you need to be different. In this case, you could definitely still do it, but you would need to find another partner or contractor to handle business operations, leaving the design duo to work their creative magic.

In our case, it looked like this: I am from generations of white Settler Canadians, right-brained, creative, and rebellious, while Suzanne, on the other hand, is a first-generation Chinese Cana- dian born to immigrants who had none of the social privilege of my ancestors. Her parents had ingrained in her that she needed to pursue a safe and steady career, and so, given her left-brain aptitude for math, she became an accountant. When I met her in 1999, she was fulfilling their dream by working at a large public oil and gas utility company, rapidly climbing the corporate ladder.

What didn't show up on her polished, authoritative exterior was the inner heartbreak and disillusionment she felt. She was working countless, exhausting hours with the goal of maximizing shareholder profit at the expense of employee well-being and environmental con- siderations, making her feel empty. By the time we met, she was in a form of existential crisis, wondering what good her personal sacrifice was bringing to the world, not to mention the significant toll it was taking on her health. The cognitive dissonance between fulfilling her parents' dream and how she actually felt inside must have been thunderous.

One day in the leadership class, we did a workshop with the larger group, overseen by a guest speaker—Deb Joy from Renewal Partners, a local startup impact investor group. From the moment she explained that the company's vision was to invest in BC-based sustainable businesses, I knew that there was hope for Lunapads's future. Deb herself went on to co-found an organic produce home delivery company and remains a friend to this day. This was a turning point for Suzanne and me because, by the end of the day, she had offered to help me prepare financial statements to pitch Renewal on investing in Lunapads. It was during these meetings that the penny really dropped that her interest went beyond that of a friend; she was destined to be a part of it.

Basically, it all came down to the fact that I needed help and she needed a new sense of purpose. Fate intervened and we took the leap. I mentioned the Visionary/Integrator model earlier in the book; I did not have that vocabulary in 1999, but looking back now, I see that this was our dynamic. Despite having very different skill sets and ways of working, we have a unique way of building on each other's ideas and picking up each other's slack.

But sometimes, these kinds of differences can cause tension. This is where the power of trust and letting go of traditional power dynamics come in. Like other close relationships, you will inevitably also need to have challenging conversations with your business partner. You will only come out the other end of these intact if they happen inside a container of respect, trust, and deep commitment. This can be hard to maintain for mature adults at the best of times, and the stakes get higher when there is money involved. We have definitely weathered some very challenging times and conversations.

Here is an example of how we have learned to work together. Prior to making big decisions, Suzanne, being more of a process geek, likes to solicit opinions from multiple people, while I tend to want to get on with things immediately and am a big fan of trusting my intuition. Both approaches have merit and have served the company at different times. When I start to think, *Can we please just get on with it?*, I remember that this is her process, that mine is different, and that she is just as likely (in fact more likely, truth be told, as my impatience is often the byproduct of laziness) to be right (whatever that means) as I am. This is a mental practice that has taken many years to build and, of course, it will not feel comfortable to everyone. What has always gotten us through the tough times is a willingness to come to the table (usually by the following day) as soon as something feels weird or tense and not letting things fester. For us, maintaining our relationship has always come ahead of purely business concerns.

One of the biggest keys to maintaining equilibrium with partners is to maintain a "whole person" perspective. I suggest that you always start meetings with an honest personal check-in. How are we *really* doing? If this does not get acknowledged, my experience is that it almost invariably gets in the way of people being fully present. Doing this also reminds us that, at the end of the day, we are just human beings. Maybe this is why the *Shark Tank* model irks me so much; it makes it so much harder to develop this key sense of trust when the setup is presumed to be adversarial and there is always a winner and a loser, rather than seeking to understand and honor whose skills fit best where.

Another important suggestion I have around partnership is to let go of the assumed need to maintain one hundred percent of control of your enterprise. It's worth considering where you stand in terms of trusting others in general at this stage. For example, are you scared that your ideas may be stolen or that prospective partners may take advantage of you financially? I'm not saying these things do not or will not happen; of course they can. What I'm pointing to here is taking a moment to check on your inner trust barometer, in case there are issues there that could use some work. A common expression of fear around trust in the case of business is the assumption that we need to maintain majority control over our ventures, an idea that I find questionable and potentially (ironically) limiting. The fact is, you are not going to be able to get far on your own, so the more self-aware you can be around how you approach relationships at this stage, the better.

I raise this in the context of the relationship with Suzanne because the opposite of this fear has proven to be true. The more skin in the game she had, the harder she worked. Another way of looking at this is to consider whether you want to own, say, eighty percent of a pie worth $100,000, or fifty percent of a pie worth $1 million. More isn't always more.

For Jacinthe Koddo, an entrepreneurial polymath whose career has taken her from holistic nutritional catering to business strategy expertise, getting comfortable with the idea of partnership was key to her success:

> *I needed to approach it slowly. I'd tried starting other businesses on my own before and failed miserably. I needed to give myself permission to have partners rather than thinking I had to do business myself. It's only now that I realize that I like working better with others, and while a partnership with others never really appealed to me, I've eased my way into one and it's been nourishing, challenging, exciting, and supportive! What originally started as a side hustle evolved into Tandem Innovation Group by trusting my intuition, surrounding myself with amazing people and asking for what I need and want. I trust in the power of serendipity and am constantly evaluating where I want to grow personally and with this business.*

What you're looking for is a dynamic where the whole is truly larger than the sum of the parts. This notion of sharing control is also creative and intellectual. How this feels to me is like having a set of building blocks that you share with someone, where you take turns adding to the structure. What this has looked like in practice for Suzanne and me is basically an endless conversation, where one idea builds on the next. To reiterate, it's not about one idea winning out over another, but a flow of ideas that build upon one another. The flow stops as soon as someone says "mine" or "wrong." The process is seldom finite and is best understood as nonlinear. Maybe the decision would be better made tomorrow, or when someone is feeling more grounded? I am also very fond of thinking outside of binary solutions: *Why not have both options? What if there's another way?*

ADVISORY BOARDS

As your network and the scale of your project expand, consider convening an advisory board. Advisory boards are a less formal version of a corporate board of directors. They are nonvoting and are there to offer you feedback and advice. If you have a mentor, definitely consider including them. Advisory boards are kind of like chess boards that you populate with diverse strategic players. One of the smartest ways I have seen to build advisory boards is getting two or three (or one will do if they are fairly well known) people, then dropping their names to attract the others. One of the main rewards that board members will receive is adding new key relationships to their own networks. Come to think of it, advisory boards are actually great places to meet prospective business partners because you have the opportunity to see how others think as you work on a project together. Again, feed and water them well and give them gifts and gratitude. Listen, deliver, and be accountable.

CHAPTER 8

Bringing Your Initiative to Life

I LOVE THE TACTILE, kinesthetic nature of this part of the book. We get to make stuff! I encourage you to be as wildly creative as possible at this stage. Your project is not real yet, which allows for maximum imagination, so don't hold back. This should be fun.

The point of this chapter is to do two things: first, to make a working model or approximation of your product, service, or initiative that can be tested; and second, to build out the financial and operational framework that will ultimately support it, also known as the business model. If this sounds like a lot, don't worry! I will break it down into steps. Let's start with prototyping.

PROTOTYPING

Prototyping is making an approximation of your product or service. It does not need to be fancy or exactly the way you imagined (part of the point here is to get a clearer understanding of what the details need to look like), so it's best to just dive in without worrying too much about getting it right. We are here to learn.

To put prototyping into context from a design thinking perspective, the work that we have done up to this point—at least in the methodology that I learned at the THNK School of Creative Leadership—is called "sensing" (looking at your personal history and other detective work) and "visioning" (translating the sensing data into a vision). It's now time to roll up your sleeves and start to shape these ideas and insights into a concrete offering.

There's obviously a big difference between designing a product and a service; however, many of the tools I'm sharing here can work for either and I will offer comments on both. A high-level observation about prototyping is that there are always endless potential iterations, so you are not looking to create your all-time perfect offering right out of the gate. You are doing this to immerse yourself in the actual user experience and see where it takes you. Curiosity is your friend; perfectionism can be invited to cool its heels elsewhere.

For starters, I would encourage you to think in terms of your desired impact, actions, and experiences. Let me break these down a bit:

- **Impact.** How will the world be different once your venture succeeds? What will it look and feel like? What are some examples of this difference?
- **Actions.** Having spoken a great deal about how we want our ventures to come from a relational—rather than transactional—space, now is the time to look at those transactional elements. What are the actions that will be taken by your users? This could be something like buying a product or service or making a donation. It could also be something nonfinancial like signing a petition, taking on a volunteer role, voting for something, subscribing to a newsletter, attending an event, responding to a survey, or spreading the word

about something on social media. What are the exact steps that need to happen in order to create the impact? Map these out carefully and then compare it with what you learn later on from actual users interacting with your prototype.

- **Experience.** How does this all feel to the different people who will be involved on both sides of the table? How will it feel to you and your team? What is the experience or journey that you are offering? What makes it special and unique? In the case of Nestworks, we want our users to feel relieved, as though their lives have just become less complicated. Easefulness is one of the core words that our team came up with in our early design discussions, which later became one of our metrics of customer satisfaction.

Another useful thing to do at this stage is to revisit the user/beneficiary profiles that we touched on in chapter 6. This can be based on a real or purely fictional person. Take some time to imagine their life and what need or value you will provide for them. You can have more than one. Write a detailed profile that includes the following:

- Their age group or life stage
- Location
- Racial, cultural, and/or ethnic profile
- Job/career/income level
- Education
- Family status (single, kids/no kids, divorced, etc.)
- Values and political views
- Pain points: what's missing for them and how can your product or service make a difference?
- If applicable, brands they like, places they shop, and other ways they spend their time, money, and attention

USER JOURNEY

Next, make a map that tells the story of their engagement with your offering. This is known as a user journey in design thinking methodology. Be sure to include what their emotional state might be at any given stage. It's okay not to know; however, empathy is a vastly underrated tool and given that you are pursuing a social change agenda, being aware of and tapping into people's emotions is a critical aspect of whatever you create. Using sticky notes or a large notepad, detail the following about your user:

- How they will learn about your offering (word of mouth, service agency, Google search, paid marketing, etc.). Feeling: curious, surprised, relieved, fed up, etc.
- What steps they will take to engage with it (visit your website, send a text, stop by a physical location, etc.). Feeling: skeptical, encouraged, inspired, hopeful, etc.
- What happens next (newsletter signup, a purchase, learning more, booking a complimentary session, downloading a free resource, etc.). Feeling: excited, anticipatory, etc.
- What happens next (email follow-up, phone call, video call, etc.). Feeling: belonging, seen, heard, etc.
- At what point is someone "converted"? If there is a financial transaction, what is it and when does it occur? If the action is, for example, dropping off donated items somewhere, where does this happen? Feeling: easeful, satisfied, connected, vindicated, empowered, etc.
- Follow-up: how do you acknowledge and retain the user? What is the quality of the relationship that you have created? What will keep them coming back and/or telling others? Feeling: connection, optimism, encouragement, virtue, etc.

GETTING READY TO PROTOTYPE

Gather anything you can easily get your hands on that may be useful. This can include:

- Arts and crafts supplies
- Lego or other small-scale building objects
- A large notepad, markers, sticky notes, etc.
- Other supplies related to your particular project
- People, if needed (role-playing can be a form of prototyping)

Thinking back to early Lunapads prototypes, I gathered many different types of materials, including raw hemp fiber, cotton batting and quilt filler material, and several types of fabric and fastenings. I used thick paper to make patterns and my trusty sewing machine to stitch together the prototypes. At the risk of repeating myself, it does not need to be perfect. The odds of creating a perfect product or experience the first time are very low. The point is to start and learn and iterate (also known as "pivoting"). Identify specific problems or aspects of what you are working on and document them. For example, in the case of Lunapads, the following key aspects needed to be solved:

- How the pads would attach to the user's underwear
- Softness, breathability, absorbency, and leak-proof capacities
- Washing and drying characteristics
- Durability
- How the pads would be stored and transported when outside the home

My first pads were a far cry from the sleek, elegant Aisle version we sell today. In fact, many of the fabrics that we now use weren't even invented at the time. Bit by bit, I tried new designs and fabrics and got my friends to test them, learning along the way what did and did not work, what was more or less comfortable, and how they stood up to multiple washes. I even had some lab testing done to understand whether there was any potentially harmful residue in the pads. (The result being that the pads were no different in this regard than everyday underwear that is repeatedly worn and washed. Phew!)

I also took the opportunity to learn about what the testers liked and disliked about their current products, asking users how much they were currently spending and what they might be willing to pay for a reusable product that would save them money in the long run. It's worth taking the time not only to understand how someone responds to your offering, but also to learn about other solutions that they may currently be using to mitigate the problem you're seeking to address. I learned that the two major barriers that users were concerned about (aside from some being too squeamish to consider the idea of a reusable menstrual product in the first place) were how to wash the pads and how to change and transport them when they were outside their homes. In other words, my task was no longer designing just the pads and underwear, but also the information and accessories to support successfully using and caring for them.

As you are doing this, keep notes and gather any data, questions, or feedback that show up, as well as keeping an eye on how long the iterations take to make and the price of the materials. Having a standard survey that you give to product testers is also a great idea; you can more easily see common trends that way. You will be making lots of them, so don't use up too many of your resources if you don't need to.

What if you're not making a product? Services are totally prototype-able, too. Start by mapping out the desired impact, actions, and experience as previously described, and then consider how you can approximate those steps. Services can often be prototyped by role-playing with friends or family members. I am not well versed in AI or simpler ways to replicate experience online, but from what I do know, it would be an ideal medium for service prototyping.

As an example of prototyping a service, let's look at Nestworks. As a reminder, the idea is a co-working space for parents with an adjacent childcare facility for their kids. To get a more precise understanding of how the space needed to be designed, I worked with some architects who did a great deal of research and made technical drawings based on our ideas. We built a website with a link to a survey that asked prospective users about their lifestyles, work, and family situations. We also hosted community gatherings and created pop-up events.

The community gatherings and pop-ups were the closest we could get to what we had in mind as experience prototyping, and I and other board members took the opportunity to engage directly with users about their needs and to get feedback on our ideas. In the case of the community gatherings, we had regular monthly meet-ups that we promoted on social media at a local café. This way, we developed a regular group of committed users who also spread the word about the project to their networks. We would spend ninety minutes once a month hearing about their struggles finding childcare and managing career and family needs. Going back to what I said earlier about the value of empathy, this is a perfect example. Nestworks is about addressing some of parents' core needs: child safety, economic sustainability, family attachment, and mental health considerations. We needed users to see that we understood their experience and were serious about addressing it. In this case, the prototype experience was about much more than simply figuring out how the space was going to work and which amenities were going to be available at what price; it was also about building trust and relationships.

The pop-up concept was more developed. We rented a co-working space and hired childcare providers. While it was not *exactly* what we envisioned for Nestworks, it offered the core basics of our value proposition: for parents to be able to bring their child to a co-working space and have them safely occupied, while they get some work done in a separate nearby space. We also took the opportunity of having a pop-up to shoot a video about our vision. On top of all this, it was an important first step in developing a relationship with our childcare partners—seeing the toys and activities that they brought, safety and cleanliness best practices, and how the children and parents responded to them.

Then again, sometimes you just have to dive in at the deep end. This is what happened with G Day. While I had been thinking about having an event for tween girls for several months by that point, I knew all along that part of its power had to be its scale. We could have started smaller and worked up to something bigger, but I felt that would deprive us of understanding the value of scale. The number I had firmly fixed in my head was 250 girls, and as it happened, that's exactly how many ended up coming. The only thing I wish I had done differently was to include parents more as participants, as we heard strong feedback after the first event that many of them would have liked to be included. We would have known this much earlier if we had done smaller events first. Bearing this in mind, we pivoted to offering first a part-day, then a full-day program for adults at future events.

USER TESTING

Whether you are building a product or a service, once you have a prototype ready, it's time to start testing it with your users. Find as many people as you can reasonably manage to see through the experience that you are offering. Abeego beeswax food wrap founder Toni Desrosiers literally made hundreds of prototypes that experimented with different fabrics, qualities of beeswax, and cleaning methods. She took the prototypes everywhere she went and tested them continually, using them with different types of food to see how well they worked over long periods of time, as well as what happened with repeated washing.

Invite your testers to join you on an imaginative ride and consider offering them incentives if you can. This can be as simple as free coffee and snacks, or something more elaborate and intriguing related to the issue that your project addresses; if it's related to agriculture, for example, you could consider giving small plants or packets of seeds as thank you gifts. Make it fun and interesting for people to participate and be sure to give them plenty of opportunities to share their needs and wants with you. People like feeling seen and heard as much as they want to feel like leaders or founders. Don't be shy about letting them know that their input and participation are incredibly valuable.

Make sure you are ready to document what happens and, above all, have the mindset that you are seeking to learn, not to prove or sell your idea. It's definitely a good plan to get help from friends and possibly even to remove yourself a bit from the proceedings. (If you are directing the testing, it may be harder for you to accurately observe user behavior or note their questions.) Knowing too much can get in the way of objective observation and you want to get as much clean data as possible. Close friends or family members are more likely to try to please you or hold back on negative feedback, so having an anonymous follow-up survey to get people's real opinions is a smart way to get constructive feedback, not just compliments.

From there, gather your learnings, tweak your prototype, and keep going. Once you have a minimum viable product (MVP), you are ready to go to market—almost. First, you need to consider the financial and operational scaffolding that's going to hold everything together. As for how you know that an MVP is ready, there is no hard-and-fast rule; however, the product or service absolutely needs to fulfill the value proposition. It's okay if it still does not have all of the bells and whistles that you would like it to, but it needs to work and provide reasonable value for the price that you're asking. Your MVP is also what will be used as a replicable sample if you are creating a product, and an offering that would be described on a website or in a brochure if you are designing a service.

BUSINESS MODELS AND CANVASSES

The next step is to build a more fleshed-out version of the brief ideas deck we discussed in chapter 6. Once upon a time, back when I started out in the early '90s, the gold standard of entrepreneurial startup bedrock was a long, detailed business plan. Onerous to research and write and seldom referenced once completed, somewhere along the line, the business plan got mercifully abbreviated to a business model canvas. Don't be put off by the "business" part; these documents apply whether you are for-profit or otherwise. You can think of it as a project canvas if you like. Plus: *canvas*, right? Think of yourself as metaphorically painting a picture of how your project is going to come to life. A business model canvas is a map of how any venture works from an operational and financial perspective. I think of a business model as kind of a flow chart of money, actions, and outcomes. I'm not saying that you don't need to write a more formal business plan (you definitely will in order to obtain significant levels of funding, should you choose to go that route), but this is an easier way to get started that touches on all of the same key elements.

If this is a new concept to you, I invite you to pause for a moment to do a quick online search for "business model canvas" and see what you get. There are now many diverse varieties, from feminist to regenerative, circular, social, and many more, so I'm sure you'll find one that works for you. What I love about this tool is that it's simple and allows you to see everything at once, kind of like one of those elevation drawings of a doll's house where you can see inside all of the different rooms. One of the better ideas I have come across recently is using a laminated, wall-sized canvas with erasable markers, which allows for quick iteration and changes. There are also some excellent online versions, many of which are free. Find one that you like and have it at the ready.

Any business model canvas you end up working with will have the same basic common elements. Let's walk through them.

Vision/Mission/Purpose/Impact Statement

This is how your venture will get us to the beautiful world we are headed to together. You have already done a ton of work on vision in chapter 5 by this stage and can likely come up with something awesome. Note that typical business canvasses do not include this; however, as a social impact venture, I like to see it at the top of a canvas as a reminder of your Why or "North Star." If you were able to come up with a mission or purpose statement based on the work we did earlier, this is a great place for it. Just a simple name and/or tagline will do if you're not completely there yet with the formal vision/mission statement. To clarify again, vision is about the longer-term big picture, or what the world will look like when your initiative has succeeded.

Value Proposition

What value does your project or venture provide that would be a compelling exchange for someone's time, money, and attention? This can be very simple and straightforward, and there can also be more than one. It's the How that will ultimately lead to the fulfillment of the vision. As an example, Nestworks's value proposition is to simplify working parents' lives by offering them a place to work while their children are cared for. G Day's value proposition is to provide a profound social-emotional learning experience for tween girls and their supporters, which will foster positive peer relationships, resilience, self-esteem, and community connection. Aisle's value proposition is that we offer best-in-class sustainable period products to menstruators of all sizes and genders. You should feel proud of and excited about your value proposition. I love Aisle's summary: "The Best Place on Earth to Have Your Period." Do not overcomplicate it; keep it as simple as possible and avoid trendy business jargon.

Target Beneficiary

This individual, profile, or avatar is also known as a target customer or user, but I prefer beneficiary because it implies social impact. Whose life are you improving? What is their challenge that your offering will solve? If you know or have read about a real person who represents this need and can share their actual story, amazing. If not, then it's perfectly fine—standard practice, even—to construct a hypothetical profile based on a mix of facts and hypothesis. The point is just that you do it—if you don't, it will become harder to differentiate your offering. If this is the case, my guess is that your offering might be too broad; for example, wanting to get rid of ocean plastics entirely or ending a widespread form of social bias. As admirable as this is, it's problematic to put "everyone" as your target beneficiary. Instead, you need to get people to care on a specific, personal level and engage them in ways that are accessible, relevant, and meaningful to their lives. In the case of reducing ocean plastics, you could target a specific group—makeup artists, hair stylists, grocery stores, or coffee shop patrons, for example. Think about age, gender, voting tendencies, and lifestyle indicators like the nutritional or exercise preferences that they might have. What's their story? What else do they care about that intersects with your offering?

As a related point, sometimes your **beneficiary** and **your customer/donor** are not the same person. If you are creating an initiative to support access to outdoor activities for children with disabilities, you are not expecting the children to fund your initiative; the stakeholders will be people like parents, governmental organizations and related charities, and granting bodies, etc. Be clear about this difference and make profiles for both of them.

Delivery Channel

What is the path or network through which your product or service travels to get to the customer, donor, or beneficiary? In Aisle's case, we abbreviate the fact that most of our sales are transacted via our website as direct-to-consumer, or D2C for short. You might also sell your product through wholesale channels (via other businesses), catalogues, consultants, dealers, and so on. Basically, this is anything or anyone that your product or service goes through in order to get to the end user.

Go to Market Strategy

How will your users learn about and be compelled to buy into your value proposition? This bullet point could literally fill volumes or be a plan unto itself. At a high level, it looks at what you have learned about your users and the landscape, and the classic "Four Ps of Marketing": Product (or service or offering); Price; Place (where your offering will be, such as a store, website, etc.); and Promotion (marketing tactics like ads and outreach). Combining these, you create a strategy and a series of actionable tactics that constitute a "marketing mix." This includes social media content, advertising, events, trade shows, and so on.

Revenue and Resources

Firstly, where will the money come from? How is value exchanged? Sales, grants, donations—anything with a dollar sign attached to it that may come your way goes here. Secondly, what do you need practically in order to do all of this? Do you need equipment to make your products, office space to work in, or specialized software? Do you need to raise capital? If so, how much and where will it come from? These can be big-ticket items. The next chapter will get into this in detail, so bullet points are fine for now.

Activities

What are the key actions you'll need to undertake in order to make all of this work? In the case of Aisle, this includes product design and manufacturing, customer service, marketing and sales, web design, and inventory management.

Partnerships and Allies

Who are these people and organizations for you, and what role do they play? This can include suppliers, industry groups, and other businesses or organizations. In the case of the Period Promise campaign, a social change initiative I am involved with that seeks to address the lack of access to menstrual supplies, the United Way is a key partner, as are local school boards, branches of civic and provincial government, student leadership associations, trade unions, and more. It's worth making a map of these relationships and how they connect to one another. In the case of Nestworks, we have a key partnership with a local social enterprise that trains newly immigrated Canadian women to be early childhood educators (ECEs), who then provide us with childcare services. Aisle's key relationships include our manufacturing partners, PR and social media agencies, sustainable apparel and textile industry groups, B Corp, and many, many more. For product people who want to mass-produce items, how will this happen? Finding a solid manufacturing relationship is critical but it can be extremely difficult, depending on what you're making. Having spent years in the sewing and garment industry, I've seen people frequently make the mistake of believing that manufacturers are there to help with design as well as manufacturing; in my experience, they are not.

Team and Leadership

Who is on your team? In addition to employees, this can include volunteers, contractors, mentors, and advisors. Depending on the scale of what you're creating, this section alone can be quite extensive and is extremely important. There are two things to think about here: 1) The roles themselves (title and role description); and 2) How the roles relate to one another. Again, this is worth mapping out. Google "organizational chart" for examples of what this looks like.

Cost Structure

Here is one of the most important tidbits that every single one of us needs to remember. Repeat after me: *No margin, no mission.* This is shorthand for the idea that whatever you are doing needs to make financial sense. "Margin" in a business sense typically refers to a profit margin, or how much money is left over after expenses are deducted. In the case of a nonprofit, you may need to think of things like salaries, office space, website development costs, and so on. The point is that, at bare minimum, you need to generate enough revenue to cover your costs, including salaries. Furthermore, you need to have a very clear understanding of what those costs are. This can be a very complex body of information, especially if you are making a product or have a large team, so unless you already have the financial skills to create this yourself, I highly recommend getting help from a cost accountant or other specialist with experience related to your product or service. This is one of the most critical aspects of the success of your venture and one that is often underestimated. Do not cut corners, guess, or overlook details. Again, if your project does not make financial sense, it will be impossible to deliver on the value or change that you seek. *No margin, no mission.*

A canvas is an invaluable tool that provides a high-level map of what you need to know to build out your venture. Bear in mind, this is an ongoing process that will continue to evolve and pivot as you learn more, iterate, and get more user feedback and experience. Rather than being a one-and-done type of exercise, think of it as a living document that you can do your best with for the time being and return to fine-tune as circumstances change. In the next chapter, we'll go into the essential resources like funding and consider different types of legal containers you'll need to address to realize your venture.

CHAPTER 9

Integration, Structure, and Funding

ACHIEVING YOUR VISION will require resources like time and money, and access to a variety of tools that must be chosen carefully and managed responsibly. The exact quantity and quality of these resources will be dictated by the nature and scale of what you propose to undertake, as well as its legal structure, if relevant.

Setting structure aside for a moment, your personal financial situation will dictate to a great extent how much time you are able to put toward your project, as well as if and when it takes shape as a hobby (an unpaid, volunteer passion project), side hustle (aka moonlighting, working on it alongside holding down a full-time job), or part- or full-time occupation. If you have a family or dependents, their needs will also have to be weighed as part of your choices. *Do not, for one moment, assume that your venture will be able to support you financially in the short term*, unless you have the good fortune to be starting with a large chunk of funding to kick things off—something which most people don't typically have access to.

It's hard to give general advice about how much time will be required to achieve meaningful results, as everyone's life circumstances are different. It's been my experience that, while projects invariably consume more time and often take longer to achieve than anticipated, life can also have a way of making space for what wants to happen. If your project is a true calling for you, something that is a deep expression of your values and creativity, then I would encourage you to give it as much time as you can without compromising your or your family's peace and financial security.

INTEGRATING YOUR NEW VENTURE

The expression "something's gotta give" comes to mind as I write this. As you consider the question of allocating your time and attention as a resource, think about the full spectrum of your current commitments. Is there anything that can be put on hold, removed, or demoted from your list of main priorities? Oftentimes, there will be something you need to let go of in order to make space for something new to come to fruition, but this is not always the case.

A big question that often comes up for folks considering starting a full-fledged venture or nonprofit startup (I group these together because, in my experience, they require equal commitment in terms of time and effort) is whether or not to quit your job, assuming you have one, or weighing the opportunity cost of looking for one. In order to determine this, you need to take a good, hard look at how much your project is going to cost to get up and running, what resources are available to you, and how much time you have to devote to it. Got savings to spare? Access to family wealth? Fantastic. A group of friends and colleagues who might care to chip in to help you out? Wonderful. Or maybe you will need to get or keep a "job job" to have the support you need until you're at a point where you can make a different choice. If you have a partner who is willing and able to support you for some time, then this is another resource; however, don't spring it on them out of the blue, and make sure that they feel safe and clear around what the expectations are for both of you.

You want a Venn diagram that includes:

- What you want to create and how much it will cost
- What resources you have to put toward creating it
- What your life looks like in terms of available time to pursue it

Is there a sweet spot in the middle where you feel that you can reasonably take action, or at least make a start? I say reasonably, not comfortably, because there is necessarily an element of risk or compromise that you need to be aware of. Almost nobody starts a major project with excess time, money, and social capital on their hands. Something will need to shift in order to make space for it in your life and it's essential that you go into it understanding that this will likely always be true, especially as your initiative grows.

In terms of funding, at a bare minimum, you need to understand how much your project is going to cost to get off the ground and where the funds to support it will come from. Beyond that, an essential part of your planning and ongoing practice will be nailing down how money will move through the organization in the form of ongoing revenue and expenses in a sustainable manner.

The topic of funding and capital can be tricky, and even triggering, for many of us—particularly folks in the social impact space. We can be a bit of a business-averse crowd, so I'm going to spend some time looking at our personal relationships with money before diving into the details of structuring and sources of funding. If you're feeling pretty clear on this aspect of your journey, then feel free to skip ahead to more relevant information. For anyone else who has any form of fear, resentment, or insecurity around money in any form, please keep reading.

MONEY AND YOU

Taking a personal look at what money means to you will help inform your choices and ensure they come from a healthy and realistic perspective, as you consider the financial aspects of your project.

What is your relationship with money like? In my years in the social change world, I have often observed that dealing with money is a real challenge for many of us, due to its inherent association with the for-profit world. I have also often detected the assumption that for-profits have more money and resources than nonprofit organizations, which, especially in the case of small businesses, is often untrue.

I cannot tell you the number of young people I mentor who start off by saying something along the lines of, "I want to make a difference, so I'm looking for a job at a nonprofit or charity." On the face of it, this makes perfect sense; however, the underlying implication that you cannot bring about positive social or environmental change by going the for-profit route is a belief that I feel needs to be questioned. I know this thinking well because I have been there. As a young feminist activist, I internalized the idea that capitalism was basically patriarchy's bank machine and that "capitalism" and "business" were basically the same thing. They're not. Capitalism, roughly speaking, is an economic and political system, whereas business is a practice. I see both in their current states as perverted versions of what they were originally designed to do, which is provide access to resources (capital) to build structures that facilitate the exchange of goods and services and the creation of employment. Our job as social entrepreneurs is to restore ethics and sustainability to these practices and ideologies, to imbue them with humanity, and to use them in service of making the world a better place, rather than exploiting it for financial profit. When we push the mechanisms of money-making away from us, we hand power to those who seek only to extract, not to restore.

And just in case you need to hear this, *it's okay to make money* (make a financial profit, pay yourself well, and build value in the equity that you own, if applicable) *while you are doing something awesome for the planet and its inhabitants.* In fact, doing this is an immensely valuable service, particularly if you employ others directly or indirectly. I would argue that it's the way of the future and an essential component of realizing a sustainable, equitable economic recovery in the post-COVID world. If you are holding onto some old beliefs about the evils of business, kindly examine them, then gently invite to leave your consciousness whatever fear or shame you may be carrying that tells you that having a profitable business is somehow immoral or makes you a "dirty capitalist."

Sometimes, our discomfort has to do with personal lived experiences with poverty or other forms of financial insecurity or hardship. When we know all too well what a lack of money looks like, it can make us risk-averse and scared to stray too far off a reliable income path, which makes perfect sense. We can also get triggered around the idea of scarcity. All of these reactions are completely understandable, yet also pose the risk of holding us back from achieving what's possible. You need to have a relatively comfortable relationship with risk, particularly if you are starting a for-profit venture; it's just part of the deal.

If money stresses you out, I suggest you take an inner inventory of your relationship to it and add it to the collection of insights that you have been gathering throughout this book. There are also some great resources out there, like the Trauma of Money Method, a counseling approach that addresses psychological trauma related to money. Ask yourself questions like:

- What is your earliest memory related to money?
- What did your parents or others who raised you teach you about money?
- During your childhood, what was your family's financial reality? How were you made aware of this?
- What feelings are coming up for you as you answer these questions?

- If you are a parent, what are the main things that you want to teach your children about money?
- What's your current relationship with money like? If it's not one of perfect comfort, how would you like it to change?
- Do you have any role models or people you admire (as opposed to envy) from a financial perspective? What makes them admirable?

If you imagine that someone as experienced as I am in entrepreneurship must have overcome all of my money issues, I'm sorry to tell you that it's simply not the case. As with so many other unresolved personal issues, I simply persist in trying to manage and heal them, with my instigator/leader self often coaxing my scared self to come along for the ride.

In fact, money and finance are among my core insecurities. I am not good at math, which has made it even harder to come to terms with finance. Honestly, it's been a massive uphill struggle for me just to achieve basic financial literacy. Whether you are completely freaked out or a math/finance whiz, unless you are miraculously able to run your initiative on a purely volunteer basis, you need to think of money as the lifeblood of your organization. The less afraid or hung up you are about it, the better off you will be. I encourage you to take this work very seriously, as not having a grip on your initiative's financial ins and outs is a recipe for disaster.

It seems obvious, but it bears pointing out that money can be dangerously tied to our feelings of self-worth. In other words, if we don't feel "valuable," it makes sense that we may then have trouble advocating for appropriate salaries for ourselves or asking for loans or other forms of funding for our initiatives, for example. I have seen time and time again situations where entrepreneurs—especially women and racialized or otherwise underestimated folks—literally discount the value of their labor. I have totally done this myself. Although we understand that this is a result of persistent systemic structures and attitudes, when we start something new, it gives us the opportunity to take a stand for a different approach. The best advice I can offer is to be as self-aware as you can when it comes to money; fear of it can rob us of the opportunity to create change and make us literally shortchange ourselves.

I now tend to think of money as water, or a form of shapeshifting, life-giving energy that can be both bad (money-laundering, greed, fraud, extortion, and blackmail come to mind) and good (freedom, generosity, abundance, pleasure, meeting unmet needs, and so on). What shape does it take in your consciousness? If you experience it as something mysterious or malevolent, is there an image or metaphor that you can apply to it to make it feel more accessible and safer, or at least more neutral?

I'm going to return to the broader topic of funding following a discussion about legal structures, because many of your funding options will be determined by the structure your initiative takes.

PROJECT, PROPRIETORSHIP, PARTNERSHIP, COOPERATIVE, FOR- OR NONPROFIT?

Assuming you are creating anything more substantial than a project, you will need to consider what type of legal entity to choose to house your initiative. If you are already clear on this question, great—carry on. If not, keep reading. The legal form that you choose should ideally be driven by your objectives, with your structure being the most effective container for achieving them and maximizing your impact. This is not a decision to take lightly, as in some cases changing it later on can be costly and time-consuming. Having said that, it's totally fine to start small and simple with choices that will give you the greatest flexibility.

The shape that your project takes is, of course, related to the sources of funding and revenue that will be available to it. Since Suzanne has more experience with the for-profit area, I'm going to share her thoughts on this:

At its simplest level, deciding what kind of legal form your project should take comes down to scale and risk. If it is a small-scale project with little risk and cost, then it can simply be just that: a project which you are doing on the side. There is no need to call it anything as long as you don't expect to own it and scale it into something of lasting value. If, however, it is something you want to scale, you then need to think about how your venture will grow and manage money, manage risk, and take on legal liability. For example, will anyone or anything be affected by your venture if something were to go wrong? Are you prepared to personally take that responsibility or risk? Limiting your liability is typically the most important reason someone will incorporate a for-profit project or create a limited liability company (LLC), because a limited company becomes its own entity, separate from the shareholder. (NB: if you end up personally guaranteeing your company debt, you can't avoid that responsibility.)

If you are just starting out and not sure, you can always begin as a sole proprietorship, which means that the business and you are one and the same, legally speaking. The advantages are that it is cheaper (no legal fees to set up an incorporated business), faster, and simpler (your business year-end taxes are due at the same time as your personal taxes). But if you plan to scale your business, having an incorporated company gives you greater flexibility in attracting investors and increasing share ownership, tax planning, distribution of earnings or profits, and sale or "exit" (the dissolution of the company or other point at which you cease to be responsible for it).

So, it's important to do some planning and get professional advice from a trusted lawyer or accountant who can help you decide if and when you should incorporate. You can DIY your incorporation but investing in an experienced lawyer to help you create the right capital structure and shareholder agreements is essential if you are planning to scale.

It's worth remembering that you can always change your mind—although this is easier said than done, depending on the change you wish to make. For example, G Day and its subsequent legal parent entity, United Girls of the World Society (UGW), started out as a personal project that I ran on the side out of Lunapads, using our office and its amenities and even hiring one of the Lunapads team members on a part-time basis to help me. A few years prior to this, Suzanne and I decided to assume responsibility for a local nonprofit entity dedicated to girls' well-being, which at the time we imagined would house Lunapads's philanthropic activities (mostly financial and in-kind product donations to marginalized people needing access to menstrual products). The entity never ended up quite fitting our corporate philanthropic needs and we found more efficient ways of processing donations through a third-party organization called MakeWay, which allows donors to get tax receipts. To cut to the chase, when we realized that G Day was more than a one-off experiment, we decided to repurpose UGW to instead house G Day's operations. When we started running into limitations around going after grants because UGW was not a registered charity, we successfully undertook the legal process for it to become one (not a small task, I should add). As another example, my first company, everyware designs, started as a sole proprietorship in 1993, then was folded into an incorporated company when Suzanne came along in 2000.

If you do not feel like you already know which option makes the most sense to you, I would consider choosing one of the simplest: a proprietorship (or partnership, if you have a partner) if you want to go the for-profit route, or a nonprofit entity if that feels like a better model for you.

Some more of Suzanne's thoughts:

A partnership is similar to a proprietorship, except there is more than one party who owns the business. The income of the business is the income of the partners, split according to the ownership of the partnership. Partnerships are like marriages and they can be a lot of work to maintain. They are also harder to unwind if things go wrong. If you can, incorporating (when legally possible) is usually a better way to go when there are multiple people involved.

I agree with Suzanne's assessment here. Even if you are starting something simple with someone who you trust, it's worth consulting a lawyer in order to get an agreement in place before entering a partnership.

Another model that is intrinsically well suited to social entrepreneurship is a cooperative, or co-op for short. This is a for-profit, shared ownership structure that serves its members, employees, or customers, rather than outside shareholders. Further to that point, the objective of co-ops is to meet the needs of its members, rather than being an investment play. This can look like addressing food security, financial services, childcare, housing, and many other needs. Generally speaking, co-ops are more democratic and accessible than traditional private for-profit companies, and as a flourishing movement, they constitute an exciting way to get closer to achieving economic justice.

If you feel that your project would be best expressed as a nonprofit or charity, that's wonderful. Do bear in mind that the process to become a registered charity is more administratively rigorous, as a charity needs to be more transparent about its activities than a for-profit. You can imagine what a haven this type of structure could become for fraud if it were easy for less altruistic operators to obtain. Being a registered charity (known as a 501(c)(3) in the US) offers more access to grant and donation funding, as it provides tax receipts. Many foundations and other grantmaking bodies (corporate philanthropy arms, for example) commonly see being a registered charity as a high-status badge that allows them to be more efficient with their due diligence—the detailed process of validating an organization's credibility. As we saw earlier in the discussion,

United Girls of the World Society started out as a nonprofit, then became a charity once it was more firmly on its feet, which is one example of an easier way to start.

If you're feeling uncertain or confused here, take the time to do some research and seek out leaders of both types of organizations to talk about why they made their choices. Also be aware that the for-profit/nonprofit distinction can be a bit of an illusion, in that if you have a for-profit entity, you do not actually have to make a profit. (This idea actually makes me laugh, as there are heaps of enormous for-profit companies that lose money.) Conversely, being a nonprofit does not prohibit you from selling products or services. Ask yourself what you want to get out of doing this; echoing Suzanne, do you want to own something that you may realize a financial gain on through building value in shares of your company? If so, definitely go the for-profit route, as this is the only way that you will be able to do this.

Your funding options will also largely be dictated by the type of organization you create. If, for example, you go the nonprofit or charity route, you will be looking for grants and/or donors, not investors seeking a return on their investment. Conversely, if you are a for-profit company, generally speaking, you are looking to sell a product or service at a profit, not receive donations. Both types of organizations are eligible for different types of loans and grants, depending on the mission and profile of the ownership.

The final consideration is philosophical: is there a way in which your choice of container can, or should, reflect your ideological standpoint? As an example, Suzanne points to why we decided to go the for-profit route when we were initially incorporating Lunapads:

From the beginning, we have been firm that Lunapads/Aisle would be a for-profit company. We believe that business is one of the most effective ways to engage people and create positive change at scale. As proud intersectional feminists, we are using the tools of business to create greater good in the world, continually reinvesting our capital to create more products for better health and for a better planet. Moreover, our business success allows us to further fuel our feminist agenda to attain greater equity and justice for everyone.

If you, like us, feel the for-profit route is a better choice for your enterprise but want to ensure that its impact is also reflected in that choice, then there are some new values-based entities and certifications that may be a good pick for you, like registering as a benefit corporation or becoming certified as a B Corp. While it's easy to get these two things mixed up, they are different. A benefit corporation is a distinct legal entity that, in addition to a simple mandate to earn a financial profit (this defines an incorporated for-profit entity), includes language that incorporates social and environmental benefit as part of its purpose. B Corp is a third-party assessment process and certification undertaken by for-profit businesses to quantify their comprehensive social and environmental impact. It's basically the ultimate "good business badge" that becomes embedded in your corporate constitution, ensuring that the company's commitment to its values will not change, even in the event of a change in ownership—so, you could be both a benefit corporation and a B Corp. Lunapads became a founding Canadian B Corp in 2012 and has proudly maintained a "Best for the World" (in the top ten percent of all B Corps worldwide) ranking for the past five years. It's a valuable community to be part of, though I would not recommend it if you're just starting out. It's an extremely onerous process (and it should be, as it exists to weed out "greenwashers"— folks making unverified claims about their product or service's social and environmental benefits) that will take time better spent, at first, on building your project. If you're serious about it and have the time and resources once your track record and systems are more developed, then absolutely go for it.

Suzanne adds:

We are proud to stand side by side with some of the most respected B Corps in the world, including Patagonia, Seventh Generation, Allbirds, Ben & Jerry's, and more. Becoming a B Corp has helped us become a better company and given me purpose as a business leader. As someone who left the corporate world disillusioned, being a B Corp has given me a North Star to help me lead with honor and create a legacy for what business can do. It has shown me best practices around human resources, sustainable supply chain management, good corporate governance, and ways to be a regenerative steward of the environment.

HOW MUCH MONEY WILL YOU NEED TO GET STARTED?

Honestly, the answer to this could possibly be none; it depends on what you are trying to achieve. When I think of, for example, projects I am part of in my community that address period poverty (lack of access to adequate menstrual supplies and education, preventing individuals who need them from fully participating in education, employment, and a dignified life in general), most of what our team of activists has done is garnered media attention, lobbied political leaders, and amassed and distributed donated products, costing us practically nothing. In my capacity as a committee member supporting various product and education drives, I also wear my Aisle hat and leverage our team's wisdom and resources; for example, asking these entities to publicize our product donation drives. There have also been few, if any, financial transactions involved due to our relationship with the United Way, a charitable entity that provides meeting space and some administrative support for us. Such an arrangement may also be possible for you; again, it depends on what you are trying to achieve. This does, however, raise the topic of non-financial, non-time-related resources. Be aware of all other forms of capital you have at your disposal and don't be afraid to use them to further your goals.

If you are feeling a bit lost on the financial front, fear not! There are some incredible people out there who love nothing more than figuring these types of things out. You do not need to be able to do it all yourself, but you must be able to understand your startup and ongoing costs and cash flow, at least at a high level. Again, get help if you need it. Once the initiative is running, you should either learn basic bookkeeping or engage a reliable bookkeeper to help you keep track of your money and records. Bookkeeping software is actually quite user-friendly (when it doesn't scare you). As your enterprise grows, you will need to either hire an accountant or outsource your bookkeeping, accounting, and financial services. For these types of accounting or legal services, ask around your networks and local Better Business Bureau for some leads. Be sure to meet them in person or via video conference to have a face-to-face conversation about your objectives. Look for a positive connection in terms of how they listen, their reputation and reviews, and sense of their over-all values alignment and integrity. If you have a nonprofit or charita-ble organization, you may be able to obtain discounted rates or even pro bono (free) services, so be sure to ask.

As I mentioned previously, most projects take at least twice as long as originally forecast to accomplish and end up costing at least twice as much. In our eagerness to achieve our impact, we can be overly optimistic about certain realities, as though the magic of our mission will somehow solve everything or make people want to con-tribute things for free (although this does usually happen, depending on it as a strategy is not advisable).

Something that's worth remembering, especially for folks with financial privilege, is that as amazing as your project is, it's not rea-sonable to expect someone to build a website, design a logo, do your social media, or other tasks for free. If they freely offer to do these types of things, then that's great, but expecting it is just not cool, so don't. However, do consider what you may have to offer in exchange for someone's time or shared resources and be prepared to barter. Remember, it's okay for you to ask and equally okay for them to say no.

Getting back to the subject of startup money, larger projects and commercial ventures where a product or service is going to be marketed will definitely involve financial costs. For some ballpark figures, recent US research indicates that the average small business requires around $10,000 in capital to get going. Obviously, this is a generalization, and the true range is far broader.

Basic things to include in your startup budget:

- A website and ongoing hosting fees
- Branding
- Incorporation costs, if applicable
- People's time for services like bookkeeping, etc.
- Space and equipment

Be sure to always track your time carefully. Your time is part of the true cost of whatever you produce and if this information is missing, it will be hard to correctly understand your costing, which can lead to building an unsustainable business model. The value of your labor can be hard to see, especially if you're doing something that you love or is just part of your regular life. As soon as there is a financial aspect to what you're doing, timekeeping is vital.

In a similar vein, if you are making a product, keep track of all materials required and used, as well as labor for assembly, packaging, and anything else that may be relevant. Marketing costs (this applies equally to nonprofits) are a bit of a wild card, because they can vary so widely. However, they must be factored in because they address a key issue: how people will hear about you. Thinking about marketing, you can see how easy it is to eat up that $10K. As advised earlier, take whatever figure you come up with and double it to be safe.

SOURCES OF FINANCING

Love Money

Regardless of what type of organization you create, startup costs are most likely to be borne by you or someone close to you. "Love money" is an adorable term that describes personal savings (in a recent poll, seventy-seven percent of small business founders said they self-financed their startups this way), as well as support from friends and family. I relied heavily on my parents for support early on, from working out of their basement to reduce overhead, to securing loans, to cash in the form of loans and equity—and I personally financed Nestworks's startup costs. They don't call it love money for nothing.

In this situation, there is often little to no expectation of repayment or making a return; people contribute because they believe in you and have resources that might not otherwise be available to you through banks or investors. If you are privileged enough to be able to access this type of funding, go for it—however, be mindful that someone else had to work for it and that you owe it to them to give it your best shot and not take anything for granted. The flip side of this involvement is that they are willing adults who understand there is reasonable risk of losing their investment. Assuming you are able to realize financial success further down the road, consider paying it forward by using some of your returns to fund someone else's dream, especially if they have not had the benefit of the same advantages.

Sales

Selling your product or service, of course, generates revenue. If you are a small business that does not take on investor capital and primarily, or exclusively, relies on personal savings and sales to reach breakeven or profitability, this is known as bootstrapping. In order to make this viable, your offering needs to be appropriately priced: finding the perfect balance between meeting your cost and margin needs while providing good value to your target customer. When an organization is able to achieve this, it's really something to be proud of. You are not weighed down by debt, nor are you beholden to investors. The downside is that, assuming you want to rapidly scale the venture, you may not have the necessary funds to do so without looking for outside capital. But this too depends on your objectives; you will always have the option of seeking investment or loans at any time.

As I mentioned earlier, being a charity or nonprofit does not preclude you from selling goods and services, a practice known as social enterprise. No matter what, you are going to have to deal with the same issues as for-profits (the topics we considered when looking at the business canvas are more or less universally applicable), although how you allocate your margin and profits will look different.

It's unlikely that you will be able to start a product-based enterprise without sufficient capital to make the product in the first place. In other words, you can't sell something before you've made it—or can you? If lack of access to the startup-required capital is a barrier for you, then your options are to either use your savings (if you have them), get your hands on some love money, take out a loan, or crowdfund your project. If your goal is to build a scalable venture (rapidly growing in a large marketplace), then you may want to consider courting investors to purchase shares in the company to provide you with the necessary growth capital. This process is commonly known as raising, which I will discuss in more detail shortly.

Debt

Debt is repayable money that you typically borrow from a financial institution as loans or lines of credit, but it can come from other sources too, including private lenders. There is a plethora of debt funding options available specifically to women, youth, racialized individuals, other marginalized groups, and local entrepreneurs, some of which may apply to you. The main advantage of debt, as opposed to equity (shares in the ownership of a for-profit company), is that you do not give up any form of ownership or control of your organization as part of the transaction. Loans are a more common source of cash for for-profits; however, nonprofits can also borrow money. The downside is that you're then in debt and will need to factor paying both principal repayments and interest into your monthly cash flow projections.

Personally, I am a fan of using debt for business needs—with the caveat that I am not talking about credit card debt, which can be very expensive and is only recommended when other avenues have been exhausted. Obtaining debt funding is faster and less onerous to organize than raising equity, but it can also be a pain and highly inaccessible, especially when you are starting out without any kind of track record. Banks are naturally risk-averse yet they enjoy talking a big game about supporting small businesses and entrepreneurs. My experience is that you need to take these early exchanges with a large grain of salt and be prepared to provide reams of detailed paperwork and hear things like, "You don't meet our risk profile," or that you don't have the right ratios, and so on.

Notable exceptions are organizations like SheEO, which offers crowdsourced interest-free loans to majority women/nonbinary-owned and led ventures that have in excess of $50,000 in annual revenue and are making the world a better place as a core part of their mission.

Another creative new option available to e-commerce entrepreneurs these days is revenue-based lending, as exemplified by the Canadian firm Clearco (formerly Clearbanc). Clearco analyzes your online sales and makes their loan offer based on predictive algorithms. According to their website, they receive a fixed percentage of your daily sales until they have recouped the loan and their flat fee, making for a fast source of nondilutive financing without personal guarantees. There are many other small business loan opportunities out there, so have a look around to see what's available.

Crowdfunding

Crowdfunding is when a group of people individually contribute funds toward a project or venture on an online platform. For a small venture, you might create an online campaign that explains your amazing idea to your prospective backers, along with what they will get in exchange for their contribution.

Crowdfunding can be used to fund the creation of any product (video games, books, and films being popular examples), to back a specific project, or to pool equity to create a business. It's often done in highly creative and compelling ways, where gifts or rewards are offered in addition to the base product/project, thus incentivizing higher-value contributions.

Variations on the crowdfunding theme include donation as well as equity models. There are several crowdfunding platforms, the best-known being Kickstarter, Indiegogo, and GoFundMe. Several innovative, newer platforms specialize in certain types of projects; for example, funding an equity raise. There are too many details about the differences to get into here, so if this is a route that appeals to you, dig into some research and, as always, ask around. Crowdfunding campaigns are also done for marketing and research reasons, to raise awareness, build community, garner publicity, and test the market for a given product or service.

These opportunities are some of the most positive examples I've seen of the democratization of access to capital due to the rise of internet accessibility. Something I've heard a lot from friends who have done crowdfunding campaigns is that you need to budget a huge amount of time for planning, and doing real-time marketing, as the campaign unfolds. Although gathering support can appear simple and almost magical from the outside, an enormous amount of work goes into these campaigns. A persuasive video is the key piece of collateral you will need to produce for a successful campaign, so bear in mind that they are not entirely free to start.

Here are some general tips "crowdfunded" by colleagues who have been there.

Kaz Brecher, one of my most treasured teachers at the THNK School, co-created OuiSi with Paul Brillinger, one of my classmates. OuiSi, a photo card–based activity designed to "foster creativity and ignite curiosity," exceeded their original goal of $15,000, raising $20,000 from over three hundred backers. Here are Kaz's tips for a successful campaign:

- Really understand your audience. If you're putting out a product, research anything in the same sphere that might use the same tags and get to know who might be funding. For example, it'll be the parents who do the funding for a kids' book, yet the product needs to appeal to kids. Research which groups of parents are using crowdfunding, who they trust, what kind of vote of confidence you need to convey, and how you might let them experience what you'll be delivering; for example, putting downloadable coloring pages in the campaign updates.

- How sure are you that you can deliver if it's a success? This is a common pitfall for first-timers and it's important to have done significant research on production, as well as being able to plan for "what if" scenarios, especially if you're trying to deliver something tied to an immovable date (like the holidays).

- The video really does matter. Giving people a deep sense of the delights and benefits of what you're offering—as well as how to use it—is what tends to land it. This can be achieved by conveying the impact on the audience as much as by showing the product itself.

- It's important to set tiers for crowdfunding that still allow people who love the idea but don't need the product to contribute; sometimes those small donations under ten dollars really add up.

Another colleague of mine, Kevin Harding, is a policy analyst and social enterprise expert. Kevin raised over $115,000, for an original campaign goal of $50,000, to fund a legal challenge to save a locally founded outdoor gear co-op from being sold to a US-based private investment firm. He was kind enough to customize his advice for this book:

- Pitch crowdfunding as the solution to a problem.
- It's good to have your campaign come out of a broader buzz around something; for example, can you tease your product or service on social media or a website and indicate that crowdfunding is forthcoming? You want to build up anticipation.
- What you effectively need to do is to build out a message calendar. For an allotted number of weeks before the campaign, you'll be hinting; during the campaign, you'll want to promote your milestones ("We've hit a stretch goal," or "We're getting there but need your help to put us over the top"), and then announce when you're at ten percent, fifty percent, etc. of your funding goal.
- Plan out your messages across your platforms. How many for Twitter? How many for Facebook? You can use a social media scheduler like Buffer to help you pre-plan and get them out the door.
- Activate your networks and have them ready to pitch with you. Can you line up a bunch of other social entrepreneurs who will lend you a tweet when you launch your project? You can help them write it or they can write it; these people are your validators.
- Rewards! Everyone loves rewards, whether it's a digital download or a dinner with a validator (who likes you and your project and would take a big donor out for dinner on your behalf, especially if you've got big names, etc.).

Grants

Grants, or free (nonrepayable) money, are a wonderful way to fund whatever it is you're up to, assuming it's legitimately in line with the grantor's criteria. Although I have less experience with this type of funding, some of the pitfalls that I have seen experienced colleagues grapple with include misalignment with the grantor's expectations, unreasonably onerous reporting, and a vulnerable dependency on this type of funding, which is often cyclical and by no means guaranteed. Organizations can often find themselves adapting their proposed project to meet grantors' criteria, sometimes to the point where it becomes disingenuous or loses the original intended impact of the project. This type of funding is a more natural fit for nonprofit or charitable entities, but some businesses can also be eligible.

Grants come with a wide variety of sizes, terms, and areas of focus. This array can be overwhelming and difficult to understand, the process bureaucratic and definitely requiring patience, if not professional services. For more complex grants, you may want to hire the services of a professional grant writer or grant consultant who can help you locate which grants you would be most likely able to access based on your goals. These types of consultants are typically paid by a percentage of whatever funding you obtain, so be sure to get that information up front, as you will need to budget accordingly. For example, if you need $50,000 to get your project off the ground and you apply for a $50,000 grant with the help of a grant consultant, you could end up with considerably less once they receive their commission (at least ten to fifteen percent of the grant amount). Another helpful place to look is government agencies (or, in Canada, the Concierge Service program) whose job it is to help you navigate government services and aid. Overall, I would advise people going this route to have patience and resilience in dealing with details.

To date, Nestworks has received two grants, totaling $50,000, to enable us to hire consultants to develop our financial model and determine feasibility. The funds came from two local foundations whose mandates include supporting community-based nonprofit initiatives. The application process was different for each one and we were turned down by the second foundation the first time we applied. The second time around, things were led by a staff member who had attended lengthy webinars about the granting process and who was further supported by two of our board members in drafting the final application. Do not let an initial no deter you. Ask for feedback and apply again if you are able to. The more you are able to demonstrate alignment between your project's aims and the larger goals of the granting organization, the more likely you are to succeed. Sometimes these relationships can take years to develop, so start early, and be patient and willing to invest a great deal of time into personal meetings and other demonstrations of your determination, leadership, and community-building abilities.

Donations

Donations are another form of nonrepayable funding common for nonprofits and charities. This money comes from individuals or organizations and is intended to support whatever activity it is that you're undertaking. If you have ever contributed to a campaign to address an issue that matters to you, this is what I'm talking about. The act of giving money without expectation of a financial return or transaction, because you want to be part of creating some form of meaningful change, can be a highly personal, emotional choice for donors. Depending on whether you are an individual, a nonprofit, or a charity, donors may expect a receipt that can be used for tax purposes. Bear in mind that only registered charities are able to offer tax receipts to donors; individuals and nonprofits do not have this power, which can be a deterrent to some donors.

The two main things I want to emphasize in terms of the success of this form of funding are transparency and gratitude. By transparency, I mean that you are clear and honest about what the funds are being put toward (no need to be overly precise, but some people can be very picky about this) and careful that there is alignment between the donors' expectations and how the funds are actually used. Gratitude is perhaps the most important aspect of ensuring the success of a donation strategy; people donate money because it feels good to support something that they care about. Showing them abundant gratitude is both their reward and an indispensable part of your strategy to maintain your donation pipeline.

Equity Investment

If you are a for-profit entity, you'll need to know that equity investment is where you sell shares in an incorporated company to investors. Investors can be individuals, groups of individuals, or corporate entities like venture capital (VC) firms or private family firms/offices. Depending on the types of shares being sold, these players will have greater or lesser degrees of control over the company, as well as a wide range of contractual options around other conditions including directorship (board membership), fund distribution, prioritization of repayment, and more. The main reason for considering investor funding is likely getting your hands on a far larger amount of capital than you would be able to borrow, thus giving you the ability to grow your enterprise faster and at greater scale. This financing model has become ubiquitous in popular startup culture. But before assuming that you *need* to go after equity funding, especially institutional, I encourage you to take a deep breath and learn as much about it as possible before diving in with pitch decks ablaze. I also counsel you to interrogate what your objectives are. What pace of growth is truly optimal for you and your organization? Are you willing to surrender partial ownership and control of your venture? And if so, on what terms?

When we hear the word *investors*, we typically think of a venture capital firm or a high-profile tycoon investor like Warren Buffett. These stereotypes obscure the fact that there is also a vast network of "Angels"—high-net-worth individuals who are accredited investors—who make personal investments, as well as private groups who aggregate their capital into funds that they then deploy collectively. Despite their counterintuitive moniker, Angels are, in fact, real, and they can be game changers. Here's a real-life example: Once upon a time, a wealthy elderly woman read about Vancouver-based impact investor Joel Solomon in a newspaper article and was inspired to reach out to him to see whether there were any female-owned ventures in his portfolio that she could support. As it happened, there was—Lunapads. This individual made a modest yet extremely helpful investment in us and subsequently passed her shares along to her extremely smart adult granddaughter, with whom we have a warm relationship to this day. They don't call them Angels for nothing.

Furthermore, there are increasing numbers of these kinds of investors and groups, many of which are impact driven; they target areas such as food security, social and climate justice, gender equity, and Indigenous and racialized founders, to name just a few focuses. You will need to do some further research into your niche, especially as things are evolving so quickly.

IS THE VENTURE CAPITAL ROUTE RIGHT FOR YOU?

For readers whose impression of VCs and their relationship with entrepreneurs is driven by TV shows like *Shark Tank*, where wily investors are pitched by entrepreneurs to make equity deals, I have news for you: if you are under the illusion that these deals actually happen, in the end, most of them don't. They also should not be taken as representative of the normal state of affairs between small businesses that do have investors and those investors themselves. As a reality check, most enterprises are privately held, and less than one percent of all businesses ever receive venture capital funding. As a bitter sidenote to the one percent statistic, less than five percent of that goes to women, and of that five percent of one percent, less than one percent goes to women of color. In other words, the world of venture capital is largely inaccessible to "everyday people." Which is not to say that there's nothing, or that it's not changing—it is.

There is a growing group—a movement, even—of values-driven individuals and organizations in the investment space. One such leader is Arlan Hamilton, a formerly homeless, young, Black, queer woman, who heads one of today's most exciting and innovative venture capital firms, Backstage Capital. Backstage is part of a growing cohort of firms and pools of people specifically wanting to correct the egregious prior state of affairs, and to tap the underserved markets of what she calls "underestimated" entrepreneurs: women, racialized, and LGBTQIA+ founders. See the resources section in chapter 12 for more impact-based investment firms.

If you decide to seek equity funding, you will need to start with the deck I outlined in chapter 8 and add more detailed financial information. Be prepared also to justify, or possibly defend, your venture's valuation (this being the total value of the company). There are many ways to ascertain this, including multiples of sales or EBITDA (earnings before interest, taxes, depreciation, and amortization), or simply an anticipated forecast (an estimated number based on sales/growth projections and market indicators). If you choose to go this route then, unless you or someone close to you is already well versed in these terms and transactions, you will need help from skilled legal and accounting professionals, or be prepared to face a steep learning curve. As we can see in the case of Arlan Hamilton, this certainly is possible with sufficient intelligence and determination. Include in the deck how much money you are looking for, what you plan to do with it, and how that will affect your revenue projections, which also need to be detailed (typically for a five-year period). This pitch deck, which will include details we reviewed earlier about your product, team, and so on, will serve as a calling card for anyone interested in learning more about you.

I would also encourage you to be clear on investors' expectations of the timing of your growth and exit. Traditional VCs are typically looking for a very short-term relationship (three to five years is common), with the expectation that you will use their capital to scale rapidly and then exit (be sold, often to a larger company), at which point the investment is paid back according to the terms of the shareholders' agreement. There are alternative models emerging that are in it for a longer term and place value on more than financial returns; for example, a social impact or gender equity lens, where investors consider these aspects along with the potential for financial returns. If social impact is your ultimate goal, you will need to consider how your venture's mission is going to be preserved if it changes hands. Being a B Corp is extremely helpful in this regard, as part of the certification process involves changing the company's articles of incorporation to include dedication to mission as part of its legally stated purpose.

Once you have a deck, start looking and asking around. By now, I hope you've started sharing your story far and wide and have looked into prospective networks, educational opportunities, and so on, as these are where you're most likely to start finding potential investors. An adage I have heard time and time again is, "If you're looking for money, ask for advice; if you're looking for advice, ask for money." This is a clever way of saying that it's not always wise to be direct, at least initially. Asking people for money can put them on the spot, whereas asking for their advice appeals to their ego first and also gives them breathing room to be curious and ask questions about your venture.

It's also worth remembering that, at the end of the day, you are the one with the power in this situation. I know that it often doesn't look or feel that way when you are someone who falls outside of the Silicon Valley tech dude paradigm of entrepreneurs seeking investment, but believe me, you are. I say this because I believe that the world is starved for ideas like yours: ones that will truly make a difference.

Remember that most traditional VCs are professionals playing a set of odds and working within a very specific, constrained model. These are the important questions you need to ask: Are their values aligned with my values for my venture? What are they bringing to the table, other than money? In other words, how can they help in nonfinancial ways? This kind of help is known as "smart money" and includes valuable contacts, knowledge, and skills. Ideally, they will want to bring these assets to bear on your venture to support its success, especially since they will also have skin in the game. Other VCs are more hands-off—it just depends.

Going back to my previous observations about the traditional investor pitch model, what is typically being assessed is your venture's ability to scale (achieve exponential growth, preferably as rapidly as possible). This expectation has become a norm in the VC startup scene, where talk of "hockey stick growth" (yes, it actually looks like a hockey stick on a graph), followed by a relatively fast exit (sale of the company) is essentially the holy grail. There is huge pressure inherent in this type of plan. Ask yourself if this is what you actually want and, if it isn't, reconsider your options or find investor partners who are more aligned with your plans and values. Here are Suzanne's thoughts on how to weigh going after VC vs. Angel funding:

Your first "round" of raising money to fund your business is called a "seed" round (and sometimes "pre-seed"). Pre-seed and seed rounds typically raise $100,000 to $2 million from friends and family, as well as accredited angel investors and syndicates. For most social entrepreneurs, doing the research and networking necessary to find Angels is a far better use of your time than preparing for venture funding. Don't be sucked into the heady headlines about multimillion-dollar raises and billion-dollar valuations; raising venture capital is the exception, not the norm, for social entrepreneurs. If, however, you have an exciting revenue-generating business that is growing quickly and is scalable (10x to 40x) and you are prepared to give up some ownership or equity in your business, then go after venture capital (i.e., series A, B, C rounds of $2 to $100 million).

Finally, bear in mind that your investor partners should be people *who you like,* or at least trust and respect. Although we are talking about a business relationship, these are people you are going to be connected with for a fairly long time—likely several years—so you want to be comfortable and confident around them. You are building something together, after all. Think of this as any human relationship; if it feels off, or like your values are not aligned, don't do it. This is definitely an occasion for a serious gut check. Not to dwell on the negative, but I have seen some business partnerships and investor relationships go totally sideways. And as with a marriage, it can be complicated, expensive, emotionally draining, and time-consuming to get a divorce. Think twice, then think again, before saying yes.

Having said that, Suzanne and I have nothing but good things to say about our long-term shareholders Carol Newell, Joel Solomon, and the team at Renewal Partners, who have been with us at Lunapads/Aisle since 2000. Renewal was among the earliest cohort of impact investors in North America, and they are the smartest, kindest, most patient investors that I could possibly imagine. People like them are gold; when you find yours, communicate with them regularly and never take their support for granted. Today, thanks to their early leadership, there is a flourishing community of impact-based funds. See the resources section in chapter 12 for more information.

As a final note about seeking equity investment, be prepared for this to be a significant area of focus for you and senior leaders on your team, which will need to happen alongside the various other responsibilities required to keep your venture going. If it's at all possible for you to lighten your workload while you are in raise mode by delegating or otherwise, then by all means, do it. In addition to creating a pitch deck, you will need to provide detailed information about your company, including a detailed business plan, financial statements and projections, articles of incorporation, supplier agreements, sales contracts, social policies, employment agreements, and so on, as part of an intensive review and verification process called due diligence. DD, as it's known in the trade, can take months and involve multiple meetings in order to make sure all questions are answered. This is a good opportunity to ascertain whether the firm or Angel in question is a good fit for you.

If you are concerned about maintaining the confidentiality of this information, you may ask your prospective investors to sign a nondisclosure agreement (NDA). This typically happens before entering the DD process, and the investor is given access to a secure online "deal room" that contains all the materials that I listed above. Be aware that not all investors (especially not sophisticated VCs) will be prepared to sign an NDA; the sheer volume of deals that cross their desks may make this impractical, if not impossible.

Researching funds and investors is another key activity that you will need to budget time for. Once you have a prospect list, you will likely have to talk to dozens, if not hundreds, of people, pitch to a fraction of that number, enter the due diligence process with a still-smaller number, soft circle (receive an informal commitment) from a fraction of them, and finally receive a term sheet (an offer to invest) from a handful of entities or individuals. The term sheet will contain what the investor wants (as opposed to what you're offering; they are not always the same thing), including valuation, type, and number of shares, voting and directorship rights, and so on. By the time you're at this stage, you are hopefully on the same page, but you never know. There is also commonly a lead investor (assuming there is more than one investor party), who typically puts in the largest portion of the funds and negotiates the terms with the business owner/shareholders; other smaller groups follow along, though they don't have as much say, as they are coming in with smaller amounts of money.

If this sounds potentially exhausting, guess what? It is! Which is not to say that I recommend not doing it—just go in with your eyes open and be ready to work your butt off, answer some very tough questions, and hear a lot of nos. That said, it can also open you up to very productive and even personally rewarding relationships. It took us years to work up to doing a major equity raise for Aisle; Rome wasn't built in a day.

CHAPTER 10

Facing Challenges and the Unexpected

I N THE PREVIOUS TWO CHAPTERS, we looked at building your product or service and business model and considered options for funding it. This chapter is about the ripples resulting from the steps you've taken toward getting the party started and what happens next. While there is no exact formula here, I can virtually guarantee you that things will not always go as planned—for better, for worse, and for weirder. As excited as you are to pursue what is calling you, there will be times of frustration, fatigue, despair, and uncertainty, and I don't just mean in terms of running your enterprise. Some of my biggest battles have been entirely internal: personal demons preying on insecurities and self-doubt. In my experience, these can have as much (or more) destructive power as a cash flow crunch or failed supplier relationship. I would also like to add that not all impediments are disastrous; some end up guiding us in unexpected ways that can be absolutely wonderful. The main thing, as I stressed earlier, is to let yourself begin and to maintain a sense of curiosity and flexibility about what happens next.

Since I believe in the power of stories, I'd like to kick this chapter off with one, along with a poem and a thematic metaphor. On the eve of the 2020 US presidential election, one of the SheEO Venture CEOs shared a post with a small group of West Coast founders on a private SheEO Slack channel. Her team was stressed about the election, as well as some major upcoming changes to the company. Morale was low and distraction high at a crucial time, and this CEO was feeling hopeless and alone.

The SheEO sisters immediately jumped in with all manner of words of support. Sonia Strobel, founder of Skipper Otto Community Supported Fishery, shared the poem "Our Real Work," written by American writer Wendell Berry, as something that she had found solace in while she navigated uncertain times.

> *It may be that when we no longer know what to do*
> *we have come to our real work,*
> *and that when we no longer know which way to go*
> *we have come to our real journey.*
> *The mind that is not baffled is not employed.*
> *The impeded stream is the one that sings.*

While I fully understand that poems may seem trivial to some in the face of the very real challenges of entrepreneurship (not to mention life), Berry's words, and the spirit in which they were shared, stayed with me. There is a reason we choose our seemingly irrational or unimaginable ventures, which can seem impossible to understand for those who choose a less uncertain path; and with good reason, since "changing the world" is a practically undoable task, which we are nevertheless called to. This chapter is about cultivating resilience, adaptability, persistence, creativity, and self-compassion as we grow our projects during particularly uncertain times, and finding ways to see ourselves as the singing, impeded stream as we navigate our journeys.

Right at the outset of the pandemic, the SheEO Ventures (there are ninety-one of us worldwide) gathered online to discuss how to support one another in the face of this extraordinary challenge. Among us were leaders of companies facing near-immediate mass staff layoffs, supply chain disruption, loan defaults, and the very real threat of bankruptcy. To call these "impediments" in our streams is too kind: these were serious rocks.

SheEO's Ask/Give practice, as discussed in chapter 1, is a fast way to solve people's immediate needs using the community's existing resources. I have never seen it at work faster than on that call. Literally within minutes, entrepreneurs with resources were offering to cover payroll for others who had been harder hit, among multiple other examples.

I was introduced to the concept of biomimicry—the adaptation of natural systems to address complex human problems—many years ago, thanks to an image that depicted a forest of seemingly separate trees, with a vast network of roots connecting them from beneath. I learned how, in droughts and other times of stress, the root network transmits information and nutrients between the trees and can even bind together to physically support them during storms. The image has always stayed with me and I often use it in presentations. The SheEO call brought this so vividly to life: it was a literal enactment of this principle. In that moment, we became the forest. We are all trees, and our network is the roots. We have everything we need to support one another *when we are connected*. Looking back to chapter 1, consider what might happen to these trees if they decided that their well-being needed to come at the expense of one another, rather than recognizing that they were symbiotic.

COVID-19 demanded that many of us mobilize our resources on a broader scale, which brought challenges as well as rewards. On March 17, 2020, Suzanne and I were asked by a friend, the leader of a social services agency that serves youth experiencing homelessness, if we could supply her team with cloth face masks. By now, cloth face masks are ubiquitous, but in mid-March of 2020, they were basically unheard of in the West. We did some quick research and concluded that in the absence of medical-grade masks (largely unavailable due to the spike in demand), well-made cloth masks could still reduce the possibility of transmission and would additionally preserve the supply of medical-grade masks for medical professionals.

Aisle's cloth menstrual pads have been proudly made in my hometown of Vancouver since the company's inception, so having immediate access to fabric and skilled labor made the mask-making task relatively easy. The activity reminded me of using regular kitchen staples to make a different dish than your usual fare; you already have everything you need, and you're just using them to make a different recipe. It's a good little mental exercise to consider what your business "pantry" looks like and how else its ingredients could be deployed.

I got out my sewing machine at home and made some samples, then got our production manager and sewing partners involved and looked at how we could use fabric that we already had on hand to make the masks. Then we got to work. One thing led to another and we ended up making and donating over six thousand masks to front-line service providers working in Vancouver's Downtown Eastside, a neighborhood facing extreme social and economic challenges. Soon, opportunities arose for us to supply remote Indigenous communities in BC, as well as racial justice community organizers across North America. Without COVID-19, we would never have discovered this additional capacity, created a multitude of new relationships, or found new ways to leverage our resources for impact.

THE GREAT PANDEMIC PIVOT

In the spring of 2020, with borders closed, flights cancelled, and gatherings curtailed, the online space was suddenly our collective solution for connection. We have all seen some incredibly creative online adaptations by now, from fundraising galas to fitness classes. But it's been about more than changing the means of delivery of our meetings and services; in the most successful cases, it's also been a change in mindset that takes COVID-19 as an opportunity to reframe or innovate.

Respected Vancouver-based yoga teacher Carine Young had to instantly pivot from in-person to online teaching, a move which could appear on the face of it to be a disappointing hassle as her practice had, up to that point, been entirely in-person. Not for Carine, though. Drawing on her empathy for her students, as well as yogic philosophy, she pivoted to deliver a service that became even more valuable in the pandemic context.

> *Sharing yoga's benefits seemed especially important during quarantine, so I created some free content to keep students engaged and feeling supported. I felt the need to keep sharing and teaching, especially when external forces were oppressive. I didn't want to feed into the chaos or fear generated by social media. I chose instead to reframe self-isolation as self-retreat and created an R&R at-home retreat to offer sanctuary for those feeling stuck in quarantine, so they could see staying put as a personal treat; to change the fear into freedom. I was driven to communicate more calmness when surrounded by the unknown. It gave me clarity and purpose. To create my own future and way of teaching was more empowering than waiting for the unknown. I embrace change; it keeps me on my toes. I had to learn all the technologies that go with teaching online. Following my initial online launch, I am ready to let go of results and accept being in the unknown— applying yoga philosophy in life.*

Like pretty much all of us, Carine adapted her business to the online space. What's remarkable about her approach is that she also reframed her language and way of thinking about it. This is an example of the soul trait "Coloring Outside the Lines"; Carine saw this challenge as a learning experience and an opportunity to amplify the value of her service, at a time when self-care and positivity were more needed than ever. Are there ways in which your current constraints offer opportunities for mental reframes, or even to expand the reach of your project? One of the things I have enjoyed about Zoom is that it's made it possible to attend events around the world that I would not otherwise have been able to afford to travel to.

Abeego founder Toni Desrosiers's business was initially devastated by the pandemic; close to eighty percent of her sales were almost instantly wiped out, forcing her to lay off most of her staff and drastically scale back production. Fortunately, her prior success had allowed her to build up enough cash reserves to prevent an outright bankruptcy. Her perspective on COVID-19 is consistent with her overall view that we need to take the good with the bad, in business as in life.

The pandemic has changed the way that I think in so many ways. It served as a reminder that you really only have right now—that's all there is. For me, the advent of COVID-19 was both the darkest and the brightest time. The dark part was all of the sales going away and having to let a bunch of people go, which was incredibly hard. The light was that it gave me space, time, and the ability to think, dream, and imagine again: to take a breath. When you are on this constant "grow, grow, grow" trajectory, you don't have room to get centered to think about whether you are actually designing the business as a place where you truly want to be. You are just swept up in a constant drive. If you look at nature, it grows, it harvests, and then it rests. We don't do that in our society. The pandemic gave me time to rest.

Assuming that a rest is a welcome and available opportunity (and in full recognition that it may not be), I invite you to consider the extent to which you may have internalized the belief that it's not okay to slow down, for either yourself or your venture. We are surrounded by a hustle culture that amounts to the idea that if you are not busting parts of your reproductive anatomy in your quest for market domination, then you're not trying hard enough. There is so much wrong with this perspective that I hardly know where to start, yet I want to be mindful that it's no small (or even always possible) matter to simply opt out of our circumstances at any given time. Toni's way of thinking is a great example of the soul trait "Impact is the New Currency." If her priorities had been traditionally growth oriented, she would not have had the wisdom to take this opportunity to nourish herself and allow her venture to recalibrate.

My point here is that there is a presumption of truth and inevitability to this culture, which is false and destructive. It's collectively hurting all of us, and I encourage you, as you make your journeys, to notice how it shows up and be aware of any opportunities that arise to challenge it. This can look like setting personal boundaries, making unapologetic self-care choices, interrogating organizational culture along social justice lines, and examining the types of benefits that you make available to your team, among other things. If our goal is positive social change, it's radically counterproductive that it should come at the expense of anyone's well-being or mental health.

As panic gave way to a process of recalibration, the most interesting example for me of letting the new constraints show the way to pivot our offering was with Nestworks. Although on the face of it, co-working spaces seem like a terrible idea in an era of physical distancing, the pre-existing and largely unmet need for childcare was becoming increasingly exposed. The work-from-home lifestyle may have been a blessing for many but working parents without access to childcare were generally not among those singing its praises. Having to manage their kids' educational needs was yet another challenge. The truth of how COVID-19 had disproportionately affected women and people of color, who form the majority of frontline workers, became glaringly apparent. Add to this living in small urban spaces where the idea of a home office is a fantasy and the loneliness brought about by missing collegial friendships, and you have a recipe for relatively ideal conditions for something like Nestworks to succeed, once we are clear of COVID-19's menace.

While it's still a work in progress, I now foresee a pared-down (no organic lunches or meditation rooms on offer—yet), hyper-local version of Nestworks as being viable. The pandemic also exposed how unnecessary most of our commuting is. What if, instead of putting on a suit and driving or taking transit downtown to a soulless office, you could wear something comfortable, bundle up your kids, and walk or bike to a place where you can quietly get work done while your kids are close at hand, engaged in fun and educational activities? While I am, of course, devastated by the damage caused by COVID-19, I am intrigued to see how people and businesses are adapting and innovating because of it.

These examples are, of course, specific to a particular crisis, yet they serve as a powerful, universal reminder that change and challenge are always with us. This raises the importance of mindset and community—those other trees your roots are connected with. It also shows us that sometimes the rocks in our stream are actually indicators or amplifiers of truth, as uncomfortable as they may be. Toni Desrosiers of Abeego shared her insights about dealing with these, as well as many other rocks that she has navigated:

> *You have to honor those dark times. It's like emotions. We think that laughing and happiness are cool, but people have problems with crying. It's like that with your business. You need to embrace the dark and the light equally. We don't want to be with negative emotions; we want everybody to be happy. It's like that with entrepreneurship—we only want to hear about success, not the hard times. When we don't validate it, it's like, "You've got to be successful all the time."*

You will not always be winning or (cringe) "killing it." Nobody is. I also strongly caution you against feeling like you need to cultivate a bulletproof image as an entrepreneur, as this perpetuates an unrealistic and potentially damaging stereotype and can make it hard to connect authentically with others. Think back to the example that I shared at the beginning of the chapter, where the CEO reached out from a place of need and vulnerability. Others responded immediately and without judgment, because they all recognized the truth of what she was sharing. It created safety and allowed everyone to emerge stronger, together.

COMPETITION

What's it like when what you thought you wanted—or who you thought you wanted to be—turns out to be less than what you had hoped for? As much as I tout "collaboration over competition," I will be the first to admit that competition is indeed a very real rock to be reckoned with before we can visualize a better way to move our economy and human needs forward. Abeego has been copied dozens, if not hundreds, of times by now. Toni Desrosiers reflects:

I never kept it a secret, I chose not to patent it, and I was transparent about my ingredients really early on because I wanted my customers to understand my product. I always knew Abeego would be replicated by another company and still, the first time I got copied, it was like I had my teeth knocked out. It stalled me creatively for two years. My ideas were frozen inside me, because I was too fearful to share them in case they were "stolen." It was the darkest time in my life as a creative, inventive person, because my strength is my ability to identify problems, invent solutions, and communicate them in a compelling way. This strength was buried and, as a result, my company stood at a standstill for almost two years with little to no growth, while I watched beeswax wrap pop up all around me. At the end of the day, however, the competitors have been beneficial to Abeego and have positively impacted our growth. I was my own worst enemy and every minute I spent wallowing in my fear and shame was a minute wasted.

Rather than presume she needed to control or otherwise "own" the market for beeswax food wrap, Toni is grateful that so many more people are using it, far beyond the numbers that she herself would realistically have been able to service. This further exemplifies the soul trait "Impact is the New Currency," because to Toni, the point of her venture is *having less plastic in the world*, even if that does not necessarily mean getting all of the market share for her product. Suzanne and I hold exactly this perspective about the enormous growth in recent years in the reusable menstrual product marketplace. Competitors have raised awareness more widely than we could have on our own and offer more product variations than we would be able to produce. This is my ideal reframe of what competition can look like; nobody needs to sink in order for all our boats to rise.

Should Toni have protected the idea legally with a patent? Maybe, and maybe not. Patents are expensive, take ages to obtain, and then only cover a very specific design. If a competitor makes something comparable but with slight variations, there is no way to stop them. The other big downside to trying to enforce patent protection is that it's a major distraction from growing your initiative through product innovation, building your team, creating an impactful brand, managing cash flow, and ensuring a top-quality user experience.

Further to this point, I would invite you to consider the extent to which you have internalized the necessity of "owning" a particular idea. Ownership, as an abstract concept, can be problematic and can risk the ethically questionable appropriation of others' ideas, even when it's "legal" (e.g., you were the first to take out a patent or other form of intellectual property protection). Taking Lunapads as an example, I was often asked in the early days whether I had "invented" washable menstrual pads and period underwear, a question that baffled me. Considering how long menstruation had been around, it seemed beyond obvious to me that countless versions of the idea had come before mine. As I shared earlier, the first Lunapads were inspired by another brand whose design didn't work for me, so I dove in to iterate on the concept with my own ideas. Failure to realize this when it's true (and it's not always) is one of my personal pet peeves. There is no shame in acknowledging that we are standing on others' shoulders—the previous work that forms the foundations from which our own imaginations take off.

RETHINKING YOUR BUSINESS MODEL

What happens when your business model is not exactly churning along swimmingly? Back in the early 2000s, when online shopping was not yet fully a thing, Suzanne and I decided to commit the funds invested in Lunapads by Renewal Partners to a high-growth strategy based on infiltrating the US natural products retail market. The classic formula was to attend major trade shows in order to get the attention of retail buyers, whose orders would in turn get the attention of distributors who would supply the retail stores from their warehouses.

It was a very expensive process, and we did not have enough capital to support additional marketing in an almost-invisible category with skinny margins. There was already one relatively well-established American company, the Portland, Oregon-based GladRags, whose wonderful founder Brenda Mallory soon became a friend. GladRags decidedly had the home turf advantage and was already listed with several major distributors, which made it hard for us to differentiate our offering. At the time, it was just Suzanne, me, and a couple of part-time team members. We worked our butts off: packing up our booth, traveling to shows, collecting business cards, and trying to get to know influential buyers, followed by weeks of follow-up phone calls and emails. There just wasn't enough of any-thing—people, money, or time—to be able to make it work. Long story short, within less than two years, we were almost out of money with little to show for it.

We went back to Joel Solomon at Renewal to share the bad news and ask for his help. I will never forget our meeting and the feeling of dread that I had heading into it. We explained the situation and he replied that he could not justify "throwing good money after bad" on a business model that was clearly not working. In other words, no further funds were forthcoming. "But," he said, "I believe in you two. Go back to the office and put your heads together and make a plan to move forward." The dread dissipated and, buoyed by his faith in us, we did precisely as he advised. What came out of our conversation back at the office was a decision to abandon any further US distributor/wholesale investments and to take our last few thousand dollars and invest them in a new e-commerce website. With the trips and their associated expenses off the table, we were able to instead focus on what was working—Canadian sales—as well as putting time and energy into generating web sales. Another important part of this strategy was that while the sales volume was lower, at least initially, the margin was far higher, thanks to having off-loaded so many expenses. We fully recovered within about six months.

In some ways, you could see us as simply lucky; however, my lesson is that if Joel had agreed to continue to help us limp along, we would never have made that timely decision. But the real gold was the reminder that, at the end of the day, his investment *was in us*, and that we had the power to change our situation if we put our heads together. This situation was just a rock in the stream letting us know that we needed to change our business model.

SELF-DOUBT

What about when your challenges are internal, not external? This can include mental health challenges like stress, depression, and impostor syndrome, and brutal unforeseen life circumstances, not to mention internally dealing with skepticism (or worse) from other people. One of the biggest challenges that I have experienced in my career is self-doubt. Also known as the "inner critic," "gremlin," and many other names (I think of mine as "the demon"), it shows up as a voice that tells me I'm a lousy leader and human with terrible ideas, who has no right to take up space. This is particularly challenging for people entering spaces where they are already underrepresented or marginalized, because those types of messages are reinforced in the bigger social picture every day. This means that your mental health is going to require additional tending in order for you to stay strong and keep going.

My esteemed colleague Elizabeth Sheehan, the founder of a carbon footprint–measuring and reduction tool for organizations called Climate Smart, shared some helpful thoughts about self-doubt; I have excerpts of these taped at eye-level in my workspace.

Self-doubt is a companion when we dare to be brave. Sometimes loud, other times quiet. Approach it with a warm, kind curiosity. Listen to it from your wise self. Ask if what you hear is true. Ask what it needs. Feed it that. Share with others you trust.

I welcome this gentle approach. Too often, self-doubt is framed as weakness or something that we need to "get over" or "crush," after which point, we will presumably be "demon-free." This has never been my experience. It's like it's always waiting in a closet for the perfect moment to wreak havoc. If this is true for you, you likely already know the types of situations where demons find fertile ground.

Elizabeth's approach does not assume that you have something wrong with you that needs to be fixed; self-doubt is a form of fear that likely starts from a place of self-protection. By offering it warm curiosity instead of contempt or scared submission, you are able to unpack and thereby begin to manage it. She suggests another helpful tip, which is to do a reality check on what the voice of your self-doubt is saying:

On reflection, where I struggled was with expectations of myself and of how things are supposed to go. This has helped me surface the out-of-reach unconscious beliefs about power, money, and intelligence in ways that have made me a better human being.

This idea raises key questions about unconscious beliefs. Are your expectations realistic and authentic, or do they stem from traditionally enforced social conditioning and beliefs? For example, is the voice using words like "never," as in "Women of color never get bank loans."? Although we do know from factual evidence that women of color have greater difficulty accessing loans than white women, and certainly far more often than white men, is it actually true that they never do? No. Should this statistic stop you from trying? Of course not. So, a good question to ask your demon right off the top is, "Is that actually true?" It's also worth remembering that to varying degrees, the challenges that come your way may be manifestations of systemic inequality. Got turned down for something? If your demon starts up about how it's your fault and your personal failure, remind yourself that it didn't happen in a vacuum, and that our systems—especially economic ones—are far from the meritocracies they attempt to portray themselves as.

I talked about Patrice Mousseau in chapter 2, as an example of the "True Grit" soul trait. Her experience of systemic anti-Indigenous discrimination is a disheartening example of what I pointed to above. She shares the double bind that she faces:

As much as there is lip service paid to women and Indigenous entrepreneurs, systemic racism is still deeply prevalent. It is not a meritocracy out there and some of the requirements can make even applying for help incredibly challenging. The system is weighted in favor of white men, but it's presented as neutral. To add insult to injury, as someone who has worked my butt off and overcome all manner of challenges to build a successful business in spite of these barriers, I am often told that I am only successful thanks to the perceived government "breaks" I receive as an Indigenous person. It's deeply hurtful to see everything that I have done just discounted like that. If anything, it's been harder, yet I'm told that I'm getting special treatment and didn't need to try as hard as others did.

Part of the reason for the persistence of self-doubt in the entre-preneurial journey is that we are in a perpetual state of doing things for the first time, giving demons ample room to play the doubt card, simply because there is no frame of reference for you doing that spe-cific thing successfully. It can be helpful, in such cases, to remember the first time that you got the hang of a skill as a kid—say swimming, reading, or whatever is true for you. Find that feeling of the initial uncertainty from the simple fact that you had never done it before, then see if you can locate the energy that kept you going to see it through, come what may. Maybe you did fail; what happened next? What you need to find is a kind of mental touchstone of an expe-rience that you had, at any point in your life, of achieving a goal for the first time. It literally could be anything, but it's especially potent if the experience was unexpected or had fear associated with it that you had to vanquish on top of the task itself.

Another common aspect of struggle for underrepresented people in the entrepreneurial space is the sheer dearth of others who look like us. I remember being at a pitch competition once and being in front of a panel of around ten white men and two white women, thinking how much I resented the feeling of the men's eyes on me and wondering how much worse it would feel to be a person of color in the same situation. Then there's the inherent adversarial framing of the pitch format itself, as discussed earlier in the book. The presumed power dynamic is that you are there to please, impress, and earn their approval. In situations like this where the demons start chattering, whether it's at a bank or a sales meeting, a helpful reframing can be that your vision is the precious commodity they are fortunate to be learning about, and possibly have the opportunity to support. If they say no, do not take it personally or as a negative reflection of the worthiness of your initiative. These people are often looking for a very specific type of enterprise, so if you don't make the cut, it's most likely because it's simply not a fit. Instances like these are precisely why we need more diverse leaders making investment decisions.

Sometimes demons may take the shape of actual people who oppose or belittle you in your life. In these cases, listening deeply to your "wise self" (borrowing Elizabeth's words) is a tip also shared by Danielle Keiser, co-founder of the Menstrual Health Hub, which is an encyclopedic online resource directory. Here are her thoughts:

When someone tells you you can't do something, that should be the fuel for your fire. When you stop and listen to yourself—like truly listen—and know that your wonderful idea has the potential to grow wings and fly, you've got to take that and run with it! You'll regret it for the rest of your life if you don't! I never, ever thought that I would end up starting an NGO and a global consulting agency. I thought I'd become an actress or maybe a lawyer. A politician, even. But here I am, making the world more aware of menstruation and the importance of the female experience. Remember, there are no plans for your future except for the ones you create yourself. Don't let anyone else hold the pen to the story of your life!

Vanessa Richards, whose leadership gifts I introduced in chapter 4, shared the concept of "staying in your corner" with me, which I suspect is born, at least in part, of her experience as a Black woman; in short, not everyone is going to be in your corner, so you have to be your own hero and protector. Her words:

Stay in your corner. Speak to yourself words you'd want a champion supporter to speak to you. Say them when it matters and when it seemingly doesn't. Just keep cheering yourself on. Be your own coach and know when to bring in other coaches to help you.

As a community engagement professional, Vanessa also highlights the power of positive relationships during times of stress and struggle:

Work with people you admire and like. They may not always be the obvious fit for what you are trying to achieve, but they may be the best company along the journey, which has its own profound value. A solid relationship can give you the room to adapt, encourage new ideas, and open up new perspectives. Trust is a solid foundation to bloom from. A solid relationship also knows when to bring in alternative or additional targeted support. If you like and admire your co-workers (the ones you can choose), your work can be a beautiful challenge and good fun along the way. Joy along the way matters. Stay in your corner. Be a cheerleader for others.

Being a cheerleader for others is a surprisingly effective antidote to the demon blues. It may seem counterintuitive to refocus our attention on others when we are feeling caught up in our own challenges, but I agree with Vanessa that it can work wonders. It's interesting to me how often we teach what we need to learn and can give ourselves what we need by offering it to others. Listen and take note of the words of encouragement and advice that you give to others, and share them with yourself internally.

OTHER CHALLENGES AND SETBACKS

What about when things go sideways, either on a personal or business level? Let's not kid ourselves—they can and will. Entrepreneurship can be incredibly stressful, especially for those flying solo. There are a heap of decisions and things that we just plain don't know or have never done before, and we often have no one to pass things off to or get support from. Like many challenges in life, there will be moments where you are going to have to take a deep breath and just make the best decision that you can with the time, information, and resources available to you.

Bonnie Foley-Wong's company, Pique Ventures, is an inclusive Angel investor fund focusing on leadership diversity and women-led ventures. Like Arlan Hamilton's Backstage Capital, Pique seeks to address the lack of funding for underestimated founders. But when you're up against patriarchy, capitalism, and white supremacy all at once—not to mention raising a young family—it's easy to understand how it was almost impossible for Bonnie. Her story is a moving mini–case study of meeting challenges of all varieties.

In 2012, disillusioned by the finance industry, I embarked on an exploration to answer two questions: How can we move money more purposefully, and where are all the women investors? I founded Pique Ventures, a boutique investment firm that specializes in ventures founded by diverse women, in response.

I tried different models for bringing investors and entrepreneurs together, being mindful of their time and wanting to create a more human and enjoyable experience. I hosted a slow-meeting event over tea at the end of 2012. From there, one of the investors I invited said she didn't have time to go to these events, but if I raised a fund, she'd invest in it. I tested that idea and received less-than-supportive feedback. Just as I was about to give up on it, I met someone who would become Pique Fund's first external investor. From there, I tried to gather enough investor interest to launch the fund. And then I was pregnant with my first child. Pique Fund launched twenty-five days before the birth of my daughter. The fund launch was smaller than my target, but I realized that starting was more important than the size. I didn't let the perfect be the enemy of the good.

I tried to scale it and raise another fund and missed a key milestone. It sent me and my company spiraling downwards. The truth is that I gained the skills, worked hard, and loved it. Still, I encountered sexism, bias, and barriers, even from people who called themselves allies. That stung. But I had the courage to make a tough decision, slow down the business, relocate to where I could get more support, and make a plan B. Although feeling sad and disheartened, I still persisted in trying to find a way to launch the fund and look for a job (that plan B) at the same time.

I should feel proud that I recognized I needed to change my situation, asked for help, and landed an amazing new role where I can continue the work and impact that I started with Pique Ventures. And since I am persistently curious and love storytelling, I'm now writing a book about the lessons I learned while raising Pique's second fund and sharing the stories of other women who beat the odds to raise venture capital funds.

One of Bonnie's strategies for coping and getting ongoing support from trusted friends was to start a private Facebook page, where she could share her experiences and get the support that she needed. As one of the members of the group, I witnessed time and time again how vulnerably sharing your messy truth with people who have your back can be medicine for us all. By modeling that it was okay to need and ask for help and feel stressed, disappointed, and uncertain, Bonnie built a community and created a safe space for us to freely share and offer support to one another.

RECONCILING CHANGE AND LOSS

Business challenges can have profoundly personal aspects, as I experienced with the Lunapads-to-Aisle rebrand in March 2020. What was supposed to have been a major media event ended up being totally overshadowed by COVID-19. We were in Toronto at the time, attending the SheEO Global Summit, and had a beautiful moment on stage sharing the news with the eight hundred attendees there, even as we realized that the launch was not likely to have anywhere the impact we had planned and hoped for.

For all my excitement about the advent of Aisle, I can't say that letting go of the Lunapads brand was easy. After all, I had created it and proudly waved its flag for over two decades. That said, I completely understood the rationale for the rebrand. We had been hearing from customers for years that they found the name confusing, as it obfuscated the fact that we sold period underwear as well as menstrual cups. (I think you'll agree that "the Lunapads Cup" just sounds flat-out odd.) Our media consultants also let us know that the brand was perceived as dated (as in "hippy/crunchy"), which made reporters reluctant to write about us.

As much as my head totally got it, it was hard for my heart and ego to not take it as a bit of a blow. As a founder, it's practically impossible to not identify yourself with your brand or product, so I internalized the rebrand decision as representing me being too old, not cool or relevant anymore, and so on. Yuck. Practically speaking, I realized—for a multitude of reasons—that while I had been the one to birth the initial vision, I was not going to be able to take it into the future. Part of this feeling is related to my uneasiness with e-commerce and social media, which play critical roles in the company's success. What really showed me that it was time to step aside was the recognition that I had already creatively moved on by starting G Day and Nestworks. I strongly felt that it was time for others more thoroughly engaged with and dedicated to the evolving menstrual awareness scene to be the architects of our next expression. As the initial conversations were starting about the new brand, with the help of a skilled, leading-edge consultant whose finger was firmly on the pulse of contemporary aesthetics and branding, I decided that it best served the company for me to largely stay out of it from then on. I retired from my role as creative director and moved out of the office in order to focus on G Day and Nestworks, essentially putting the rebranding process out of my mind.

I should add that I kept in regular and, as always, amicable contact with Suzanne about the business overall, attended advisory board meetings, retained the title of co-founder, and did not exit the company as a shareholder. I just didn't want any of my feelings to negatively influence the incredible work that the team was doing, and I committed to be unequivocally supportive of the outcome they had poured their hearts and souls into.

A few weeks after the launch and in the context of COVID-19, we conducted a workshop session led by the exceedingly skilled Sarah Dickinson, one of my treasured THNK teachers and an Aisle advisory board member. In the workshop, Sarah shared with us that change is challenging because it feels like loss, something that, in the case of COVID-19, was brutally true for so many. In our case, it felt like the pandemic had basically stolen Aisle's launch; the big, special project that the team had been working on for the past two years was suddenly a nonevent. How could it not feel like a crashing loss on top of everything else?

Sarah asked us to take a few minutes to journal about what had been hardest for us personally, and why, since the pandemic began. I started to write and, to my surprise, discovered a well of grief about the Lunapads brand. My insight was that I had been so busy trying to stay out of the way of the rebrand process that I had skipped a critical step: honoring and grieving the past. Looking back, I think I was scared that showing any sadness about the loss of Lunapads might be perceived as not supporting Aisle. The lesson here is to give yourself permission to fully process your feelings, especially when they're hard. I did not feel like I deserved to have them, thinking that they were trivial or insecure, or that they amounted to some sort of betrayal. As I shared previously, ritual is a great tool for processing this type of change, and I for one was grateful for this unexpected experience of closure.

HUSTLE CULTURE

Sometimes challenge comes in the form of a story or image of ourselves that needs to shift. Sonia Strobel, of Skipper Otto Community Supported Fishery, was holding herself to a completely unrealistic ideal of what the work of an entrepreneur was supposed to look like and was in turn neglecting her family and compromising her company culture.

Coming into entrepreneurship, I would hear people talk about how busy they were all the time, being really stressed out and working all hours. I thought that's what I needed to do in order to be successful.

I really fell for hustle culture and believed that if I wanted to change the world, I was going to have to wear myself to the bone to do it, have zero boundaries, and say yes to everything. I realized that I was very worried about how people would perceive me, like if I wasn't seen to be at my limit all the time, then I didn't deserve to have success. As though my sense of self-worth came from how busy I was.

My breaking point came in October 2018. I was in the office being my usual strung-out busy. I was so raw, not sleeping properly, my mind filled with endless chatter, and suddenly felt an overwhelming urge to cry. There was just no way around it, so I went into the bathroom and had a big sobfest. Then I got mad at myself for crying, basically telling myself, "Leaders don't cry—I don't have time for this!"

I came out of the bathroom and my business partner asked me if I would come into the boardroom to speak with him. I immediately thought that he was mad at me about something I had forgotten to do and became mad at him too. I was just projecting stuff all over the place, all the while thinking, I don't have time for this; can't you see that I'm busy?

In the boardroom, he sat me down and gently called me out on my perpetually stressed-out behavior and the impact that it was having on the team. I burst into a fresh round of tears. We both had a good cry, in fact, and then he suggested that I take a month off. Coming from busy land, I found this outrageous and impossible; however, I couldn't deny the truth of what he was saying.

But I started to think about it, wondering whether the wheels would in fact completely come off the business if I wasn't there. Would everything sink? Would I die? I decided to go for it, on the condition that I sit down and make time to truly understand what was happening for me. It started me on a journey of inner awareness and questioning my beliefs about what success means.

Doing the inner work of meditation and mindfulness, and slowing down, has made it really clear to me that the company's vision is about promoting wellness for everyone who is part of it, myself included. I am so fortunate to have grown a company for the past twelve years and now I get to choose how I want to be. If I come into the office and am freaking out all the time, that will be my company culture. I need to be aware of that for myself and for everyone else.

There are so many important points in this story, including the perils of hustle culture, the toll that unchecked stress can take on us, our teams, and our families, and taking responsibility for one's self-care and mental health. Personally, I feel better just knowing that other people who I look up to also share my bad habits of social comparison and self-criticism. Honest sharing is always healing.

These are some suggestions for what to do when you are feeling stuck, stressed, or out of steam:

- Be aware of perfectionism. Don't let the perfect be the enemy of the good.
- Ask yourself whether, in your attempt to make the world a better place, you may perhaps be overloading yourself.
- Check in on your aspirations. Are they realistic, meaningful, and true for you?

- Are you being gentle with yourself? Whose voice are you listening to—yours, or your demon's? Check in by placing your hands over your heart and taking a few deep breaths. Literally wrap your arms around yourself and give yourself a hug. I wish that I had given myself more support around the rebrand process in this way, rather than dismissing my feelings as wounded ego.

- Consider another time in your life when you met a challenge of any variety and came through it. Remember the experience and the feeling that it gave you. Consider journaling the story or sharing it with a friend. What lessons did you learn then that you may be able to draw upon now?

- Is it possible to break what you're working on into smaller steps, even something as simple as the next email or phone call?

- Ask yourself, "Do I need to make this decision right now, or can it wait until I have more information and feel more ready?" If it does not need to be done immediately, put it down and stop fighting with whatever it is, especially if it involves self-doubt or self-criticism.

- *Ask for help.* This is astonishingly hard for some of us to do. Seek out a trusted friend or mentor and ask for their time to help you process whatever is happening. Please, just do it. We all need this sometimes; it's not weakness.

- Find a physical way to express what you need and then create it. Making a list of things you want to let go of that are no longer serving you, then burning it, is another powerful move that can take you from mulling something over in your head to taking action. Is there a way that you can give yourself what you need by making something, or otherwise physically creating it?

- Have a good cry (or whatever processing grief, sadness, disappointment, anger, etc. looks like for you) and just be present with whatever comes up. Sometimes things take their own time to resolve or achieve clarity and that time may not be now. Metaphorically put down whatever is weighing on you and find something else to do that nourishes you and feels useful.
- Press pause on thinking about your own needs and pull your focus back to the bigger picture. Is there a way you could be of service to others?
- Stay in your corner (as Vanessa Richards recommends).

All of these stories represent why I believe that, in the entrepreneurial world, we social types have an edge: our mission and our Why. Have there been days when I have been terrified of losing my business? For sure. Regular uncertainty, stress, fatigue, and so on? Absolutely. So, what has kept me going every single time? My Why and the people who are on this journey with me. Knowing that I am fulfilling a deeply personal calling that matters in some way makes me feel my most human, like a more fully expressed individual who is aligned with whatever it is that brought me to this planet. While I do wonder at times whether I should be doing what I'm doing, I never question whether it matters. This never fails to bring me solace, strength, and the courage to keep going. So, my advice for this section is to draw from the place that we explored together in chapters 3, 4, and 5. These lessons are not just there to shape your vision, but also to give you the mojo to keep going when it's far from easy. Hang in there, be gentle with yourself, and go back to that original feeling of inspiration when you need help to take the next step forward.

Massive caveat alert: your mission and Why alone will not get you where you want to go, and can even end up obscuring very real problems, toxic relationships, and unhealthy compromises you may be making. This is a hard thing to admit and a tough subject to tackle. The reality is that things don't always work out, even with the awesomeness of what you're seeking to create and the best of intentions.

Longtime SVI community member and SVI Women producer Martha Belcher, one of the wisest souls I have the good fortune to call a friend and mentor, cautions:

> *A difficult but emerging reality within the frame of social enterprise—especially for people of our generation who were at the forefront of the movement—is the belief in mission as a magic cure-all or an excuse for subpar, or even discriminatory, behavior. Don't hang out too long in toxic work environments, even if the mission is a good one.*

WHEN ROCKS CREATE RIPPLES

To go back to the poetic allusion at the beginning of this chapter, I believe that not all "rocks" are equal. Some of them may look like obstructions but are really disguised indicators of opportunity. I'm going to close this chapter with a story about an out-of-left-field opportunity for impact beyond our wildest dreams, which became a life-changing experience. Before diving into this story, I invite you to consider how you might respond if someone, albeit at a great distance, asked for your help to essentially replicate something that you had created.

In 2000, Lunapads was freshly incorporated and trucking along with Suzanne and me as partners, when one day, we received a letter from a Zimbabwean-Canadian woman called Isabella Wright. Until that day, if you had asked me what I imagined that menstruators in the Global South (formerly euphemistically known as "the developing world" by people of my generation) used to manage their periods, I would have had zero idea: I had never thought about it.

Isabella Wright let us know that the situation for people with periods in Zimbabwe was, in fact, dire. The economy was in a tailspin thanks to the infamous Robert Mugabe's corrupt leadership and as one consequence, menstrual supplies were either astronomically priced or flat-out unavailable. As a result, adults were missing work and students were missing school, on top of having to deal with a dangerously shifting mix of violence and economic instability. We immediately shipped out several hundred pads and went on to send hundreds more over the next few years. Little did we know that this was just the beginning of one of the brightest aspects of Lunapads/ Aisle's impact.

The years went by and the donation practice continued, branching out to seventeen countries across the Global South. One particularly impactful ripple of this activity came when Carrie-Jane Williams, a Vancouver-based university student, fundraised to purchase a suitcase load of Lunapads to take to Uganda, where she was working on a youth literacy project, in 2008. Already aware of the menstrual health and hygiene (MHH) relationship with girls' education, she was close to the end of distributing the Lunapads when she met a couple of other student volunteers, who were also aware of the issue. Inspired by the Lunapads that she showed them, Paul and Sophia Grinvalds were hit with the brainwave to remain in the country and start a pad-making company. Being the responsible, thoughtful people of integrity that they are, they wrote to us in 2008 to be fully transparent about their objectives and ask for our support. Suzanne and I remember the moment we received their email and considered what to do. Never once did we hesitate or consider their invitation as anything other than an exciting opportunity to be part of something incredible, as opposed to a competitive threat. So began one of the most remarkable relationships in the Lunapads/Aisle journey.

We set up a series of monthly Skype calls to mentor Paul and Sophia's startup and were thrilled to watch the rapid growth of their enterprise from a distance. In 2012, we had the opportunity to visit Uganda and, of course, made plans to meet Paul and Sophia (known as Sonia) and visit the AFRIpads factory. I cannot overstate what an important experience it was for us. The feeling of walking into the factory and seeing two dozen women sewing pads on treadle (foot-operated, nonelectric) sewing machines was one of the most moving experiences of my life. After pursuing this improbable idea, for which I had weathered skepticism and even revulsion for almost twenty years, to see it flourishing and being welcomed as an important innovation for supporting youth reproductive wellness and life-changing education, moved us to tears.

We loved spending time with Paul and Sonia and their team, who gave us a hearty and generous welcome. During this time, we decided to create a TOMS shoes–inspired buy-one-give-one (BOGO) program that has, to date, provided over thirty thousand girls with AFRIpads. The following year we went a step further and made an equity investment in AFRIpads, supporting the building of a ten-thousand-square-foot factory.

There are some moral lessons to this story: the importance of trusting, letting go, and relinquishing control, and saying yes even when you are not sure how something may go. These are the ripples that sing as they dance between the rocks.

CHAPTER 11

Radiance

A s my career has unfolded through the years, I have come
to think of growth patterns and impact in an increasingly expansive, nuanced way, which feels, well, *radiant*. Radiance is a beautiful
word that implies transcendence, as well as multidimensional impact
that may extend beyond your initial vision or—as we saw at the end
of the last chapter—into ripples that you never imagined.

The key aspects of radiance that I want to explore in this chapter
include ways of understanding and assessing our impact; alternative
ways of looking at endings; and a deep conviction of mine that to truly
succeed as social entrepreneurs, we need to consider the integrity of
our leadership practice as much as that of our product or service.

EXAMINING IMPACT

Starting an initiative that creates positive social and/or environmental impact—making the world a better place in some way, shape, or
form—is the most inspiring, light-filled aspect of radiance. It's what

has led you to where you are right now and inspired you to roll up your sleeves, pick up your sword, and be willing to transform. It's everything. Until this point, we have taken the concept of impact as a given, but it's now time to take a harder look at exactly how you are going to make a difference, the ways and means of measuring this, and how to ensure that it's not a misfire in the first place. For a reality check, let me say that embedding impact into entrepreneurship is taking something already difficult and complex several notches up in terms of the challenge. Just because it feels good does not necessarily make it easy.

As in all of life, when it comes to making a difference, we risk our intentions and our impact falling out of alignment with one another. For all our care and desire to help, things can go horribly wrong if we're not clear and careful, especially when there are social power imbalances present. This can appear in as many different ways as there are people and forms of oppression in the world. For example, people from the Global North wanting to help Global South communities can unconsciously come from a place of presumed superiority and potentially create, or perpetuate, a culture of disempowerment and dependence. The legacy of colonialism runs deep and there are a multitude of assumptions and microaggressions that can inadvertently surface under the auspices of charity. In addition to making sure that what you are offering is genuinely needed and is being delivered in a culturally respectful and sustainable manner, one also needs to be sensitive to unconscious racism and "white saviorism."

These concerns can be equally valid for issues closer to home, like housing insecurity, racial justice, and health- and ability-related causes. If you are not a member of the population whose needs you are seeking to serve, interrogate how this distance might be shaping your perspective and assumptions. This is not to say you shouldn't do it; just be aware. Allyship—playing a conscious, supportive role to oppressed groups that one is not a member of—is an essential part in bringing about social change; however, it requires ongoing self-awareness, clear communication, and willingness to accept and act on feedback. On that point, an excellent article on the topic is "The Characteristics of White Supremacy Culture," from *Dismantling Racism: A Workbook for Social Change Groups* by Kenneth Jones and Tema Okun. Rather than being about racist or nationalist organizations, the article highlights culturally transmitted traits and attitudes that show up across organizations, social dynamics, and individual behaviors, often on an unconscious level. It's exactly these types of unconscious biases and assumptions that can thwart good intentions and create an unintended negative impact. If you are a person with social privilege and any of these terms and concepts are new to you, I strongly encourage you to investigate them.

This discussion surfaces a tricky double edge to our sword of social entrepreneurship, which is essential to consider as we develop our initiatives. When we seek to make a difference, we are, by definition, seeking to hold ourselves to a higher standard of behavior and transparency. By being out there as changemakers, we are putting ourselves in a position where we can be uncomfortably (and even unfairly) scrutinized, which can obviously be time-consuming and irritating. When this happens, you need to catch yourself and remember that this is part of what you signed up for as a social change leader, and that things like psychological comfort and one's assumed right to it can be indicators of social privilege, which need to be examined. If you want others to uphold a higher ethical standard, it goes without saying that questions may come your way about your own choices, actions, levels of privilege, and accountability. On top of the fact that this takes time, it can also necessitate doing some significant inner work—especially for those of us coming from places of social privilege—which I contend is absolutely essential, not to mention deeply rewarding. Whatever issue you are seeking to address with your initiative, some form of research and self-examination will almost certainly be necessary, depending on where you stand within an intersectional (multifaceted) understanding of social power dynamics.

In addition to the personal aspect of the double edge, there is often a real financial cost to doing good that you will need to factor into your plans. We have faced this again and again at Lunapads/Aisle. Our products cost more than our competitors' due to our extreme diligence and commitment to the sustainability of our textiles, our labor standards, and B Corp compliance, among other things. All of these things cost money, which in turn impacts our margin. This presents a conundrum from a values perspective, as we would like our products to be accessible pricewise to as many people as possible. As a small business, we often find ourselves balancing our desire to offer the highest quality, most sustainable products with how much we charge our customers, how we compensate our team members, and how much money we are able to contribute to our company's impact initiatives. These are incredibly tricky decisions that are seldom easy to make.

THE PERILS OF PERFECTIONISM

This trickiness raises the issue of perfectionism. If you have read the article that I mentioned above, you will have noticed that "perfectionism" shows up first on the list of characteristics.

In the social impact space, it is possible to easily fall down an endless rabbit hole of what I'll call "moral perfectionism," which presents another conundrum, especially in view of the advice from the beginning of this section; to recap, you absolutely need to do your homework around verifying your impact and take steps to be self-aware around which forms of social privilege you may hold. The tricky part is that this work is potentially endless and, as I alluded to in the Lunapads/Aisle example above, there is not always a perfect solution. You are going to have to make hard choices at some point along the way.

The best advice that I can offer on this front is to be prepared to be *completely transparent* about your decision-making process. Working yourself into a state of ill health or bankrupting your enterprise is not going to serve anyone. Accept the idea that your project and leadership are part of an ongoing process of learning and improvement, rather than a fixed goal of being "done" once you have completed JEDI (justice, equity, diversity, and inclusion) workshops, have raised a certain amount of money toward a worthy cause, are a B Corp, or whatever other ways you choose to validate your impact. I suggest getting really good at listening, accepting feedback, taking responsibility, being accountable, learning from experience, forgiving yourself, and moving on.

Another aspect of this discussion is the personal toll that perfectionism can take on ourselves and others. This is not to say, "Hey, take a day off being such a do-gooder," or "Go ahead, cut some corners." Rather, don't lose sight of the fact that as humans we are imperfect by nature. In our desire to make our world—a product of human imperfection—a better place, we are bound to make mistakes and not be able to do everything that we want; there aren't enough hours in the day, for one thing. I believe this is a particularly important point for your average person and especially for women. We are already inundated by messages about how we fall short or need to improve ourselves to meet cultural expectations about beauty, body shape and size, and acceptable "feminine" behavior. Never feeling like we are "enough" is a typical way that misogynist oppression manifests. Be mindful of ways that it may be showing up in your practice as a social entrepreneur. Pick your battles and priorities, and do not lose sight of the importance of self-care and creating strong personal boundaries.

ASSESSING IMPACT

So, how do you know when you're actually having the impact that you want to have? In addition to questioning your assumptions and doing solid research, the most important place to look is to your beneficiaries—the people and communities whom you serve. Look for ways to solicit anonymous feedback that is accessible to them; do not, for example, assume that filling out a form is the easiest way for them to communicate. Ask. Also, make sure that you are getting the full picture of their needs and that they feel safe and empowered to give you honest feedback.

For example, in the early days of donating Lunapads to organizations supporting girls' education in the Global South, we just sent pads because that was what we understood that they needed, without asking for further information or context. When we got feedback that they also needed underwear, that was the key to the success of the program; they needed them to be able to use the pads in the first place. Being the affluent, well-intentioned Global North leaders that we were, it never occurred to us that they might not have underwear—a great example of how, when we are unconscious of our privilege, we can make assumptions that thwart our goal of being helpful. In addition to the underwear question, we subsequently developed a nuanced intake process, through which we were able to learn about cultural norms around menstruation in each community. Would it be socially safe, for example, for a girl to wash and dry her pads in an outdoor place that was publicly accessible? If she needed to dry them inside or hide them, were they made out of fabric that would dry quickly in an indoor environment? Did she have access to soap and clean water?

THERE IS A CRACK IN EVERYTHING

Radiance, by definition, goes in all directions and can illuminate less-than-beautiful corners. As I suggested earlier, misaligned intention and inconsistent personal integrity can sabotage even the strongest of impact ideas. That said, in picking up our swords, we will almost certainly fall on them at some point. How can we gracefully learn and grow from these experiences? There is a line in the classic Leonard Cohen song, "Anthem," that goes: "Forget your perfect offering. There is a crack, a crack in everything. That's how the light gets in."

I'd like to share a bit of history of the natural menstrual care industry as an interesting, real-time case study of the amazing possibilities—and co-existent potential pitfalls—of social entrepreneurship.

Who would have ever thought that periods would be a modern gold rush? When I started making washable cloth menstrual pads and period underwear in 1993, there was a mere handful of commercial brands: Lunapads, Feminine Options, GladRags, Sea Pearls natural sea sponges, The Keeper (a natural rubber menstrual cup) and the DivaCup (the first silicone menstrual cup). As I mentioned earlier, Lunapads had an explicit eco-feminist social change agenda that used business as the vehicle to proliferate its impact.

Remember when I said that your Why can keep you getting out of bed every morning, even when things are less than easy? That was us. In the face of thousands of "Ew, gross!" and "Seriously? You actually wash them?" moments, we persisted, knowing the awesomeness that lay on the other side of social conditioning, skepticism, and squeamishness. And bit by bit, things came around, thanks to customers who wanted alternatives to wasteful disposables and trusted us to deliver something that worked, was comfortable, and respected their diverse needs.

Lunapads grew steadily but modestly as the years went by, until around 2015 when, all of a sudden, people became willing to talk about periods and even (gasp!) to embrace different ways of managing them. It was then that our hard work, and that of our many aforementioned colleagues and activists, started paying off. I should add that the founders of these groundbreaking companies had come to be cherished friends. We never felt like traditional competitors; we would have dinners at trade shows and follow-up calls to check in and offer support to one another, knowing that competition between us was essentially pointless. After all, why turn against one another when there were endless green pastures of opportunity to cultivate? To revisit the Underdog archetype, we were the collective David to the Goliath of disposable manufacturers. It would have been counterproductive, to say the least, to have framed each other as adversaries.

Given that consumer interest and the general zeitgeist were catching up to what we had always known about the unique opportunities and appeal around menstruation, it's no surprise that a crop of new startups started to enter the space. Initially this excited us, as we assumed that the new entrants would be like the others in our cozy gang: all boats rise! But we soon noticed a troubling new trend. As feminism became increasingly co-opted for marketing purposes during this era (an entire brilliant book has been devoted to this topic in Andi Zeisler's 2016 *We Were Feminists Once: From Riot Grrrl to CoverGirl®, the Buying and Selling of a Political Movement*), media sources began superimposing the brash Silicon Valley entrepreneurial stereotype onto this emerging group of new menstrual health leaders. The background story for each of them became oddly repetitive: they had entered a space where there had been no innovation for decades and spotted an opportunity to "disrupt" it with their "new" reusable product idea. Some of these leaders embraced the hype, successfully pitching the narrative to investors to create slick brands with big social media marketing spends. Although it was, in a way, exciting to see big-money investors and even mainstream disposable manufacturers investing in this new crop of reusable brands, we were skeptical about whether "bigger" would necessarily translate into more impact and sustainability. Based on our experience up to that point, we were hopeful that together, we would be able to not only grow the overall market for reusable products substantially, but to do it in a way that defied the competitive, scarcity-minded, winner-takes-all mentality that defined normative business practice in other established industries.

Sadly, it was not (or not yet) to be. While it's impossible and, moreover, unfair to generalize, our observation has been that an injection of big capital into progressive products combined with media hype does not lend itself to a progressive way of doing business. It was, and continues to be, challenging to take the high road when confronted with disappointing or questionable behavior; however, that is what we have steadfastly chosen to do—until now. As an example of less-than-ethical behavior in our sector, Suzanne shares the following story:

> We started Lunapads with the belief that a for-profit business like ours could use the tools of capitalism to improve the experience of menstruation while doing less harm to the planet. We have always held a "blue ocean" perspective when it comes to competition (there is room for everyone!) but my quiet tolerance for ethically questionable, competitive behavior hit a breaking point in December 2020, when a large, direct competitor brazenly tried to purchase (using a credit card with the name "R&D" and a shipping address to their corporate headquarters) the entire size range of one of our styles of period underwear. The timing of the purchase immediately followed the publication of an article in a major outlet about Aisle's product development team taking the time to work with (and pay) plus-size individuals to make body-affirming underwear that truly fit, as part of Aisle's equitable design principle. In my open letter to the CEO (I did not name them or the company), I not only called out their unethical behavior, but also their lack of integrity and willingness to do

the real work of listening and responding to plus-size people in a genuine manner, instead defaulting to building off our work. Many companies these days are paying lip service to size inclusion and body justice, but few actually walk the talk, which takes meaningful effort. I suggested that they should take the money they intended to spend on our products and spend it instead on hiring plus-size models and design specialists.

Going back to what I said about the sheer size of the market negating the need for this type of behavior, the global menstrual care market is currently sitting at forty billion US dollars annually. Not only is forty billion a mind-bogglingly large number—which is being spent by people who have no choice about whether or not they need menstrual products—but beyond that, *reusable products only represent around ten percent of the total market.* If ever there was a case for competition essentially being pointless, this is it—this is literally one of the most potentially abundant markets in the world.

Perhaps the most troubling phenomena in our sector are the arrival of cheaply made products and the greenwashing of goods that make less-than-transparent claims about their "ethical" supply chain. As leaders who intimately understand ethical supply chains, including the importance of paying a fair wage, Suzanne and I can't help but think that someone—likely female factory workers—is being taken advantage of when a T-shirt retails for five dollars and period underwear for ten dollars. Like fast fashion in general, this form of "low-road capitalism" only serves to teach consumers that the lowest cost is best, ignoring the fact that cheap goods often mean harm for the workers who make them. The fast fashion approach to reusable menstrual products is also resulting in misleading claims about their performance and durability. What's the point of making a "sustainable" product that does not meet its performance claims or last long enough to reasonably replace disposable products? And yet, I can certainly appreciate that not all people can afford to pay for more expensive, ethically made products, despite the fact that they are more economical in the long run. I would argue that in this case, the solution is looking for creative ways to leverage crowdsourcing, interest-free layaway technology (Aisle uses Sezzle) and making donations to help ensure that quality products are accessible to as many people as possible. Given that menstruation is an inevitability, we believe that employers, governments, and educational institutions should be taking responsibility for providing products—reusable and disposable alike—to their team members, students, and citizens. Rather than expending energy on turning a quick profit or making a media splash, my wish is that leaders wanting to make a difference in the menstrual equity space would seek creative, collaborative ways to make quality products as accessible as possible.

All that being said, in most ways, I am incredibly grateful for, and humbled by, the way the natural menstrual health market has grown so robustly. Although Suzanne and I, along with other early leaders of the aforementioned companies, were certainly the groundbreakers, the space is where it is today thanks to scores of other sincere, values-led, inclusivity-minded voices who have joined us.

For all the concerns I have about some of the newer actors in the natural menstrual health movement, I would say that we are overwhelmingly surrounded by generous, inclusive, like-minded colleagues who are simply incredible. We cannot say enough good things about the Menstrual Health Hub team as a shining example of a globally uniting force, as well as, of course, our beloved friends at AFRIpads. Technology has also played a positive role in helping users better understand and track their cycles through apps like Clue, while diverse social impact nonprofits like #HappyPeriod, No More Secrets Mind Body Spirit Inc., Days for Girls, The Period Purse, and many others are making a huge difference.

If the global menstrual health movement has an ambassador or spokesperson, it would have to be Jennifer Weiss-Wolf, a tireless lawyer-turned-activist-turned-author whose 2017 book *Periods*

Gone Public: Taking a Stand for Menstrual Equity was a tour de force defining a cultural turning point. Heck, she even coined the term "menstrual equity"! Her excellent book traces the contemporary movement's origins on a global scale, and her tireless work as an activist has resulted in menstrual products becoming tax-exempt in a majority of US states. Although we may have been the ones to get this particular ball rolling, we have been joined by a host of heart-led, visionary leaders who are helping make progress that we could never have imagined.

Yet it feels as though something is potentially being lost along the way: an opportunity to do an inherently good thing—making reusable menstrual products—in a genuinely innovative, socially impactful way. An opportunity this big has the potential to be a leading light on the road to a healed version of capitalism. Again, I do not question the impulse for growth, as long as what and how we are scaling is done with integrity. My issue is with initiatives that have an impact-based product or service that defaults to traditional, competitive "low road" codas. We need to examine the How of what we are doing, not just the What and Why. Green products and services being marketed in ways that do not promote progressive, ethical, inclusive leadership and operational practice is going only halfway in terms of what's possible. When we go all the way, making our leadership and work practice as awesome as our products and services, we put the "greater" into greater good.

As I shared earlier, I call this kind of alignment and its impact "radiance." Lunapads/Aisle's impact has been in social and environmental benefit, seeding and supporting the growth of other like-minded ventures through mentorship, public speaking, and positive relationships with "competitors," as much as in financial returns. While there may have been some years of (financially) flat growth, our radiant impact has consistently been shining.

MEASURING IMPACT

So, what does radiant impact look like? Since 2000, **200 million disposable products,** and counting, have been diverted from landfills thanks to customers switching to our products. Here are a few more examples derived from Lunapads/Aisle.

AFRIpads

Lunapads/Aisle has made over $100,000 in cash donations to AFRIpads and is a proud shareholder in the internationally recognized, groundbreaking venture, whose products (originally inspired by Lunapads) have reached over 3.5 million girls. We directly donated over $225,000 worth of pads, cups, and underwear to communities in need throughout Canada, the Caribbean, Asia, and Africa, reaching over thirty thousand girls.

In 2016, our team collaborated with AFRIpads to co-produce a booklet about menstrual health called *Girl Talk!*. On my previous point about understanding user needs from a holistic perspective, we identified a major gap and opportunity in the form of providing materials to support not only the successful adoption of AFRIpads, but furthermore as a springboard for critical sexual and reproductive health education. *Girl Talk!*—illustrated, I should add, by a then-eighteen-year-old female artist—is a full-color twenty-four-page booklet that tells the story of Sandra, a twelve-year-old Ugandan girl living in an urban area, as she starts her period. Since its launch in 2016, forty thousand copies have been distributed to girls in Uganda, Kenya, and Malawi, and it's been translated into Kiswahili and French. *Girl Talk!* has since been expanded into a full curriculum that has reached over thirty-two thousand NGO educators in nine countries, who have in turn educated over 110,000 women and girls about the menstrual cycle, reproductive anatomy, and personal hygiene practices.

Dignity Kits

Another longstanding Global South impact relationship that we are deeply proud of is with Rachel Starkey, one of the most passionate leaders that I have ever met in the field of global menstrual health. We first met Rachel, who is Canadian, in the early 2000s and have been collaborating ever since. Rachel and her family have been living in Egypt for many years, where they operate a garment manufacturing business. Being in this business showed Rachel the need and opportunity to upcycle fabric waste at scale, making it into useful items like blankets (an enterprise she dubbed Transformation Textiles), which were then donated to communities in need. While I was visiting her in 2012, she and I created a size-adjustable underwear design that could easily fit into cutting markers for T-shirts, which could yield thousands of pairs. Inspired by classic Lunapads, we added bands in the gusset to hold liners for use during menstruation. For our first test of this idea, we sent fifty thousand "Dignity Kits," comprising three pairs of underwear and nine liners, to multiple communities in Malawi, with Lunapads funding the shipping costs. Thanks to feedback from the recipients, we realized that the underwear could easily be replicated on a local level, so we created easily shareable and printable instructions that we have been freely sharing ever since. In just over a decade, this innovative solution has been shared with dozens of organizations both large and small, ministries of health and education, refugee camps, war zones, prisons, and other garment factory facilities in over fifteen countries throughout Africa, the Middle East, India, and Southeast Asia. Lunapads/Aisle also partnered with Transformation Textiles during the Middle East refugee crisis in 2014/2015 by again covering the shipping costs for thousands of Dignity Kits, which were distributed in refugee camps in Egypt, Greece, Jordan, Iraq, and Syria.

Equitable Design

Suzanne and the Aisle team developed an inclusive design process that considers equity and impact as integral parts of product design. The principles of equitable design are considering underrepresented users, inviting diverse perspectives as a way to improve design, and being curious about how a single solution coming out of this process may have the potential to benefit many. As I highlighted in chapter 2 as an example of the soul trait "Gifts from the Margins," the Aisle boxer brief was originally conceived with a transmasculine user in mind. Upon launch, it quickly became Aisle's number one selling product—and not only because its unique style lines appealed to a gender-nonconforming user, but because it offered a body-affirming experience of comfort and performance for bodies of all shapes and sizes.

Lunapads/Aisle has been championing the inclusion of transgender, nonbinary, and genderqueer individuals in the menstruation conversation since at least 2011. As one example of our impact on that front, here is a note that we received recently:

> *Just a quick note to say how happy I am that companies like yours are making my life and my trans teen's life so much more comfortable. When your teen really needs men's period underwear—not women's boy shorts—it was so amazing to find that you offer exactly what we were searching for. To whoever realized this need and pushed forward to make it available—thank you, thank you, thank you. Give that person a hug.*

—*H, mom of a trans boy teenager*

One-to-One Impact

I have lost count of how many early-stage social entrepreneurs Suzanne and I have mentored in the past twenty-plus years, but I would guess that it numbers in the hundreds. Examples of ventures whose founders we have mentored include a line of gender-inclusive work safety garments, four lines of organic skincare products, a bamboo and organic cotton infant clothing collection, a chain of physiotherapy clinics for children, and a line of zero-waste reusable-fabric food storage containers. My guess is that they have further extended this practice to mentoring others to do the same, thus creating ripples upon ripples of impact.

When I think back on the thousands of customer service calls and in-person customer interactions that I have either been part of or witnessed, I am deeply moved by the quality of trust, emotion, and vulnerability that has been at their core. From support for teens struggling with their first period to customers enduring painful menstrual conditions like endometriosis, as well as individuals living through pregnancy loss, birth trauma, and gender dysphoria, our team members have provided so much more than just information and product recommendations. We have brought meaningful compassion to experiences that are often dismissed, diminished, or ignored. I cannot even begin to hazard a guess at how many lives we have touched in this way.

Environmental Impact

Aisle is the first menstrual product company to conduct a comprehensive cradle-to-grave analysis to calculate the amount of waste, CO_2 emissions, and energy saved by each of our products compared to standard disposables. This is displayed by a live ticker on our website. As examples, our 2020 life-cycle assessment (LCA) shows:

>100,000 kg of waste diverted
(equivalent to 10,000,000 disposable pads)

>300,000 kg of CO_2 emissions avoided
(equivalent to >1,000,000 km of driving)

>6,000,000 kWh of energy saved
(equivalent to >25,000,000 days of LED light bulb energy)

LETTING GO

Up until this chapter, reading this book has been, at least potentially, a real-time exercise. By now, you may be starting, considering starting, or fully engaged in developing the vision you feel called to pursue. This chapter could have been an infinite exploration, given the potential situations that might transpire in the course of growing a multitude of diverse ventures. One thing that all initiatives have in common is that they will end, or at least go on without the founder(s) at the helm. You might decide to sell or hand over control of your venture to others; there may be an ending or dissolution, or even something as big as an IPO (initial public offering, or stock exchange listing).

What if my venture doesn't work out? you may be wondering. It still puzzles me that failure is viewed as such a fearsome, shameful outcome. Did you "fail" if you were inspired, found the courage to take a risk, learned something, and made new relationships? Failure can be a learning and personal growth experience, or even something that leads the way to "success." There can absolutely be very real financial consequences, which may be hard to bear; however, there is always something else to follow next. Google "famous failures" and you will find surprising names like Walt Disney, Oprah Winfrey, and Stephen King among the top results.

It's actually fairly unusual in business circles to talk about endings in any context other than failure or exit (selling the company or your shares in it). As we know from personal relationships, not all breakups are bitter; sometimes, it's just mutually understood that it's time to move on. I would like to propose a new mindset around crafting our exits as mindfully, creatively, and gracefully as possible.

Let's look at some basic assumptions about what exit looks like, at least in a for-profit context. Although this may not be relevant to readers embarking on social change projects, as opposed to large-scale incorporated or charitable entities, the standard trajectory for ventures is a linear three-step process: startup, scale, and exit. If you are starting a for-profit entity and seeking investment, be prepared to be asked what your exit strategy is. (As strange as this may feel at startup, who knows what will end up happening?) What's strange to me is how obsessed we are with the "startup," to the exclusion of what happens at the other end—much as we celebrate life and fear death, rather than revering death as an essential part of a meaningful cycle. My experience is that any and all of the things that happen following the initiation of a project or venture, measured or otherwise, can also be wonderful, surprising, and liberating.

What happens when we question the inevitability of this trajectory? For example, what if our lives and ventures are actually (like practically everything in nature) cyclical? This is not just the menstrual cycle–geek in me talking; it's an incredibly rich way of looking at things that actually makes a heap of sense and, I would argue, points us to the future. The concept of the circular economy, which is the notion that we need to consider every product's waste and end-of-life as much as its inception, is consistent with this thinking. How can we design our ventures and products to be upcycled? Or perhaps to have many cycles of change and growth? I think you will agree that this nontraditional (and dare I say, feminine) way of looking at organizational growth persuasively reimagines fundamental concepts like endings and exits.

It's worth pondering what the true difference is between something changing, ending, and "failing." These labels feel increasingly arbitrary and unhelpful to me and, in many ways, exist only in our own minds. I would argue that they're not as different as we commonly believe and that the story is ultimately ours to frame. I am further inspired by some creative new approaches to endings that are currently emerging in the social impact space. Let's consider some developing ways of thinking about letting go.

UPCYCLING: THE END, OR A NEW BEGINNING?

The onset of COVID-19 precipitated the "hibernation" of G Day (consistent with the views I just shared, I won't say "ending"), along with a poetic real-life example of upcycling. We were in the midst of gearing up for events in Vancouver and Toronto in 2020, including a fundraiser. All of them were cancelled. It would be years before we could hold the same types of events that we had in the past, typically attended by between one hundred and three hundred people in a very nonphysically distanced manner. I flirted briefly with the idea of creating a Zoom-adapted version of G Day but quickly abandoned it, as I just couldn't wrap my head around it. It was time to let go.

The Zoom calls I had with our team and the board to share my decision were full of emotion, as we each shared what G Day had brought to our lives. What came up repeatedly were recollections of how G Day's ethos had supported our inner girls, as well as bringing us unique joy and connection. Deep friendships have been founded through G Day ties and everyone expressed regret when we considered the loss of in-person connection and ritual in the COVID-19 (and likely post-COVID) era.

An interesting opportunity came out of this moment in the form of Fire & Flower, another local organization offering programming highly aligned with G Day's, yet very different in its expression. Whereas G Days were big one-off events, Fire & Flower's programming happens in smaller groups over several weeks and includes camps. I had known the group's founder, Elisa Lee, for several years through our shared interest in rites of passage and supporting adolescent girls' well-being, as well as via the Groundswell network (an alternative business school where I act as a mentor and advisory board member), where she had been a student. She and I had talked in the past about whether Fire & Flower would be better as a for-profit or nonprofit organization, so when the decision was made to discontinue G Day, I approached her about taking over United Girls of the World Society (UGW), a registered charity that is G Day's parent organization, and using it to house Fire & Flower. Obtaining charitable status is onerous, time-consuming, and expensive to do from scratch, but it's relatively simple to reassign leadership once obtained, especially between organizations who are closely aligned in purpose. Once obtained, charitable status has huge benefits, including the ability to issue tax receipts for donations and being eligible for a far wider array of grants. I loved the idea that UGW could effectively be upcycled into a wonderful organization doing similar work, and Elisa's board was similarly excited by the opportunity. Long story short, we undertook the necessary legal paperwork and made it happen. This was followed by a beautiful online celebration attended by G Day and Fire & Flower leaders and community members to honor the transition.

I love this story as an example of cyclical change taking the place of an ending. Yes, G Day as we knew it was over, at least for the foreseeable future. And yet, through the transfer of its legal entity to another values-aligned partner, rather than ending, it was being transmuted and transformed. The impact would still be there and could even radiate in different ways.

ALTERNATIVES TO TRADITIONAL EXIT

As we observed earlier, traditionally, an exit (or to get fancy, a "liquidity event") means either liquidating your company's assets, selling the company as a whole to another company or individual, or creating an initial public offering (IPO) on a stock market. If you are a for-profit company with shareholders, then this is where everyone gets paid out and moves on. Either way, you are relinquishing control and responsibility, and perhaps realizing a financial gain. As sensible and relatively straightforward as this may sound, to see it as the best or only option potentially misses the opportunity for a radiant solution. There are a few other possibilities worth considering, which I've laid out below.

Social Impact Mergers and Acquisitions

Although mergers and acquisitions (M&A) are typically associated with the large-scale for-profit world, they are not unheard of in the nonprofit and social venture space, and their ability to produce cost efficiencies (larger earnings for shareholders achieved by paring down duplicated functions) applies equally to less financially minded motives. Merging with another initiative can bring lots of benefits alongside the opportunity for founders to move on, knowing that their legacy will be continued. Are there organizations that align with your values, which may offer services complementary to your products, or vice versa? Another potential synergy could arise if your entity has a strong online presence while the other is strong in different channels or related communities. Perhaps a charitable entity may wish to acquire a social enterprise to generate revenue. This kind of outcome is yet another reason to reconsider holding a strictly competitive mindset as you contemplate others pursuing similar visions to yours.

Employees Stock Option Plans (ESOP)

ESOPs have existed for some time as a way for employers to reward team members for their loyalty by giving them shares in their company, in addition to their salaries. While ESOPs are partial in most cases, it is absolutely possible to fully transition a company to being completely employee-owned through a large-scale ESOP transaction. A heartening example of this is Bob's Red Mill, a producer of whole-grain flour and other foods. In 2010, after rejecting multiple takeover and sale opportunities from large competitors, founders Bob and Charlee Moore decided to create an ESOP to protect their workers' jobs and the brand's values. After a gradual transition period of ten years, the company became one hundred percent employee-owned as of April 2020.

Cooperatives

Cooperatives are communally owned, for-profit legal entities that are less expensive to create than ESOPs. (Fun fact: Zebras Unite is a co-op and also has a separate nonprofit.) The key differences between an ESOP and a co-op are the governance structure, as co-ops give each head one vote irrespective of the total amount they have invested in the business, and their incorporation falls under different legislation (in British Columbia it's the Cooperative Association Act). This option offers the organization direct access to collective decision-making. While I have not undertaken the process, transitioning from a for-profit entity into a co-op appears to be standardized and relatively straightforward from a legal perspective. Co-ops are a natural fit for social ventures such as childcare, housing, and food-related services, but are increasingly present in more traditional business sectors, including consultancy groups. In such cases, the co-op offers a structure in which people can work together and rely on each other without having to answer to anyone but themselves.

Exit to Community

Exit to Community (E2C) is a new, highly imaginative, impact-minded line of inquiry around exit that is emerging out of the Zebra herd. E2C is a collaborative project created by Zebras Unite and the Media Enterprise Design Lab (MEDLab) of the University of Colorado Boulder. E2C seeks to imagine an alternative to the limited startup-scale-exit model—one that centers founders, customers, suppliers, workers, and other stakeholders as the primary beneficiaries of the venture's success, as opposed to just financial shareholders. Although similar to the idea of co-ops in terms of values, E2C seeks to explore different structures and ownership models than are currently reflected in the co-op model.

E2C is an exploration of potential ways for anyone connected to a company (a stakeholder) to gain the ability to reach an ownership position, where community members can become shareholders, or even assume full ownership of the company. Part of why I am excited about E2C is that it's designed to be more accessible to regular people than traditional models, where money and power continue to be disproportionately concentrated in the hands of a privileged minority. E2C promises opportunity for members of underrepresented groups to become founders, owners, and leaders by democratizing the founder-shareholder model.

As a final observation, I want to simply encourage you to stay curious and open about the trajectory of your initiative, knowing that the future will obviously be different from now and there will likely be options available that do not presently exist. Who knows; perhaps you will create an alternative ending, beginning, or upcycling of your own design.

A RADIANT FUTURE

I am far from alone in dreaming of more creative and humane ways to approach growth, economics, and entrepreneurship. In fact, I feel as though I am just one ray among a glowing cluster of others articulating their own versions of radiance. For as much as the bigger-better-faster-more growth model continues apace in the mainstream, there are burgeoning voices and movements exploring a plethora of creative, sustainable, regenerative alternatives.

An entire book could be devoted to the following people and their amazing ideas, which have all shaped my thinking, but here I will only touch on them briefly. If you're not already aware of this growing group of thinkers, writers, and activists, you will enjoy researching them. Kate Raworth and Denise Hearn are among a new generation of regenerative and embodied economists disputing the dominant models of infinite, exponential growth in favor of models of sustainability inspired by the natural world. adrienne maree brown's brilliant concept of "emergence" deeply informs the way I've embraced organic, nonlinear, and bodily ways of knowing and seeing. Melanie Rieback's post-growth entrepreneurship movement and Charles Eisenstein's sacred economics are also very inspiring to me. All of their ideas point to better, more inclusive, and humane ways of conceptualizing new social and economic models.

Other leaders I am following include Carol Anne Hilton, whose book *Indigenomics: Taking a Seat at the Economic Table* posits Indigenous wisdom as being central to building a better world. Jennifer Armbrust's business school, Sister, is an unapologetically feminist take on entrepreneurial practices and business models. Kelly Diels is another leading-edge thinker in feminist entrepreneurship who pens a mighty "Sunday Love Letter" every week and has a soon-to-be-released book. A few other favorite go-to sources of inspiration, connection, and hope are CV Harquail's brilliant book, *Feminism: A Key Idea for Business and Society*; the excellent online magazine *LiisBeth ¤ Field Notes from the Feminist Economy*; and its sister network, the Feminist Enterprise Commons (FEC).

The aforementioned "renegade economist" Kate Raworth speaks of businesses' healthy functioning as "thriving"—similar to a tree, whose development levels off to a steady state after an early growth spurt, giving off oxygen and ultimately dropping seeds to support new growth. She points out that the only place in nature where the VC-friendly model of endless exponential growth is reflected is, alarmingly, in the spread of cancer.

Whether Lunapads/Aisle and our colleagues are the ones to achieve it or not, the times we are in are both demanding and creating the conditions for widespread change. In the case of the natural menstrual care industry, my feeling is that the opportunity to create amazing products and social movements—and to do it in an abundance-minded way that respects, includes, and celebrates our peers—still very much exists.

So, friends, where does all of this leave us? As I write today in the early, wintery beginnings of 2021, the world feels at once more precarious and more hopeful than ever. COVID-19 vaccines are being distributed, the US presidency (and vice presidency!) has changed hands, remarkable and previously unthinkable changes are happening on the reproductive justice front in South America, and orca whales are being born in the Salish Sea, near where I live. What all of this tells me is that the future is in our hands, and it needs us to be humble, proud, and brave; to trust ourselves and to relinquish the bigger-is-better, winner-takes-all values that have put us in the dubious situation in which we now find ourselves. As an alternative, it is my deepest hope that we can collectively open ourselves up to imagining, exploring, and co-creating a new, inclusive, and radiant approach to entrepreneurship—and to life, for that matter—in the name of the greater good.

PARTING THOUGHTS

We have been on quite a journey together so far, and if you're anything like me, remembering details can be a challenge. This is a recap of some of the central ideas that I have tried to impart, which you can refer to later for a quick hit of inspiration as you continue on your quest.

- See whatever you pursue as a deeply personal and creative form of self-expression, or even an art.
- Seek first to collaborate, not compete. Saving the world is not a zero-sum game. Playing by the old rules will not get us where we need to go.
- Remember Melody Biringer's wisdom: relationships are the true currency.
- Treasure your outsider or "margin" qualities. Please read Arlan Hamilton's *It's About Damn Time: How to Turn Being Underestimated into Your Greatest Advantage*—especially if your experience is as a person who falls outside the dominant power paradigm.

- Be aware that you are likely conditioned toward linear forms of thought and try to start unlearning them. Ask yourself what other forms of knowing and intelligence might also be real, worthy, and available. Read adrienne maree brown's *Emergent Strategy*.
- Consider which lessons we might learn from nature as we consider models for our initiatives. Check out Kate Raworth's TED talk, "A Healthy Economy Should Be Designed to Thrive, Not Grow," as well as Melanie Rieback's TEDx talk, "Post-Growth Entrepreneurship."
- Honor transitions with care and intention. There is power in ritual that can literally work magic and transform our efforts into the quest they really are.
- Reframe transactional thinking as relational thinking. Cherish the human moments at times that just feel like paperwork.
- Be attuned and open to diverse, creative ways of understanding agency, partnership, and planning. Think collectively, rather than individually.
- Cultivate a possibility mindset. What if the regular rules didn't apply? What if you could set your own terms?
- Do not take positive impact as a given; be mindful, self-aware, and diligent.
- Consider the principle of equitable design; how might this be relevant to your product, service, or initiative?
- Consider how your initiative can support widespread, progressive systems change, not just its own (or your) success.
- Ask yourself whether there is an opportunity to level up your initiative from "good" to "greater" by infusing values into the How, not just the What and Why.
- Think beyond existing or traditional concepts of scale and success.
- Lift as you rise. Respect and make room for others, especially if you carry social privilege.

- No margin, no mission.
- Move gracefully and nurture things.
- Stay in your corner.
- Be the singing stream.
- Practice radiance.

CHAPTER 12

Next Steps and Resources

WE'VE COVERED A LOT OF GROUND ALREADY and you may already be feeling clear on your goals and have them well underway—wonderful! Or you may still be sifting ideas, doing research, and reviewing the activities discussed here. That's equally good.

A question to those of you who have not already taken action: is there something that you need to let go of in order to move forward? Contrary to some, I do not necessarily believe that you *can* "have it all"—or if you can, probably not all at once. Life is busy and you are probably working, dealing with family and community demands, and so on. Some recalibrating may be necessary in order to make space in your life for the new venture or pursuit you choose to embark on. Like clearing out a closet, I find that making space in life often invites in what wants to happen next.

I also have a few words to add about so-called "work/life balance," which I believe to be a bit of a myth that can have the unpleasant added effect of making us feel grossly inadequate for not having everything perfectly "balanced" in a world not designed to support such a thing. Make peace with yourself. Avoid burnout. Consider your boundaries. Ask for support. You cannot be all things to everyone—and that's okay.

If you are caught up in one of these ideas and feeling overwhelmed or like you are falling short then, before going any further, please cut yourself some slack, take some deep breaths, and tell yourself that you are amazing just as you are.

I would also add that it's okay if it just doesn't feel right to take action at this moment. Remember my earlier words about the oppressive limitations of either/or thinking, urgency, scarcity, and hustle culture. Maybe it's time for you to rest, consider the possibility of other options, take stock, tend to other aspects of your life, or simply be still. Perhaps, instead of taking action, it might feel better to *just receive* whatever comes next, or simply trust in the wisdom of the present moment. It's okay—in fact, it's sometimes essential to be in this liminal space: the threshold or the messy middle. This is usually most fruitful when experienced without resistance or the urge to "get on with it." Some of your best ideas and insights may come from this period.

When I'm in a lull or feeling stuck or uncertain, I will sometimes ask myself, *What if everything is already perfect? What if the only thing I actually need to do right now is just breathe?* Remember that what you are looking for is likely looking for you too, so trust in that and do whatever the next right thing appears to be, no matter how simple or seemingly insignificant it is. Take care of yourself, then consider how you can serve or support others.

I would encourage you to continue to read, research, follow, witness, join, and otherwise take in the amazing conversations, organizations, and initiatives unfolding out there in the "blue ocean"—and online. Sooner or later, a moment of inspiration or a new relationship will show up and you'll know that it's time to get moving.

RESOURCES

The following is a smattering of places to look for further support, education, and kinship. A strange plus to the pandemic is that so much more content is available online. Courses and conferences that were previously only accessible in person are now just a few clicks away. This is not, of course, a comprehensive list. The field of social entrepreneurship is evolving rapidly, so enjoy surfing around out there to see what's new and resonates with your expression of it.

You can also join the Greater Good community! I would love to hear how you enjoyed the book and your feedback on other ways that I might be able to serve you. Sign up for my newsletter at www.greatergood.work or get in touch at www.madeleineshaw.ca.

Books and Magazines

This is writing I have enjoyed and that has influenced my thinking as a social entrepreneur in some way. There are, of course, more excellent titles out there—I just haven't read them yet!

- *The Blue Sweater: Bridging the Gap Between Rich and Poor in an Interconnected World* by Jacqueline Novogratz
- *Let My People Go Surfing: The Education of a Reluctant Businessman* by Yvon Chouinard
- *The Art of Non-Conformity: Set Your Own Rules, Live the Life You Want, and Change the World* by Chris Guillebeau
- *It's About Damn Time: How to Turn Being Underestimated into Your Greatest Advantage* by Arlan Hamilton
- *Leapfrog: The New Revolution for Women Entrepreneurs* by Nathalie Molina Niño and Sara Grace
- *Emergent Strategy: Shaping Change, Changing Worlds* by adrienne maree brown
- *Body and Soul: Profits with Principles—The Amazing Success Story of Anita Roddick & The Body Shop* by Anita Roddick

- *The Ecology of Commerce: A Declaration of Sustainability* by Paul Hawken
- *The Clean Money Revolution: Reinventing Power, Purpose, and Capitalism* by Joel Solomon
- *The Boss of You: Everything a Woman Needs to Know to Start, Run, and Maintain Her Own Business* by Emira Mears and Lauren Bacon
- *The Fire Starter Sessions: A Soulful + Practical Guide to Creating Success on Your Own Terms* by Danielle LaPorte
- *Periods Gone Public: Taking a Stand for Menstrual Equity* by Jennifer Weiss-Wolf
- *What Matters Most: How a Small Group of Pioneers is Teaching Social Responsibility to Big Business, and Why Big Business is Listening* by Jeffrey Hollender and Stephen Fenichell
- *We Were Feminists Once: From Riot Grrrl to CoverGirl®, the Buying and Selling of a Political Movement* by Andi Zeisler
- *Think Like a SheEO: Succeeding in the Age of Creators, Makers, and Entrepreneurs* by Vicki Saunders with M.J. Ryan
- *Big Magic: Creative Living Beyond Fear* by Elizabeth Gilbert
- *The Soul of an Entrepreneur: Work and Life Beyond the Startup Myth* by David Sax
- *Good Company* magazine by Design*Sponge (www.designsponge.com/goodcompany)
- *LiisBeth ¤ Field Notes from the Feminist Economy* (www.liisbeth.com)

Organizations and Communities

Once again, this is not intended to be a comprehensive list; there are likely local versions of these kinds of organizations in your community. Be sure to follow organizations and leaders that resonate with you on social media, especially Twitter and LinkedIn. For the sake of accuracy, I have, in several instances, taken organizational descriptions directly from their websites.

Social Venture Institute (SVI)

As discussed in the book, SVI is my spiritual home as a social entrepreneur. It is a community dedicated to social justice, sustainability, and all manner of impact. It's a series of conferences and related social events, as well as a vibrant and very useful email list that goes out to its like-minded alumni. Readers may also enjoy connecting with its sibling, Social Change Institute (SCI), which is more oriented toward nonprofits. SVI Women is equally highly recommended.

www.hollyhockleadershipinstitute.org

SheEO

I cannot say enough good things about SheEO as a resource and community for women and nonbinary entrepreneurs, and those who wish to support them. Even better, SheEO is international, not just in Canada, and there is a massive amount of content available online. If you have a spare $1,100, I encourage you to become an Activator. Your contribution—although not a traditional investment or loan, in that you don't get financially "paid back"—forms a critical part of the interest-free loan funding that helps to grow Ventures, not to mention countless other networking and content benefits. If you have a for-profit or nonprofit venture that generates over $50K in annual revenue, is majority women- or nonbinary-owned and led, and is improving the world in a demonstrable way, then I strongly encourage you to apply for Venture funding. Even if you are not ultimately ranked as a top Venture to receive funding, being part of the process will expose your Venture to smart, helpful Activators across whichever country you apply in (currently open to citizens of Canada, the US, the UK, New Zealand, and Australia).

www.sheeo.world

B Corp

B Corp is for mission-driven, for-profit ventures who have plans to grow their impact. It's a highly respected, international certification only available to ventures following a rigorous assessment of their social and environmental impact. Becoming a B Corp is not a small undertaking and you need to be serious and meticulous about all aspects of your business practice. Highly recommended, but not for the faint of heart from an information and process perspective.

www.bcorporation.net

Groundswell

Billing itself as an "Alternative Business School," Groundswell is how I imagine SVI being if it had a permanent home. I feel deeply aligned with their philosophy that entrepreneurs are built from the inside out; in other words, it's not just the soundness of someone's business idea, but the inner process that needs to be considered first as the foundation for a successful venture. Another way I would frame Groundswell is as an "incubator for the 99%." Their approach has a deeply human quality and makes a point of addressing the needs of immigrants, people of color, women, LGBTQIA+, and gender-nonconforming individuals. Folks outside Vancouver are in luck, as the entire program is now online.

www.groundswellcommunity.ca

Spring

Spring bills itself as a "global incubator, accelerator, and advisory firm that helps impact entrepreneurs, investors, and entrepreneurial ecosystem-builders build thriving communities." While my experience has been fairly limited, Suzanne has participated in several of its programs, and found it to be particularly helpful around raising capital.

www.spring.is

Zebras Unite

Zebras Unite was the first group I became aware of that thoroughly articulated the case for championing "small" business, flipping the classic paradigm of the unicorn entrepreneur/venture in their groundbreaking article "Zebras Fix What Unicorns Break" (essential reading, if you have not already seen it). These folks are creating a dynamic community that is

generating all kinds of amazing conversations, funding avenues, and overall thought leadership related to all things impact entrepreneurship, especially on the smaller (yet mighty) end of things.
www.zebrasunite.coop

Centre for Social Innovation (CSI)

How I wish we had one of these in Vancouver! If you're in Toronto or New York, though, you're in luck. They are basically hubs where you can connect with like-minded community ventures for events, desk/office space rental, mentorship, and more.
www.socialinnovation.org

THNK School of Creative Leadership

THNK is an Amsterdam-based executive education institute that seeks solutions to global challenges through applying business tools and design thinking methodology. It attracts global cohorts composed of an intentional clash of corporates and other senior professionals, creatives, and entrepreneurs (social and otherwise), with the stated goal of "supporting leaders to develop innovative solutions to the world's greatest societal problems."
www.thnk.org

Kanuu Indigenous Innovation

Kanuu is an Indigenous-led social enterprise that "provides skill development, coaching, and ongoing support in entrepreneurship for Indigenous peoples in Canada and beyond."
www.kanuu.ca

StartOut

StartOut's mission is to "increase the number, diversity, and impact of LGBTQIA+ entrepreneurs and amplify their stories to drive the economic empowerment of the community."
www.startout.org

Black & Brown Founders

This organization provides "community, education, and access to Black and Latinx entrepreneurs, allowing them to launch and build tech businesses with modest resources."
www.blackandbrownfounders.com

Common Future

Common Future (formerly BALLE) is a "network of leaders (re)building an economy that includes everyone." Initiatives—including Social Entrepreneurs in Residence and Fellowship programs—are designed to shift capital into communities, uplift local leaders, and accelerate the development of equitable economies.
www.commonfuture.co

WEConnect International

WEConnect International "helps drive money into the hands of women business owners by enabling them to compete in the global marketplace." It "connects member buyers to women-owned sellers based outside of the US, enhances their capabilities to transact business, and instills confidence that sellers meet buyers' standards for women-owned businesses."
www.weconnectinternational.org

Women Entrepreneurship Knowledge Hub

The Women Entrepreneurship Knowledge Hub (WEKH) "shares research and resources on women entrepreneurs in Canada. Made up of ten regional hubs, WEKH . . . includes a network of over 250 organizations, reaching more than 100,000 women entrepreneurs."
www.wekh.ca

The Fireweed Fellowship

The Fireweed Fellowship is "the first national accelerator program for Indigenous entrepreneurship in what is currently known as Canada. The program consists of a ten-month-long, immersive, cohort-style fellowship program combining online educational sessions, self-directed on-the-land learning, and leadership development. Additionally, the program offers peer support, one-on-one coaching, mentorship, and pro-bono professional services, as well as investment-readiness prep."
www.fireweedfellowship.com

Women's Enterprise Centre

Women's Enterprise Centre is a "nonprofit organization devoted to helping BC women to start, lead, and grow their own business." WEC also provides "business skills training, personalized business advice, mentoring, practical business resources, and a supportive community to help women business

owners gain the skills, mindset, financing, and networks they need to realize their business potential."
www.womensenterprise.ca

Women's Enterprise Organizations of Canada

Committed to the growth of women's entrepreneurship, the Women's Enterprise Organizations of Canada (WEOC) "works with women's enterprise support organizations to champion innovation, broaden expertise, and enhance collaboration. WEOC members support women entrepreneurs by providing an array of services, including business skills development, access to financing, networking, and export opportunities."
www.weoc.ca

The Forum

The Forum is a Canadian charity that "educates, mentors, and connects women entrepreneurs. From raising capital to developing a pitch to growing your HR, sales, and leadership skills, The Forum supports women entrepreneurs leading business at any stage, of any size and industry, anywhere in Canada."
www.theforum.ca

Ashoka

Ashoka "identifies and supports the world's leading social entrepreneurs, learns from the patterns in their innovations, and mobilizes a global community that embraces these new frameworks to build an 'everyone's a changemaker' world."
www.ashoka.org

Accelerating the Accelerators

Accelerating the Accelerators (AtA) is a network "dedicated to increasing the effectiveness of impact accelerators, incubators, fellowships, and business plan competitions. It is a structured program designed to support impact entrepreneurs in launching and scaling social enterprises."
www.conveners.org/accelerating-the-accelerators-home/

Hello Alice

Hello Alice is "the first machine learning technology to help business owners find their path by matching them to personalized opportunities and resources. Whether you've owned a business for years or you just had a brilliant idea in the shower, Hello Alice works by matching you with opportunities, locally and online, that will help you start and grow a business."
www.helloalice.com

League of Innovators

League of Innovators "aims to bring youth aged 15-25 out-of-the-box experiences that will build and sharpen their entrepreneurial skills. Building their confidence, empowering them to create and take charge of their future, and recognize the power that they hold as innovators and entrepreneurs in our ever-evolving economy."
www.theleagueofinnovators.org

Development Impact & You

This organization offers a veritable bonanza of practical tools to help shape your ideas. This is a perfect place for social entrepreneurs to look for business canvas models and more as they flesh out the How of their projects. Bonus: it's free!
www.diytoolkit.org

Impact Hub

The Impact Hub Network is a "community (16,000+ members) and accelerator for positive change with 100+ locations across five continents, in more than 50 countries. Impact Hub supports building ecosystems to drive collaboration and entrepreneurial innovation around the Global Sustainable Development Goals (SDGs) through locally rooted Impact Hubs, as well as with partners and allied networks."
www.impacthub.net

The DO School

The DO School "offers a unique approach to innovation by curating a diverse group of startups, experts, and internal teams that collaborate to quickly develop and implement new solutions to company and government challenges. It empowers impact entrepreneurs from around the world to

solve the big challenges of our time, providing the tools, skills, and network they need to scale their impact."
www.thedoschool.com

SOLVE

Solve is an initiative of the Massachusetts Institute of Technology (MIT) with a mission to "solve world challenges and is also a marketplace for social impact innovation. Through open innovation challenges, Solve funds and supports select tech-based social entrepreneurs to help them drive lasting, transformational impact."
solve.mit.edu

Hella Social Impact

Further to my comments in chapter 11 about how unchecked social power imbalances can inadvertently thwart impact projects, this is an excellent tool for assessing how your initiative may be unconsciously upholding systemic racial biases.
www.hellasocialimpact.com

Feminist Enterprise Commons

Feminist Enterprise Commons is a "brave, Zuckerberg-free co-working, mutual aid, and learning space for feminists who aim to build anti-oppressive, anti-racist, socially just, generative enterprises or community projects that challenge patriarchal business culture, extractive capitalism, white supremacy, colonization, and straight lines."
feministenterprisecommons.mn.co

Slow Factory Foundation

Slow Factory is "a public service organization operating as an open education institute, independent research lab and new media platform, and a granting and empowerment fund. Primarily but far from exclusively fashion-based, their initiatives and programs focus on circular design, material innovation and addressing social inequity."
www.slowfactory.foundation

Slow Entrepreneur® Movement

When one of the hottest entrepreneurial magazines is called *Fast Company*, you know that these folks have a distinctly different take. As their website states, "*Slow Entrepreneurship* is rooted in the belief that, as the founder of your company, your well-being is your greatest priority. When you make your well-being your top priority, you go farther, faster. We promote a set of values + practices intended to fuel your engine as you build a business that thrives."
www.slowentrepreneur.com

EMgirls

EMGirls (the EM is for EMpower) is "a youth-led nonprofit organization that aims to empower girls by continually challenging them to step out of their comfort zones. EMGirls aims to bridge the gender gap in the entre-preneurship field and acts as a catalyst for girls to hone their confidence, resilience, and critical thinking."
www.emgirls.org

Post Growth Entrepreneurship

Post Growth Entrepreneurship (PGE) "reframes business as a form of activism, art, spirituality, and creative expression. This business model embraces flat growth curves and rejects the need for investors, scaling, and exits. PGE questions entrepreneurial 'common wisdom' and re-envisions business as a vehicle for pure positive impact. It also offers events, research, education, and community to (aspiring) post-growth entrepreneurs."
nonprofit.ventures

Entrepreneurs with Disabilities Program

This program is designed to "make it easier for entrepreneurs with disabil-ities or ongoing health conditions to pursue their business goals by provid-ing access to a network of business professionals and resources."
www.communityfutures.ca/edp

Criterion Institute

Criterion is "a nonprofit think tank that works with social changemakers to demystify finance and broaden their perspective on how to engage with and shift financial systems."
www.criterioninstitute.org

Cooperatives for a Better World

Cooperatives for a Better World is a "not-for-profit, mission-based organization focused on sharing cooperative identity with the world and the difference it makes in local, national, and global communities."
www.betterworld.coop

Start.coop

Start.coop "accelerates the growth and development of the next generation of co-operative entrepreneurs with the knowledge, tools, and financing necessary to build businesses that share prosperity among the many, not just the few."
www.start.coop

Black Innovation Alliance

The Black Innovation Alliance (BIA) is "composed of support organizations that serve Black innovators. Their mission is to ensure that Black ownership is increasing through equitable participation in the innovation economy."
www.blackinnovationalliance.com

Echoing Green

Through Fellowships and other innovative leadership initiatives, Echoing Green "spots emerging leaders and invests deeply in their success to accelerate their impact. Echoing Green provides seed-funding and leadership development to a new class of Fellows every year and welcomes them into a lifelong community of leaders."
www.echoinggreen.org

Social Venture Circle

Social Venture Circle (SVC) "connects, empowers, and finances entrepreneurs, investors, capacity-builders, and policy makers in a powerful, diverse, and inclusive network."
www.svcimpact.org

Community-Wealth.org

Community-Wealth.org "offers a cornucopia of information about innovative community wealth building strategies throughout the United States, including ESOP, impact investing, co-ops, Community Development Corporations (CDCs), and much more."
www.community-wealth.org

Global Impact Investing Network

The Global Impact Investing Network (GIIN) is "dedicated to increasing the scale and effectiveness of impact investing around the world. By convening impact investors to facilitate knowledge exchange, highlighting innovative investment approaches, building the evidence base for the industry, and producing valuable tools and resources, the GIIN seeks to accelerate the industry's development through focused leadership and collective action."
www.thegiin.org

SOCAP Global

SOCAP "convenes a global ecosystem and marketplace—social entrepreneurs, investors, foundation and nonprofit leaders, government and policy leaders, creators, corporations, academics, and beyond—through live and digital experiences that educate, spur conversation, and inspire investment in positive impact."
www.socapglobal.com

Impact Investment Firms

Renewal Funds

Renewal Funds is "a mission venture capital fund investing in early growth stage companies to accelerate the transition to a sustainable economy. They invest in innovation that will advance the sustainability of food, water, and climate, contributing to a safer and cleaner planet for future generations."
www.renewalfunds.com

Backstage Capital

As the Backstage Capital website states, "Less than ten percent of all venture capital deals go to women, people of color, and LGBTQIA+ founders. Other VCs see this as a pipeline problem. We see it as the biggest

opportunity in investment. Backstage Capital has invested in more than 170 companies led by underrepresented founders."
www.backstagecapital.com

SecondMuse Capital

SecondMuse Capital "considers entire economic and social systems and not only companies and their products and services. We strategically influence and deploy capital across sectors and regions to help create new economies that are growing, resilient, and inclusive."
www.secondmuse.com

ACKNOWLEDGMENTS

I NEED TO START WITH MY PARENTS, as they were, of course, my earliest supporters. You know the type of parents who tell their kids that they can do *anything?* Those are my folks. I cannot imagine two more patient, supportive, generous, and loving parents than Duncan and Pat Shaw. I love you so much.

My warmest thanks go to the Goodell family for their decades of friendship. Without their encouragement, I don't think I would necessarily have developed the self-belief to become an entrepreneur in the first place.

My participation in the Venture Program at BCIT in 1994 was a critical first step on my journey as an entrepreneur. I was thoughtfully supported there by Ken Takeuchi, Lynne Larson, and the late, great Peter Thomson.

Other early supporters and collaborators include Andrea Gray-Grant; Sian Pairaudeau; Christian Prekratic; Shah Hirji; Henry Faber; Judy Ho; Megan Thomas; Madeleine Nelson; Lana Underhill; Tim MacDougall; Noel, Valerie, and Kate Roddick; Kathleen Staples;

Eric Boelling and Gary Smith; Dolly Scarr; Andrew and Melanie Graham; Ed and Mariette White; Sean and Daphne Hodgins; Cameron Rolfe and Mary Letson; Joe and Michelle Bridle; Rod Hyslop; Lisa Wolverton; Andrea Horton; Kim Martin; Juliette Sale; Trish Dolman; Gabriella Corter; Jackie Greenizan; my brother Keith Shaw; and our late, deeply missed cousin Jamie Shaw.

Once I started selling Lunapads, it wasn't long before I met Signy Wilson, who was at the time using her prodigious facilitation gifts and budding coaching skills to educate menstruators about the wisdom of their cycles. She remains one of my greatest champions and all-time closest friends to this day.

I operated my store, everyware designs, from 1996 to 1998, and during that time I had the honor of working with Kathleen O'Grady, Lan Tran, Amy Ko, Mai Pham, Bronwyn Chambers, Tamara Rauliuk-Dunn, Kereem Al Rubaii, and Amy Meissner. I learned so much from each of these skilled, hardworking, and deeply creative souls.

It was during the everyware designs days that I developed an irresistible crush on a longtime friend named Tim Roddick. I could not possibly have maintained my energy without his continued unfailing belief in me, his supporting me by handling a multitude of life's critical background details, and, most importantly, being a wonderful husband and the best dad to our daughter I could imagine.

I met Suzanne Siemens in 1999. There is no single individual who has made more of an impact on my journey as an entrepreneur than she has and I continue to marvel at her skill and integrity, as well as the immense bounty of her friendship. Without exaggeration, none of this would have happened without her belief in the Lunapads/Aisle dream. Pursuing it has been one of the most rewarding adventures that I could imagine sharing with anyone. Suzanne was also a profound role model to me as a mom. Having the privilege of watching and supporting her when her first child, Aiden, arrived in 2002 was one of the greatest gifts of my life. I'm not sure that

I would have had the confidence to imagine the radically different approach to work-life balance that ultimately became Nestworks without the benefit of this experience—let alone the confidence needed as a working parent when Gigi arrived. I literally cannot say enough good things about this remarkable woman and the relationship that we share.

I would be remiss in not also heartily thanking Suzanne's devoted husband, Craig Siemens, as well as her faithful and hardworking brother, Henry Jew, for their unstinting support.

The Wu family—Wendy, Thomas, and Doris—have been making Lunapads/Aisle pads since 1999. I cannot overstate my gratitude and respect for this wonderful family and their vital role in our success.

Suzanne and I were introduced to Renewal Partners and its founders, Joel Solomon and Carol Newell, in 2000. Joel has been one of our most valued advisors and mentors, and Carol is a tireless, full-hearted champion. I feel beyond honored to have the benefit of their trust, friendship, and support.

The connection to Renewal brought us to the Social Venture Institute (SVI) community, where I was welcomed with open arms by a vast network of like-minded and supportive peers, including Pam Chaloult and Deb Nelson, and Breakfast Clubbers Sarah White, Denise Taschereau, Toby Barazzuol, Donovan Woollard, Mike Rowlands, Louise Schwarz, Maggie Leithead, Emily Murgatroyd McCann, Annalea Krebs, and the late, greatly missed Doug Burgoyne.

Suzanne also brought some of her most ardent and valuable supporters along with her—notably her longtime mentor, Bob Elton. When I first met Bob, he represented everything that I mistrusted about "big business"; however, he gently plucked the chip off my shoulder and generously extended his friendship to me as well. He has acted as the Lunapads/Aisle advisory board chair since its formation, marshaling diverse voices to focus on our deepest questions and trickiest challenges skillfully, kindly, and with immense care and respect. He has also been a generous supporter of our projects in collaboration with AFRIpads.

I met Emira Mears for the first time when she came into my store, everyware designs, in the late '90s. Her feminist politics and general braininess and our shared interest in DIY fashion made us fast friends, and it wasn't long before she became an entrepreneur herself, co-founding Raised Eyebrow Web Studio with Lauren Bacon. They designed and built several versions of the Lunapads website, including the one that saved our failing business model in the early 2000s. They subsequently co-authored an indispensable book for women entrepreneurs and generously chose to feature Suzanne and me in it: *The Boss of You: Everything a Woman Needs to Know to Start, Run, and Maintain Her Own Business* (listed in the resources section).

Hilary Mandel is one of my greatest collaborators and friends and played a key role in G Day as a board treasurer, volunteer coordinator, and all-round operational troubleshooter, as well as being a founding board member of Nestworks. Her wise, loving energy and "we'll figure it out" attitude have always grounded me and improved my ideas.

I am beyond grateful to everyone who has ever worked at Lunapads/Aisle. At this point, there are too many to name, but special thanks are due to our longest-standing team members: Lisa Fabbro, Morgan Martin-Wood, and Gonie Abella. Lisa has broadened my definition of feminism in so many ways, patiently bringing this tail-end-of-the-second-waver into the twenty-first century with persistence and respect; I am a better person thanks to them. Morgan is one of the most committed, creative problem-solvers I have ever met, while Gonie is quite possibly the hardest-working, full stop. In addition to working with Suzanne and me for over twenty years, she also helped us to raise Aiden, Gigi, and Garret alongside her own children, Gleanne and Lloyd.

Other Lunapads/Aisle team members, advisory board members, and supporters who have contributed to our success include Krisztina

Kun, Marie-Genevieve Lane, Sandra Allen, Christa Trueman, Tiffany Ng and her mom, Wanny Tang, Britta Wein, Josh Kremer, Mark Wong, Bernard Lo, Andrea Korens, Anika Yuzak, Evan Clow, Megan Beveridge, Jane Hope, Jody Higbee, Lisa McCord, Morgan Hodgkinson, sisters Karen and Kitty Wong, Jennifer Lipka, Shayla Williams, Hayaat Stuart-Khafaji, Ariane Bell Vila, Nanda van der Meer, Gayle Thom, Tara Wilkinson, Hilary Samson, Yvette Wu, Sarah Dickinson, Kristi Miller, Tania Lo, Jaz Poole, Anna Hutchinson, Paul and Sonia Grinvalds, and, of course, Bob Elton.

As I described in the book, G Day would likely never have come to pass—at least, not as quickly and with such space to grow—without the generosity of Susan Gibson. Other stars in the G Day constellation include Alysha Seriani, Madeline Ell, Vanessa Richards, Megan Sheldon, Carmen Spagnola, Catherine Runnals, Amanda Palmer, Tiffany Ng, Amanda Kao, Sandra Nomoto, Megan Chen, Tamara Cotton, Nikiah Seeds, Saleema Noon, Michelle Wilson and her daughter Tru, Nicole Aleong, Roberta Price, Emily Rose Antflick, Kathryn Meisner, Angelique de Montbrun, Erin Blanding, Dayna Holland, Andrea Shillington, Lea Cheverie, Karen Kobel, Kristen Sharp, Jocelyn MacDougall, Monica Morong, Tamara Taggart, Orane Cheung, Jason Aune, Sapna Dayal, Karen Lam, Navi Gill, Theresa "Tree" Walsh, Stina Brown, Marnie Goldenberg, Anna Soole, Elisa Lee, Wendy D, my cousin David Rain, Elizabeth Ross and her colleagues at the Squamish Nation, Claire Booth and the Lux Insights team, and so many more. Thanks to all of you for sharing your magic so unstintingly.

I learned so much about social entrepreneurship from my time at the Groundswell Alternative Business School as an advisory board member and mentor. Many thanks to Sanja Simic, Gilad Babchuk, Paola Qualizza, Elena Yugai, and other team members, for the opportunity to collectively nurture the spirits of dozens of early-stage social entrepreneurs.

In addition to Hilary Mandel, brilliant former and current

Nestworks board members include Michelle Hoar, Janet Moore, Hilary Henegar, Jennifer Sandoval, Dayna Holland, Shayna Rector-Bleeker, and Jessica McIlroy, ably supported by our talented and committed communications coordinator, Sandra Nomoto. Thank you for holding this dream with me, and here's to it coming to life as the post-COVID world emerges.

Massive thanks go to everyone who completed surveys for this book, including Leisa Hirtz, Norm Smookler, Sandra Nomoto, Richard Brubaker, Henri Allegra, Wumi, Trusha Govende, Mikaela Jade, Jennifer LeBrun, Shannon Loutitt, Daniela Kelloway, Zahlen Titcomb, Mark Vernooij, Nita Tandon, Hilary Henegar, Mahsa Keikha, Boma Brown, Milena Bacalja Perianes, Emily Weltman, Nikiah Seeds, Ashley Wiles, Gilad Babchuk, Petra Kassun-Mutch, Sam Mills and Surya Govender, Sabrina Rubli, Debra Joy, Bryan Buell, Marc Wandler, Loretta Laurin, Mike Winterfield, Lyn Brooks, Zoe Currelly, Golnaz Golnaraghi, Julie Nowell, Laure Dupuy, Sarah Howell, Kyle Empringham, Robin Rivers, Irina McKenzie, Toby Barazzuol, Wendy Kelly, Urszula Lipsztajn, Amy Romer, Deanna Simone, Sandy Manj, Peter Holgate, Reena Lazar and Michelle Pante, Carlene Lewall, Sarah Dickinson, Amanda Laird, Catherine Marot, and Kelly Maguire. You are all heroes to me.

Special thanks go to those whose stories I was able to feature: Mary Letson, Jeeti Pooni, Vanessa LeBourdais, Amy Robinson, Jacinthe Koddo, Vanessa Richards, Megan Sheldon, Kai Scott, Debbie Roche, Elizabeth Sheehan, Wendy Armbruster, Anthonia Ogundele, Sofia Ashley, Danielle Keiser, Bonnie Foley-Wong, Carine Young, Martha Belcher, Caroline Thibault, and Dr. Selina Tribe. Your courage and candor brought color and truth to the book that I could never have provided on my own.

Kaz Brecher, an esteemed THNK School of Creative Leadership faculty member, generously shared her crowdfunding tips for the book, as did Kevin Harding. Many thanks go to Karen Lam, Wendy Palmer, and Signy Wilson, for sharing their exercises and invaluable expertise so generously. Elvezio (Elvy) Del Bianco helped sharpen my understanding of the cooperative model.

I will be forever grateful to my original SheEO sisters, Nadia Hamilton, Sonia Strobel, Toni Desrosiers, and Ilana Ben Ari (Suzanne is also on this list!) for their incredible visions, courage, unconditional support for one another, and for sharing their stories in the book.

Other SheEO Venture founders who showed up for *The Greater Good* include Margaret Magdesian, Jodi Huettner, Brianne Miller, BE Alink, and my treasured soul sister, Patrice Mousseau. Thank you also to SheEO team members past and present, particularly Leah Meers and Jessie Wang, who, I should add, generously lent their brains and hearts to G Day Toronto. I would also like to thank SheEO supporters extraordinaire Abby Slater and Richard Ford for their generous hospitality and support. Thank you, Vicki Saunders, from the bottom of my heart, for your extraordinary vision and courage; it's changing the world into a place that I feel hopeful about.

I am incredibly grateful for the time and thoughtful feedback delivered by early readers Joel Solomon, Jill Earthy, M.J. Ryan, Paola Qualizza, Suzanne Siemens, Bob Elton, and my parents.

The patience and wisdom of my editor, Allison Serrell, and my publisher, Maggie Langrick, were essential blessings to this project, ably supported by Jesmine Cham.

Saving the best for last, I would like to thank my daughter Gigi for being, well, everything. This is a kid who has almost never known a day in her life when I was not working (or thinking about it) on one out-there project or another and was often literally brought along for the ride. She has helped out alongside Gonie packing orders at Lunapads/Aisle, has been a stellar G Day volunteer, and was the second test case for what later became Nestworks. I could not be prouder of her, or more hopeful for her and her peers as they take the future into their hands. You are my heart.

INDEX

ABOUT THE AUTHOR

Madeleine Shaw is a multiple award–winning social entrepreneur with over a quarter-century of experience launching for- and nonprofit ventures with social change at their heart. In 1993, at the age of twenty-five, she founded her first company, the precursor to Lunapads (rebranded as Aisle in 2020)—a founding Canadian B Corporation whose groundbreaking sustainable menstrual care products are sold in more than forty countries. Lunapads was one of the first ventures in the world to commercialize natural menstrual care, now a thriving industry. In 2014, Shaw founded G Day, a registered charity that produced rite of passage events for tween girls across Canada until 2020. In 2017, she launched Nestworks, a family-friendly co-working community. She has mentored dozens of early-stage entrepreneurs, is a sought-after public speaker, and is featured in the documentary films *Not Business as Usual* and *The Social Shift*. She is grateful to be living and working on traditional unceded Coast Salish territory near Vancouver, BC, with her husband and daughter.